Just Off the Interstate

EXPLORE AMERICA

Just Off the Interstate

Reader's Digest

THE READER'S DIGEST ASSOCIATION, INC.
Pleasantville, New York / Montreal

JUST OFF THE INTERSTATE was created and produced by St. Remy Multimedia.

STAFF FOR JUST OFF THE INTERSTATE
Series Editor: Elizabeth Cameron
Art Director: Solange Laberge
Editors: Alfred LeMaitre, Elizabeth Warrington Lewis
Assistant Editor: Neale McDevitt
Photo Researcher: Geneviève Monette
Cartography: Hélène Dion, Anne-Marie Lemay, David Widgington
Research Editor: Robert B. Ronald
Researcher: Jennifer Meltzer
Copy Editor: Judy Yelon
Index: Christine Jacobs
System Coordinator: Éric Beaulieu
Technical Support: Mathieu Raymond-Beaubien, Jean Sirois
Scanner Operators: Martin Francoeur, Sara Grynspan

ST. REMY STAFF
PRESIDENT, CHIEF EXECUTIVE OFFICER: Fernand Lecoq
PRESIDENT, CHIEF OPERATING OFFICER: Pierre Léveillé
VICE PRESIDENT, FINANCE: Natalie Watanabe
MANAGING EDITOR: Carolyn Jackson
MANAGING ART DIRECTOR: Diane Denoncourt
PRODUCTION MANAGER: Michelle Turbide

Writers: Adriana Barton—Pioneer Illinois
Lee Foster—Golden State Drive
Fiona Gilsenan—The East Coast
Rod Gragg—The High Plains
Jim Henderson—Chisholm Trail
Rose Houk—Through the Rockies
Steven Krolak—Desert Discovery, Panoramic Northwest
Margaret Locklair—The Old South
James Wamsley—Appalachian Adventure

Contributing Writers: Dolores Haggarty, Rob Lutes, Neale McDevitt, Enza Micheletti

Address any comments about *Just Off the Interstate* to U.S. Editor, General Books, c/o Customer Service, Reader's Digest, Pleasantville, NY 10570

READER'S DIGEST STAFF
Editor: Jill Maynard
Art Editor: Nancy Mace
Assistant Production Supervisor: Mike Gallo

READER'S DIGEST GENERAL BOOKS
Editor-in-Chief, Books and Home
Entertainment: Barbara J. Morgan
Editor, U.S. General Books: David Palmer
Executive Editor: Gayla Visalli
Editorial Director: Jane Polley
Art Director: Joel Musler
Research Director: Laurel A. Gilbride

Opening photographs
Cover: Arches National Park, Utah
Back Cover: Appalachian Trail near Blackrock, Shenandoah National Park, Virginia
Page 2: West Entrance, Colorado National Monument, Colorado
Page 5: Big Oak Tree State Park, Missouri

The credits and acknowledgments that appear on page 144 are hereby made a part of this copyright page.

Copyright © 1996 The Reader's Digest Association, Inc.
Copyright © 1996 The Reader's Digest Association (Canada) Ltd.
Copyright © 1996 Reader's Digest Association Far East Ltd.
Philippine Copyright 1996 Reader's Digest Association Far East Ltd.

Library of Congress Cataloging in Publication Data

Just off the Interstate.
        p.   cm.—(Explore America)
    Includes index.
    ISBN 0-89577-895-5
    1. United States—Guidebooks.   2. United States—Description and
travel.   3. United States—Pictorial works.   4. Automobile travel—
United States—Guidebooks.   I. Reader's Digest Association.
II. Series.
    E158.J9   1996
    917.304'929—dc20   96-17469

Printed in the United States of America

CONTENTS

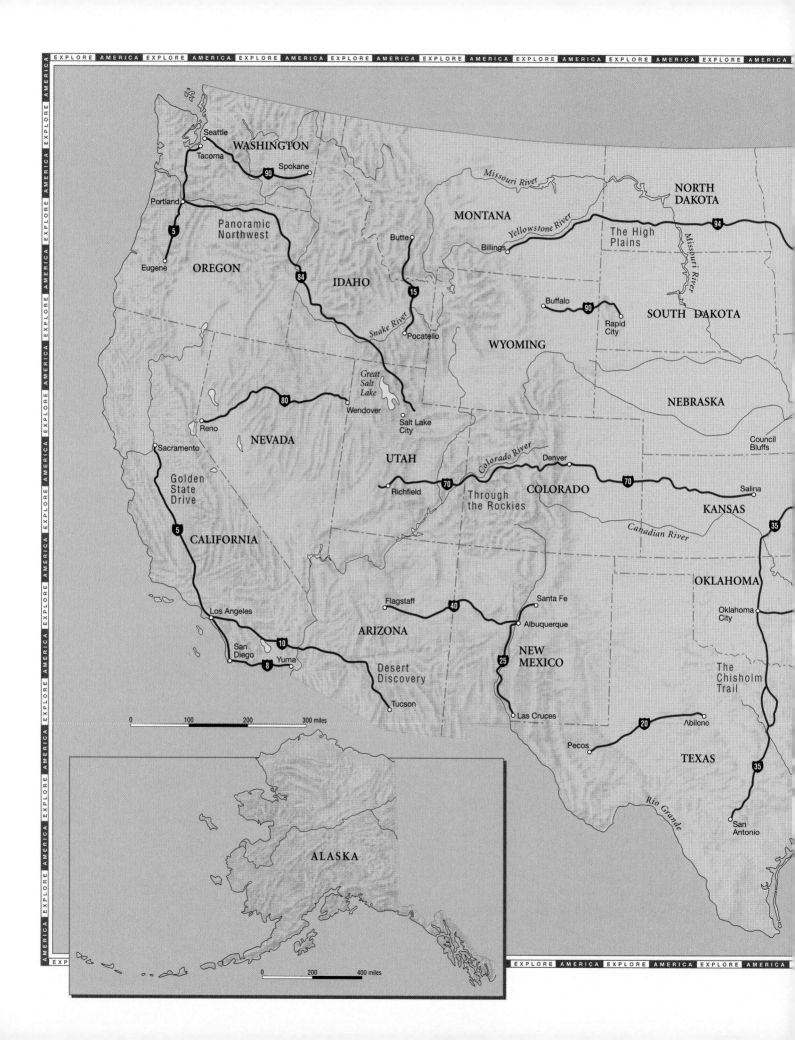

WASHINGTON

Seattle
Tacoma
Spokane
90

Portland
5

Panoramic
Northwest

Eugene

OREGON

84

IDAHO

Butte

15

Snake River

Pocatello

Great
Salt
Lake

MONTANA

Missouri River

Yellowstone River

Billings

WYOMING

Buffalo
90
Rapid
City

The High
Plains

Missouri River

NORTH
DAKOTA

SOUTH DAKOTA

NEBRASKA

80

Wendover

Salt Lake
City

Reno

Sacramento

NEVADA

Golden
State
Drive

UTAH

Colorado River

Richfield
70

Through
the Rockies

Denver

COLORADO

70

Canadian River

Council
Bluffs

Salina

KANSAS

35

5

CALIFORNIA

Los Angeles

San
Diego
10
8
Yuma

ARIZONA

Desert
Discovery

Tucson

Flagstaff
40

Santa Fe

Albuquerque

25

NEW
MEXICO

Las Cruces

Pecos

20

OKLAHOMA

Oklahoma
City

The
Chisholm
Trail

Abilene

TEXAS

Rio Grande

35

San
Antonio

0   100   200   300 miles

ALASKA

0   200   400 miles

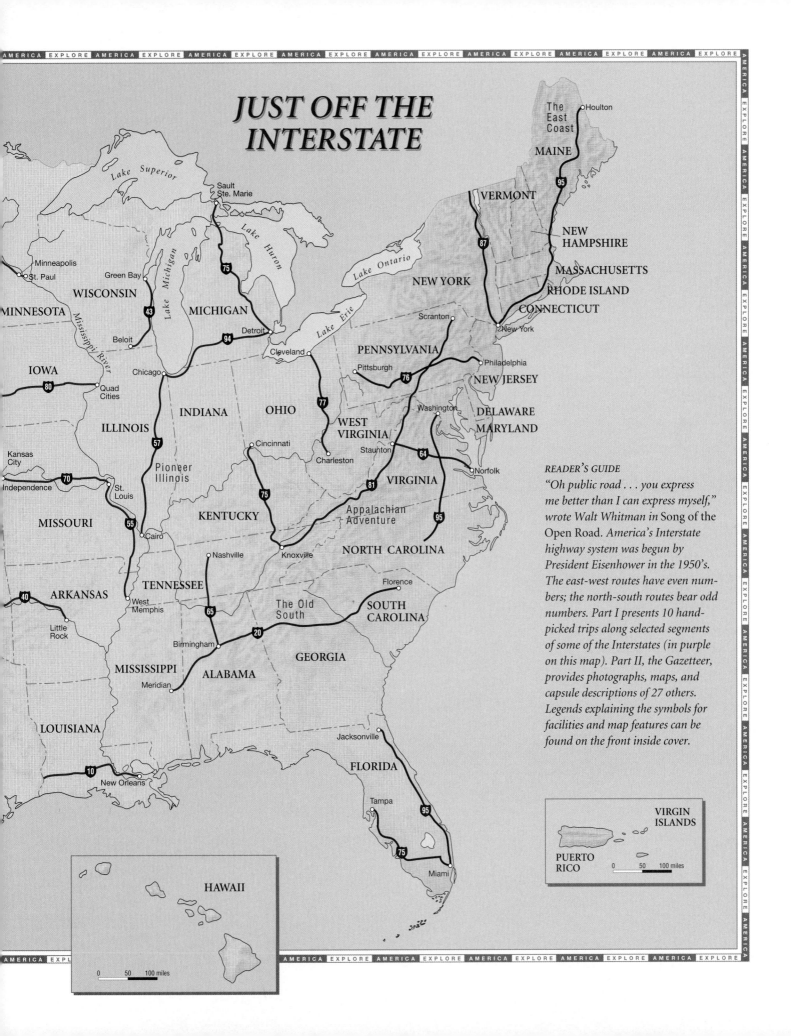

JUST OFF THE INTERSTATE

READER'S GUIDE

"Oh public road . . . you express me better than I can express myself," wrote Walt Whitman in Song of the Open Road. *America's Interstate highway system was begun by President Eisenhower in the 1950's. The east-west routes have even numbers; the north-south routes bear odd numbers. Part I presents 10 hand-picked trips along selected segments of some of the Interstates (in purple on this map). Part II, the Gazetteer, provides photographs, maps, and capsule descriptions of 27 others. Legends explaining the symbols for facilities and map features can be found on the front inside cover.*

The East Coast

Houlton

MAINE
95

VERMONT
87

NEW HAMPSHIRE

MASSACHUSETTS
RHODE ISLAND
CONNECTICUT

NEW YORK

Scranton

New York

Sault Ste. Marie

Lake Superior

Minneapolis
St. Paul

Green Bay

WISCONSIN

MINNESOTA

43

Beloit

Lake Michigan

MICHIGAN

75

Detroit
94

Lake Huron

Lake Ontario

Lake Erie

Cleveland

PENNSYLVANIA

Pittsburgh
76

Philadelphia

NEW JERSEY

DELAWARE
MARYLAND

Washington

Mississippi River

IOWA
80

Chicago

Quad Cities

INDIANA

OHIO

77

WEST VIRGINIA

Staunton

64

ILLINOIS

57

Pioneer Illinois

Cincinnati

Charleston

81

VIRGINIA

Norfolk

Kansas City

70

Independence

St. Louis

KENTUCKY

75

Appalachian Adventure

95

MISSOURI

55

Cairo

Nashville

Knoxville

NORTH CAROLINA

ARKANSAS

40

Little Rock

TENNESSEE

West Memphis

The Old South

Florence

SOUTH CAROLINA

65

MISSISSIPPI

Birmingham

20

ALABAMA

GEORGIA

Meridian

LOUISIANA

10

New Orleans

Jacksonville

FLORIDA

Tampa

95

75

Miami

VIRGIN ISLANDS

PUERTO RICO

0   50   100 miles

HAWAII

0   50   100 miles

THE EAST COAST

Slicing through five New England states, I-95 reveals the taproot of an infant nation.

For colonial New Englanders, travel routes along the East Coast left much to be desired. In the late 1600's there were only two established highways in the nation, both of them post roads owned by the government and constructed to ensure the safe delivery of mail. One of them, the Boston Post Road, wormed its way through the rivers and swamps along the shoreline, linking together the cities of New York and Boston. There were few bridges and the journey was laborious. "The roades all along this way are very bad . . . incumbered with Rocks and mountainous passages which were very disagreeable," lamented one traveler, when the road had already been in use for a century. Because few colonial New Englanders lived more than 70 miles from the sea, they preferred to travel the coastal waterways and network of inland rivers in order to avoid the difficulties of land travel.

Today Interstate 95 traces much of the same route as the original Boston Post Road, providing business travelers with a direct route between two

PATRIARCH OF LIGHTHOUSES
Overleaf: Portland Head Light, located in Two Lights State Park, is the oldest lighthouse in Maine and considered to be the most classically beautiful of the state's navigation beacons. Completed in 1791, the structure towers 80 feet above the rocky shore.

of the nation's busiest metropolitan areas—Boston and New York. But for the motorist who takes time to drive from New York City to the Canadian border, the 40-year-old highway provides an intriguing sample of the East Coast's riches.

Wending its way north from Miami, I-95 crosses from New Jersey into New York via the double-decker George Washington Bridge. Millions of commuters and visitors cross the bridge each year on their way to and from the island of Manhattan. The highway cuts straight across the city, then hugs the north shore of Long Island Sound. Many communities along this stretch of the route are suburbs of the metropolis. Just inside the Connecticut state line lies Fairfield County, a well-preserved enclave of old-money estates accessible mainly by winding, wooded country roads.

The city of Stamford, which dates back to the mid-1600's, is a center of commerce, with a skyline of glass and concrete office buildings visible from the highway. The Stamford Museum and Nature Center is located in a rustic setting just north of the city. This 118-acre woodland, where peacocks and geese strut across walking trails and otters cavort in a small pond, is a haven for nature lovers. The Overbrook Natural Science Center, the hub of nature activities at the Stamford Museum and Nature Center, includes a 300-foot-long boardwalk ideal for strollers, wheelchairs, and the elderly. There is also an early New England farm where

SEAFARING HERITAGE
A bronze statue, above, of a fisherman at the helm is one of Gloucester's landmarks.

BARNUM'S FOLLY
The Barnum Museum, near right, is topped by a large, red-tiled dome and decorated with intricate terra-cotta friezes that depict various periods of history in the Bridgeport region. This impressive structure was built in 1893 and houses a collection of circus memorabilia amassed by P. T. Barnum.

INFORMATION FOR VISITORS

There are toll sections of I-95: the Blue Star Tpk. between Smithtown and Portsmouth, NH, and the Maine Pkwy. Car ferries are available to Yarmouth, Nova Scotia, from Portland and Bar Harbor, ME. Visitor information offices are located in Hope Valley, RI; Mansfield, MA; Seabrook, NH; and just after exit 3 in Maine. For more information: New York State Travel Information Center, 1 Commerce Plaza, Albany, NY 12245; 800-225-5697. Connecticut Vacation Center, 865 Brook St., Rocky Hill, CT 06067; 800-282-6863. Rhode Island Tourism Division/Dept. of Economic Development, 7 Jackson Walkway, Providence, RI 02903; 800-556-2484. Massachusetts Office of Travel and Tourism, 100 Cambridge St., 13th Floor, Boston, MA 02202; 800-227-MASS. New Hampshire Office of Travel and Tourism, P.O. Box 1856, Concord, NH 03302; 603-271-2666. Maine Office of Tourism, 59 State House Stn., Augusta, ME 04333; 800-533-9595.

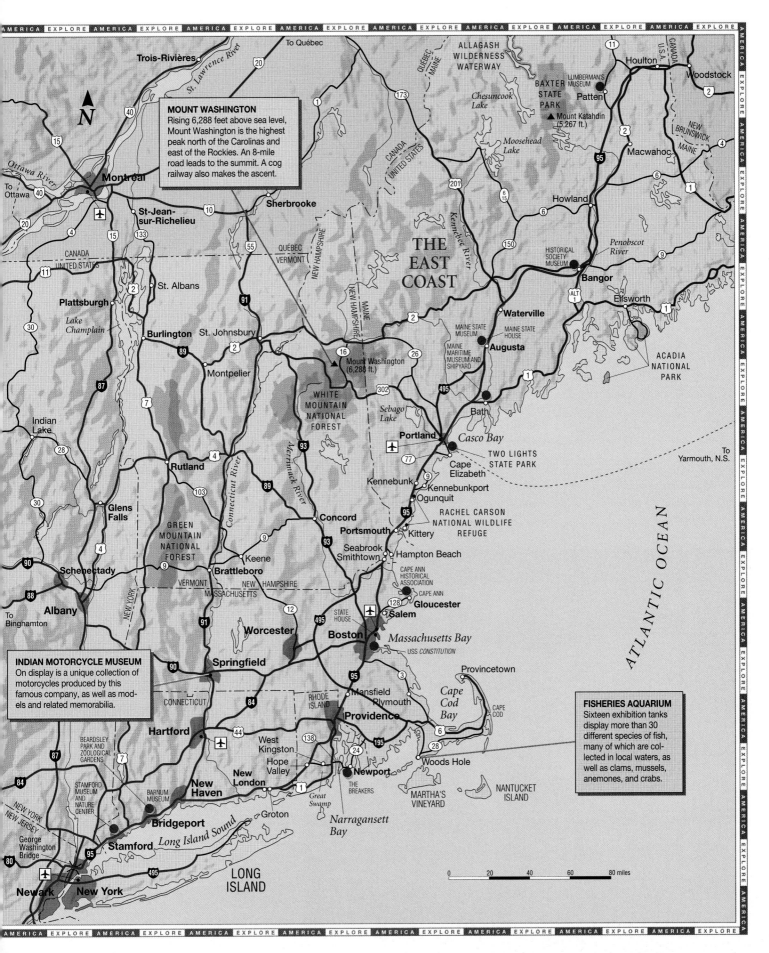

N

To Québec

Trois-Rivières

ALLAGASH
WILDERNESS
WATERWAY

Houlton

Woodstock

MOUNT WASHINGTON
Rising 6,288 feet above sea level,
Mount Washington is the highest
peak north of the Carolinas and
east of the Rockies. An 8-mile
road leads to the summit. A cog
railway also makes the ascent.

LUMBERMAN'S
MUSEUM
Patten

BAXTER
STATE
PARK

Chesuncook
Lake

Mount Katahdin
(5,267 ft.)

NEW
BRUNSWICK

Macwahoc

Moosehead
Lake

Montreal

St-Jean-
sur-Richelieu

Sherbrooke

QUÉBEC
VERMONT

THE
EAST
COAST

Kennebec River

Howland

Penobscot
River

To
Ottawa

Ottawa River

St. Albans

Plattsburgh

Lake
Champlain

NEW HAMPSHIRE

Burlington

St. Johnsbury

MAINE

HISTORICAL
SOCIETY
MUSEUM

Bangor

Ellsworth

Montpelier

Mount Washington
(6,288 ft.)

WHITE
MOUNTAIN
NATIONAL
FOREST

Waterville

MAINE STATE
MUSEUM

MAINE STATE
HOUSE

Augusta

ACADIA
NATIONAL
PARK

Indian
Lake

Rutland

Merrimack River

MAINE
MARITIME
MUSEUM AND
SHIPYARD

Bath

Sebago
Lake

Casco Bay

To
Yarmouth, N.S.

Glens
Falls

GREEN
MOUNTAIN
NATIONAL
FOREST

Connecticut River

Concord

Portland

Cape
Elizabeth

TWO LIGHTS
STATE PARK

Kennebunk

Kennebunkport

Ogunquit

RACHEL CARSON
NATIONAL WILDLIFE
REFUGE

Schenectady

Keene

Portsmouth

Kittery

Seabrook

Smithtown

Hampton Beach

ATLANTIC OCEAN

Albany

VERMONT

NEW HAMPSHIRE

MASSACHUSETTS

Brattleboro

CAPE ANN
HISTORICAL
ASSOCIATION

CAPE ANN

Gloucester

To
Binghamton

NEW YORK

Worcester

STATE
HOUSE

Salem

INDIAN MOTORCYCLE MUSEUM
On display is a unique collection of
motorcycles produced by this
famous company, as well as models and related memorabilia.

Springfield

Boston

Massachusetts Bay

USS CONSTITUTION

Provincetown

CONNECTICUT

Hartford

BEARDSLEY
PARK AND
ZOOLOGICAL
GARDENS

STAMFORD
MUSEUM
AND
NATURE
CENTER

RHODE
ISLAND

West
Kingston

Providence

Mansfield
Plymouth

Cape
Cod
Bay

CAPE
COD

FISHERIES AQUARIUM
Sixteen exhibition tanks
display more than 30
different species of fish,
many of which are col-
lected in local waters, as
well as clams, mussels,
anemones, and crabs.

NEW YORK
NEW JERSEY

New
Haven

Hope
Valley

New London

Newport

THE
BREAKERS

Woods Hole

NANTUCKET
ISLAND

BARNUM
MUSEUM

Bridgeport

Groton

Great
Swamp

Narragansett
Bay

MARTHA'S
VINEYARD

George
Washington
Bridge

Stamford

Long Island Sound

Newark

New York

LONG
ISLAND

0   20   40   60   80 miles

visitors see colonial barns and fencing, various farm animals, herb and organic gardens, a farmer's tool exhibit, and a country store. Seasonal events include Winterfest in January, maple sugaring in March, spring on the farm—complete with sheep shearing, weaving, and gardening—in May, and Harvest Day in September. A Tudor mansion contains five galleries with changing exhibitions that include Americana, natural history, and fine art, as well as a permanent exhibit on Native American culture.

A CIRCUS COMES TO TOWN

Bridgeport is Connecticut's largest city, located approximately 20 miles up the coast from Stamford. Founded in 1639 as Newfield, the town was renamed when it became the site of the first drawbridge across the Pequonnock River. Legendary 19th-century showman and impresario P. T. Barnum lived here and made Bridgeport the headquarters for the Greatest Show on Earth. He was at one time the mayor of the town and built several homes, including an exotic mansion named Iranistan, modeled after the Royal Pavilion in Brighton, England. The house features unusual innovations such as a magnetic alarm system. Bridgeport was also the birthplace of the man who later became one of Barnum's most lucrative attractions: the three-foot-tall Tom Thumb.

The Barnum Museum is housed in a whimsical three-story building that dates back to 1893. Its red sandstone blocks, columns, towers, domes, and terra-cotta friezes are an exotic and eclectic stew of Romanesque, Byzantine, and Gothic architecture. The exhibit halls house a collection of Barnum memorabilia; a scale model of a three-ring circus with 4,000 hand-carved wooden performers and animals; a 2,500-year-old Egyptian mummy; and Tom Thumb's tiny brown velvet suit. Baby Bridgeport, a six-foot, eight-inch elephant that weighed 700 pounds, was born in Bridgeport and was the smallest performing circus elephant. The pachyderm now graces the museum's main lobby. Both P. T. Barnum and Tom Thumb are buried in Bridgeport's Mountain Grove Cemetery.

Bridgeport is also the site of 30-acre Beardsley Park and Zoological Gardens—Connecticut's only zoo—which is home to more than 350 species of animals. The park boasts an indoor rain forest, a children's zoo, and shady picnic gardens. The Discovery Museum, located nearby, is also well worth a visit. More than 100 hands-on exhibits allow children of all ages to explore the fascinating world of science. In addition, the museum houses an art gallery, a planetarium, and a display devoted to the space shuttle *Challenger*.

New London, once a busy whaling port with a deepwater harbor, now draws visitors eager to savor the region's maritime flavor. Whale Oil Row, visible from the highway, is composed of four identical Greek Revival houses said to have been built by a sea captain for his four daughters. Across the Thames River is the combined submarine yard and shipyard at Groton, where the world's first diesel and nuclear submarines were built.

After leaving the Connecticut coast, I-95 veers northeastward, passing the site of one of the nation's bloodiest Indian battles, which pitted British settlers against the Narragansett Indians at Rhode Island's Great Swamp in 1675. A monument to the dead stands near West Kingston. The highway also bisects Providence, the state's first settlement, which was given the name Providence Plantations. Founded in 1636 by the liberal religious leader Roger Williams, who was ousted from the Massachusetts Bay Colony in part for his sympathy for the Narragansetts, the fledgling community at the head of Narragansett Bay had a fine harbor. The town prospered as a shipping center until the 19th century, when railroads became the vital lifeline of commerce.

Rhode Island enjoys the distinction of being the smallest of the 50 states. Like most of New England, it has a deeply pocked shoreline, whose sandy beaches and fresh ocean breezes attract boaters and bathers alike. Situated at the mouth of Narragansett Bay, Newport is a major yachting center whose protected harbor is dotted with sailboats during

GILDED COTTAGE
The ocean facade of The Breakers, below, displays the scale and sumptuousness of Newport's famous summer homes.

Moored in Boston's Charlestown Navy Yard, the frigate USS Constitution, left, is the oldest fully commissioned warship in the world. Old Ironsides, as it is fondly called, is maintained in mint period condition, right down to its ropes, above.

the summer months. The town uses the pineapple as a symbol of welcome to visitors. This tradition began when sea captains of old displayed the exotic fruit outside their homes to indicate a safe return from a long sea voyage.

Before the turn of the century, a number of railroad, mining, and business magnates constructed vacation homes in Newport as ostentatious displays of their wealth. These magnificent estates contain a treasure trove of artworks and furnishings, lavish ballrooms, and fanciful topiary gardens. Visitors can view both the mansions' exteriors and grounds from the three-mile Cliff Walk, which meanders along the coast. Six of the mansions are open to the public, including Cornelius Vanderbilt's The Breakers, designed in the style of the Renaissance palaces of 16th-century Turin and Genoa. A self-made millionaire, Vanderbilt began his career in the early 1800's operating a ferry service between Manhattan and Staten Island, and later turned to shipping and railroads. When Vanderbilt died in 1877, he had accumulated a fortune of more than $100 million. Vanderbilt's summer "cottage" in Newport was designed by architect

MINIATURE TREASURE
The Maine Maritime Museum in Bath showcases the state's enduring ties with the sea. The finely crafted miniature ship model, above, is among a collection that is on display. Other exhibits include full-scale traditional wooden boats.

Richard Morris Hunt. The house contains 70 rooms—33 of which were set aside for the resident staff and the maids and valets of visiting guests—that include a mosaic-tiled loggia, stables, greenhouses, and a colorful parterre garden. The magnificent Great Hall is dominated by a Flemish tapestry, completed in 1619 and lit by a 33-foot-long stained-glass skylight.

BOSTON'S TREASURES If Newport is a testament to those who became wealthy during the industrial revolution, the echoes of a different revolution resonate throughout downtown Boston and its harbor. The city's buildings and monuments recall the landmark events of the American Revolution: the Boston Massacre, the Boston Tea Party, the first musket shots fired between British and American troops at nearby Lexington and Concord, and Paul Revere's historic midnight ride. Reminders of the city's past include the golden dome of the Old State House, Boston Common, and Faneuil Hall—the Birthplace of Freedom. Sightseers can catch a glimpse of some of the tea that was thrown into the harbor at the Boston Tea Party at the Old South Meetinghouse and visit Charlestown Navy Yard, berth of the USS *Constitution,* familiarly known as Old Ironsides.

The U.S. Navy's oldest commissioned warship earned its moniker by virtue of its seemingly impervious wooden hull that withstood tremendous volleys from enemy cannons. It's easy to envision this magnificent vessel, with its soaring masts, complex rigging, and fluttering flags, circumnavigating the globe and trouncing the British navy and Barbary pirates. Indeed, she never lost a battle. The timber used in the ship's construction came from as far south as South Carolina, and her masts were originally felled in the woods of Maine.

The Charlestown Navy Yard, one of the country's oldest dry docks, is a National Historic Site. It was here that the USS *Constitution* was renovated, first in 1833 and then again a century later. The USS *Constitution* Museum, located just a few yards from the ship, provides visitors with details of the frigate's past and a computer simulation that allows would-be mariners to captain the ship. Centuries-old naval documents and detailed model ships are also on display. During the summer, costumed scrimshanders, coopers, and nautical knot-tiers demonstrate their maritime crafts.

From the Boston area, I-95 continues past the historic North Shore towns of Salem and Marblehead, heading toward Gloucester on Cape Ann at the tip of Massachusetts Bay. The oldest fishing port in the state, the town has had remarkable and sustained success as a fishing port. Even

though boats have harvested these waters for more than 350 years, Gloucester's offshore banks are still fertile enough to attract whales and dolphins. From early spring to late fall, whale-watching expeditions leave from the downtown wharves. Broad-beamed lobster boats continue to haul in respectable catches, as they have for generations. At the entrance to the town stands one of the East Coast's most enduring maritime symbols: a 70-year-old bronze sculpture of a New England fisherman titled *Man at the Wheel.*

The best place to begin exploring Gloucester's seafaring past is at the museum of the Cape Ann Historical Association, located at the junction of Pleasant and Federal streets. The museum houses memorabilia, artifacts, historic photographs, and intricate ship models. Many of the town's quaint streets are flanked with buildings that have been standing since the 1700's. Gravel trails along the bluffs provide sightseers and artists alike with views of the harbor, which French explorer Samuel de Champlain admired so much that he dubbed it Beauport, or "beautiful port." St. Peter's Park hosts the annual St. Peter's Fiesta in honor of the patron saint of fishermen. Down at the docks, visitors can tour an original 121-foot-long fishing schooner called the *Adventure,* which has been designated as a national historic landmark.

HOMEWARD BOUND
Surrounded by a flock of gulls,
fishing boats, left, cut through the
water toward Gloucester Harbor.
Founded in the 1620's, Gloucester
has always relied on the sea
for its livelihood.

STATELY ABODE
The Isaac Farrar Mansion, below,
was built in 1833 by a wealthy
merchant and banker as a wedding
gift to his wife. The interior con-
tains elaborate wainscoting and
carvings made of solid mahogany
that came from Santo Domingo
in the Caribbean.

After leaving Cape Ann, the route crosses the Merrimack River to briefly enter New Hampshire. The state has 18 miles of coastline composed of sandy beaches that are a geographic gift left by retreating glaciers. Fully half the New Hampshire coastline is public land, and summer weekends find visitors flocking to spots such as Hampton Beach and Seabrook.

MARITIME MAINE When I-95 enters the state of Maine, a succession of exits leads visitors to resort towns such as Kittery, Ogunquit, and Kennebunkport. Farther up the coast lies Portland, a medium-size city with small-town charm. The city was rebuilt several times over the years, after being razed by the Indians, French, and English. Portland's busy port sends out dozens of fishing boats daily, and brightly colored lobster buoys bob in its offshore waters. Ferries convey visitors and residents to several Casco Bay islands, passing rocky outcrops that house the ruins of both Revolutionary and Civil War forts. Portland was also the boyhood home of poet and lighthouse lover Henry Wadsworth Longfellow.

Maine's rockbound shores were perilous for mariners, and more than five dozen lighthouses were erected to warn ships of dangerous headlands, ragged shoals, and hidden coves. Portland Head Lighthouse, commissioned by George Washington, is a familiar sight to visitors, who have seen it on postage stamps and in picture books. The lighthouse was originally illuminated on January 10, 1791, by its first keeper, Capt. Joseph Greenleaf, who was appointed by President Washington. Two other lighthouses of note are located within Two Lights State Park in the Portland suburb of Cape Elizabeth. Completed in 1828, the twin beacons were once run by Marcus Hanna, a Civil War hero and Congressional Medal of Honor recipient. Although one of these wonderful lighthouses is no longer functional, the other still sends out the coast's most powerful beacon.

Bath is a major shipbuilding center that has launched thousands of seafaring vessels in the past two centuries. The town is an appropriate home for the Maine Maritime Museum, fetchingly situated on a gently rising slope on the banks of the Kennebec River. In several exhibition buildings and in the adjacent Percy & Small Shipyard, the museum presents a look at Maine's seafaring past. Visitors are even offered the opportunity to take a scenic cruise, complete with a narrated history, during the warmer months.

One of Maine's two great rivers, Kennebec tumbles from Moosehead Lake at a speed white-water rafters find exhilarating. Farther upriver is the state capital of Augusta. Here the Maine State Museum presents an illuminating overview of the state's natural, industrial, and social history, including one exhibit that highlights the state's major industries: lumber, fishing, shipbuilding, and granite quarrying. A 40-foot section of the square-rigged

Downeaster *St. Mary* stands as a vivid reminder of Maine's maritime past. Other displays, including arrowheads, ancient tools, baskets, and beadwork of the state's Native Americans, trace 12,000 years of Maine's history and prehistory.

Traveling upstate, I-95 heads for the Penobscot River—Maine's other notable waterway—and leads to Bangor. Gateway to the deep forests of northern Maine, the town has a rough and rugged legacy of lumberjacks and woodsmen. American essayist and poet Henry David Thoreau called Bangor "a shining light on the edge of the wilderness." Until the 1870's, Bangor was the lumber capital of the world, and many industries sprang up here to serve the lumber trade. Foundries were built to make stoves for the lumber camps and the machinery to run the sawmills, and ships were built to transport lumber to distant ports. Today Bangor's seven historic districts showcase the elegant architectural heritage of the city, including the many mansions that were constructed by the prosperous local lumber barons.

Several walking tours of the city have been mapped out by the Bangor Historical Society. Housed in a Greek Revival building constructed between 1834 and 1836, the Historical Society Museum was once the home of businessman and lawyer Thomas A. Hill. Designed by renowned English architect Richard Upjohn, the graceful house has a three-sided portico complete with Ionic columns and is listed on the National Register of Historic Places. The downstairs has been completely restored and contains a grand double parlor furnished with Victorian period pieces, Corinthian columns, an arabesque frieze, gilded

BEAR COUNTRY
Black bears, above, inhabit the wilderness of northern Maine. Blueberries, which thrive on the barrens, attract black bears to the area.

mirrors, and ornate chandeliers. The second floor is used for exhibits of paintings, household utensils, and 19th-century memorabilia.

EDGE OF THE WILDERNESS

Spreading out north of Bangor, Maine's wild interior encompasses the Allagash Wilderness Waterway—one of the country's great wilderness rivers in a protected area populated mainly by moose, bears, and an occasional park ranger or skilled canoeist. The 92-mile-long waterway lies amid 8 million acres of pine, spruce, and fir trees that are now the private property of lumber companies and are accessible only by private roads. At its southern end is Baxter State Park, home of mile-high Mount Katahdin. The park's 314 square miles of forest-draped mountains, lakes,

and streams were donated to the state by former governor Percival C. Baxter. The lifeline of Maine's modern lumber industry, Shin Pond Road brings visitors to the Lumberman's Museum in Patten. Here the clock is turned back 160 years to the time when thousands of woodsmen used oxen to haul their booty of freshly cut pine and spruce trees along this rough road from the upper valley of the East Branch of the Penobscot River. Housed in nine buildings, the museum displays an extensive collection of tools and equipment that the 19th-century lumbermen used in their day-to-day work. One building is fittingly constructed of 200-year-old rough-hewn logs. Open sheds house the sleds, tractors, and trucks used to haul the logs. A blacksmith's shop displays the tools used by farriers, wheelwrights, and blacksmiths. Another building contains a portable sawmill, a shingle-making machine, and authentic tools used to shape shingles by hand. Also on display are models and dioramas of an 1820 Maine logging camp, as well as photographs and paintings that evoke the rugged and colorful lives of the lumbermen.

The formal establishment of a border with Canada was delayed until 1842, following 60 years of competing land claims and what one senator termed "a solemn bamboozlement." Today I-95 crosses the border into New Brunswick. In the words of writer Erskine Caldwell, "A man never knows what's going to happen next in the State of Maine," and visitors may indeed be surprised to come across a Potato Feast in 200-year-old Houlton—the last American town that the Interstate passes before it leaves the country for good.

DOMED SPLENDOR
The Maine State House, below, with its impressive 200-foot-high dome, is a landmark building in Augusta. The dome is topped with a gold-covered statue titled Wisdom. *A Greek Revival portico frames the entrance to the building. The city has served as the state capital since 1831.*

Appalachian Adventure

In a span of less than 500 miles, a colorful kaleidoscope of the American past unfolds.

There is a scenic majesty about the mountainous road that sweeps northeasterly up the tumbled valleys of eastern Tennessee and southwestern Virginia into the fabled Shenandoah Valley, then rolls through the Alleghenies into fertile Pennsylvania. The mountains never really disappear. Sometimes they loom so close as to tower above the roadside, only to retreat into blue haze, tracing a dark brooding mass beyond a vista of rolling fields and small, historic towns. Along this highway, through the nation's premier cave country, beauty may be found even under the ground. But for a visitor with any sense of American history, the irresistible allure of this stretch of Interstate 81 may be its reminders of adventure and struggle, of settler and Shawnee, of Stonewall Jackson and Philip Sheridan.

Some of the most compelling sites are world famous, such as Gettysburg; others are relatively little known. Among them is a town tucked into the northeastern corner of Tennessee where Andrew Jackson began his legal career and

OLD AND NEW
Along Main Street in Jonesborough, above, stand buildings erected more than a century ago. The nation's first anti-slavery periodicals were published here.

CASCADING CATARACT
Overleaf: Stately hemlock trees rise above the tumbling twin streams of Lewis Spring Falls in Shenandoah National Park. Some 2,000 people were moved from their cabins and relocated outside the park's boundaries before it opened in 1935.

fought his first duel, and where frontiersmen organized a fledgling state that quickly became a fiasco. Founded in 1779, Jonesborough is Tennessee's oldest town. Its rich historic district, enhanced by a successful restoration movement that got under way in 1969, landed the downtown area a place on the National Register of Historic Places. The Jonesborough History Museum, located in the town's visitor center, covers the high points and directs attention to such landmarks as the Chester Inn of 1797, the town's oldest public frame structure, and the Christopher Taylor Log House, where Andrew Jackson once boarded. The birth and death of the state of Franklin, a pre-Tennessee creation that lasted four years, are duly related.

The old frontier seems ever present in this region, where mountain passes led colonial Virginians into what is now Tennessee and Kentucky. The 690,000-acre Jefferson National Forest reminds visitors of the original timberland that greeted the pioneers. In this sprawling wilderness lies the 119,000-acre Mount Rogers National Recreation Area—a bean-shaped tract that parallels I-81 south of Marion and Wytheville. The area offers a variety of outdoor activities including horseback riding, camping, hiking, cross-country skiing, trout fishing, and trail biking. The topographical star is Mount Rogers, the tallest mountain in Virginia at 5,729 feet. Natural history buffs flock here for the rich inventory of plants and wildlife. Birders can spot more than 100 types of songbirds, and anglers can catch trout in the New River.

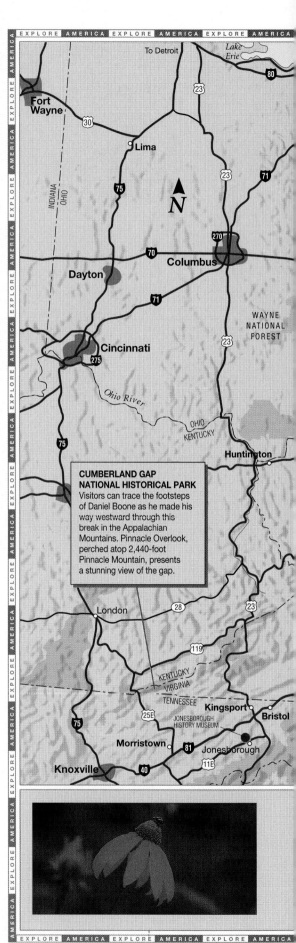

**CUMBERLAND GAP
NATIONAL HISTORICAL PARK**
Visitors can trace the footsteps of Daniel Boone as he made his way westward through this break in the Appalachian Mountains. Pinnacle Overlook, perched atop 2,440-foot Pinnacle Mountain, presents a stunning view of the gap.

20

APPALACHIAN ADVENTURE

STATE MUSEUM OF PENNSYLVANIA
An extensive collection of pewter, ironwork, and needlework, as well as one of the world's largest framed paintings, depicts the state's colorful history.

NATIONAL RADIO ASTRONOMY OBSERVATORY
State-of-the-art equipment, including a huge radio telescope, scans the universe in search of new particles. Public tours are given.

BOOKER T. WASHINGTON NATIONAL MONUMENT
The national monument contains a replica of the cabin where Washington was born. A museum traces his rise from slave to influential man of letters and displays his handwritten speeches.

SIPPING NECTAR
A ladybug enjoys the soft bedding of a green-headed coneflower, left, in Virginia's Mount Rogers National Recreation Area. Here visitors can hike along the Virginia Creeper Trail, which began as a Native American footpath and was later used by Daniel Boone.

INFORMATION FOR VISITORS

State information centers on I-81 are located in Bristol, TN; at the Tennessee–Virginia border; in Harpers Ferry and Charleston, WV; and a half-mile north of Newville, PA. For more information: Tennessee Dept. of Tourist Development, P.O. Box 23170, Nashville, TN 37202-3170; 615-741-2258.

Pennsylvania Dept. of Commerce, Office of Travel and Tourism, Forum Bldg., Room 453, Harrisburg, PA 17120; 800-VISITPA. Virginia Division of Tourism, 901 East Byrd St., 19th Floor, Richmond, VA 23219; 804-786-2051.

AMERICA EXPLORE AMERICA EXPLORE AMERICA EXPLORE AMERICA EXPLORE AMERICA EXPLORE AMERICA EXPLORE AMERICA EXPLORE AMERICA EXPLORE AMERICA EXPLORE

APPALACHIAN ADVENTURE 21

Roanoke, southwestern Virginia's major urban center, has managed to preserve the flavor of a small town. The downtown area hums with activity, much of it generated by the historic market area, with its numerous food stalls, shops, and restaurants. In the heart of the market, among clusters of renovated commercial buildings, stands Center in the Square, a major cultural complex that houses the Science Museum of Western Virginia, the Arts Council of the Blue Ridge, the Roanoke Valley History Museum, and the Mill Mountain Theatre.

Among the city's other attractions are the Mill Mountain Zoo and the Virginia Museum of Transportation. The zoo is a three-acre gathering of 45 species of animals, ranging from a Siberian tiger to prairie dogs, on top of a small mountain within the city limits. The Virginia Museum of Transportation houses a renowned collection of railroad locomotives, as well as vintage transportation equipment.

From the early days of the Conestoga wagon to construction of I-81, the main highway of the Shenandoah Valley—successively called the Indian Road, the Wagon Road, the Valley Pike, and finally U.S. Highway 11—rolled over one of the nation's premier geological wonders, the Natural Bridge. Located deep in a rocky vale, the span was carved from limestone by a determined stream. At 215 feet in height, it is an awe-inspiring spectacle, indescribably peaceful and soothing. High on one wall, a young surveyor named George Washington carved his initials.

Another natural landmark—House Mountain—looms over the western horizon to mark the town of Lexington. Here a wealth of historic architecture, much of it a distinctive form of Greek Revival, stems from Lexington's role as a center for the industrious Scotch-Irish who settled the valley during the 18th and 19th centuries. The campus of Washington and Lee University is a prime example. Adjoining it is the equally historic campus of the Virginia Military Institute, which features Gothic Revival architecture.

In the Victorian Lee Chapel on the Washington and Lee campus, a famous recumbent statue in white marble marks the last resting place of Gen.

Robert E. Lee. The Confederate commander is actually buried in the Lee family crypt, just below. A museum of family artifacts, as well as the office Lee used when he was postwar president of the college, are also on the lower level.

Gen. Thomas J. "Stonewall" Jackson taught at the Virginia Military Institute, and his home in Lexington is the only house that he ever owned. The brick town house is open to the public and contains some of Jackson's furniture and personal items. His grave is located in a cemetery on Main Street, beneath a notable statue. On display at the institute's museum are Jackson's relics, including his war horse, Little Sorrel. The campus is also home to the George C. Marshall Museum and Library, which traces the career of the great alumnus who served as U.S. Army chief of staff in World War II, and sponsored the postwar Marshall Plan for European Recovery, for which he received the Nobel Peace Prize in 1953. Military scholars and World War II buffs alike find the Marshall Library a superb resource.

Horse fanciers of all kinds flock to the Virginia Horse Center, a modern facility on 400 lush acres outside Lexington. Nearby is fabled Goshen Pass, where the rock-strewn Maury River tumbles down from the Alleghenies in a series of crystal pools.

The drive from Lexington to Staunton is one of the most beautiful along I-81. The mountains squeeze in, narrowing the Shenandoah Valley. This was the domain of rugged Scotch-Irish settlers. Sam Houston was born to one such family in the village of Fairfield. Near the town of Staunton is the tidy farm where Cyrus McCormick invented the mechanical reaper in 1831. His log shop, situated beside a gurgling stream, may be visited today.

HISTORIC CROSSROADS The town of Staunton (pronounced Stanton) lies at the junction of I-80 and I-64. Already 130 years old at the time of the Civil War, it was an important transportation center during the conflict. Unlike many Southern towns, it flourished in the postwar era. The result is a rich variety of architecture, both commercial and residential, that spans many styles. Walking tours of its five national historic districts

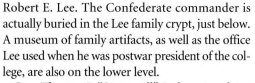

CURIOUS COLT
A wild foal, right, peers out at the world while staying close to its mother in the Mount Rogers National Recreation Area. More than 150 miles of trails let riding enthusiasts see the surrounding scenery on horseback.

PLACE OF WORSHIP
Built at the request of Gen. Robert E. Lee, the Lee Chapel on the campus of Washington and Lee University, opposite page, was completed in 1868. Lee attended daily services here with students until his death in 1870.

uncover numerous hidden treasures. There's an intriguing bank museum in one venerable, still-functioning financial institution, and country music's Statler Brothers have their own museum. In one stately Greek Revival town house, future president Woodrow Wilson was born in 1856. Today the "birthplace," as it is simply called by local people, provides an accurate representation of upper-middle-class life in 19th-century Virginia. Nearby, in another massive former residence of the 28th president, a museum recounts Wilson's career as lawyer, academic, and politician. One of the collection's most popular pieces is his elegant black Pierce-Arrow limousine.

Also in town is a major new outdoor museum, the Museum of American Frontier Culture. Three antique European farmsteads—one each from England, Ireland, and Germany—have been moved and erected on the rolling fields outside the town, along with a 19th-century log house and barns from Virginia. All four farms, complete with period furnishings, animals, crops, and costumed interpreters, depict rural lifestyles in Europe and America during the 17th, 18th, and 19th centuries. These predominant ethnic groups of the Virginia frontier merged to form a new American culture.

SKYLINE
DRIVE

To experience the Shenandoah Valley's geography in all its sprawling beauty, visitors should jump off I-81 and meander along the 105-mile-long Skyline Drive, the main route through Shenandoah National Park. The highway is the capstone of the Blue Ridge Parkway, which winds its way for 470 miles from the Great Smoky Mountains in North Carolina to Waynesboro, Virginia. Here it becomes the Skyline Drive. Besides the Waynesboro entrance, there are three other gateways: Swift Run Gap, Thornton Gap, and Front Royal.

Skyline Drive takes national park visitors to 75 breathtaking overlooks. More than 500 miles of hiking trails, including 105 miles of the Appalachian Trail, lead to jewel-like clifftops and waterfalls. Although the park encompasses an area of 300 square miles, it ranges from 1 to 13 miles in width. Naturalists have tallied 200 species of birds, 100 varieties of trees, more than 900 species of flowering plants, and a black bear population of about 300. Campers find both campgrounds and backcountry opportunities here, and sportsmen fish for trout in 30 different streams. Concession-operated lodges offer dining and pleasant overnight accommodations, often with spectacular views of the Shenandoah Valley.

HISTORIC BATTLE-GROUND

Stonewall Jackson first riveted the world's attention here. In 1862 the Confederate general outwitted Union forces in a series of lightning marches and attacks in the Shenandoah Valley. Several of these battle sites are virtually unchanged since the war. But the most famous battle occurred two years later, in 1864—one year after Jackson's death—at New Market. It was one of the South's last victories.

Today those who fought here are remembered at the fascinating New Market Battlefield Military Museum. It presents a dramatic and authoritative view of the battle, an excellent account of Jackson's valley campaign two years earlier, and an overview of the entire war in Virginia. The museum has the largest collection of original Civil War memorabilia on display in Virginia and is an essential stop for history buffs. After touring the exhibits, which also include artifacts from other U.S. military conflicts, visitors may wander through the battlefield. A walking path leads through both Union and Confederate troop position markers and provides views of the curving Shenandoah River below.

The Shenandoah is known for its scenic bends, carved through the limestone bedrock that underlies the great valley. Water has also done its share of underground carving throughout the entire region. Traveling along the highway, motorists can spy telltale sinkholes in adjoining fields, indicating caves down below. A few are so beautiful that they have been developed as public attractions.

Luray Caverns has been one of the world's most famous grottoes since its discovery in 1878. There seems something almost miraculous about this king of caves, with the brilliant sparkling colors of its formations, odd stone shapes, underground chambers that plunge up to 164 feet below the surface, massive chambers laden with ancient stone formations, and glass-clear pools.

Skilled human hands have successfully gilded the underground lily through the addition of a unique musical instrument called the Stalacpipe Organ. Stalactites at the bottom of the cave system were tuned by grinding them to precise musical pitch. Electronically controlled plungers strike the rocks on command from a big organ keyboard.

Traveling north again toward Winchester, visitors are reminded of the Shenandoah Valley's grim

year of 1864, when Gen. Philip Sheridan's Union cavalry made a smoking wasteland of what had been the Breadbasket of the Confederacy. Near the bustling village of Middletown, the handsome stone plantation house Belle Grove was the center of a furious battle that was the culmination of Sheridan's Ride—a dramatic 10-mile dash down the Valley Pike from Winchester to rally his troops to win the crucial Battle of Cedar Creek.

Winchester changed hands more than 70 times during the war, including 13 times in a single day. Here the gabled Gothic house where Stonewall Jackson was headquartered in the winter of

PRESIDENTIAL BIRTHPLACE
The handsome Woodrow Wilson Birthplace and Museum, above, houses a variety of rare artifacts and photographs that offer an intimate look at the man who led the nation during World War I.

1861–62 seems to wait for his return. Artifacts on display include Jackson's camp chest and a battle flag of the ferocious Stonewall Brigade. When the war began, the house was lent to Jackson by its owner, a Confederate colonel named Lewis T. Moore—the great-grandfather of actress Mary Tyler Moore. She contributed gilded wallpaper for

A few miles north of Winchester, I-81 leaves Virginia and enters the easternmost tip of West Virginia's panhandle. Here the landscape is rich and rolling, with low mountains on the horizon. The region's most compelling natural feature is the sweeping confluence of the Shenandoah and Potomac rivers at Harpers Ferry.

CELEBRITY'S OFFICE

Situated on a spectacular rocky point, with a view that Thomas Jefferson declared worth crossing the Atlantic to see, Harpers Ferry seems, at first glance, a somnolent old village lifted right from a 19th-century engraving. But that is a somewhat superficial impression. The town preserves the memory of a complex, turbulent, and tragic past. An abundance of waterpower led to the construction of the town's first mill by the

the house's renovation and also served as grand marshall of the Shenandoah Apple Blossom Festival. The town is surrounded by apple orchards, which burst into blossom in the spring.

A TRAGIC PAST

Winchester also has strong ties to George Washington, who as a young man served as the representative for the region in Virginia's pre-Revolutionary House of Burgesses. The log-and-stone building he used as an office in 1755–56, while supervising construction of frontier fortifications against the French and Indians, now houses a small museum. The oldest house in Winchester is a stone structure called Abram's Delight, built in 1754. Now a museum, the house features period artifacts.

JACK FROST'S ARRIVAL
Following a brilliant display of reds, yellows, and oranges in the fall, Thornton Gap in Shenandoah National Park is blanketed by the wintery white of a gentle snowfall, right. Cross-country skiers use the park's many fire roads to tour this beautiful region.

1740's. As the industrial revolution advanced into the 1790's, a United States armory and arsenal was established at the suggestion of President Washington. The U.S. Armory would be the economic driving force at Harpers Ferry for more than 60 years. On the eve of the Civil War, its complex of 20 brick structures formed a 600-foot-long double row along the waterfront, employed 600 men, and turned out more than 10,000 weapons a year.

In 1859 the firebrand abolitionist John Brown made his famous abortive raid, hoping to seize enough weapons to arm a slave insurrection. His attempt failed, but Brown had dramatically underscored the slavery dilemma. Less than two years later the Civil War began, and it raged through Harpers Ferry like an angel of destruction. Caught in the wave of devastation, the armory was obliterated and never rebuilt. As decades passed,

SITTING ON TOP OF THE WORLD
A red-breasted nuthatch, left, surveys the landscape of Mount Rogers. Fearless around humans, these comical forest dwellers are fond of recycling abandoned woodpecker nests to use as their own.

PANORAMIC PERCH
Maryland Heights, above, offers a spectacular view of Harpers Ferry. Among the notable people who left their mark on this town are George Washington, Thomas Jefferson, Abraham Lincoln, George Custer, Robert E. Lee, Stonewall Jackson, and Frederick Douglass.

STEPPING BACK IN TIME
Interpreters in period clothing promenade through the picturesque streets of Harpers Ferry, right. Living-history programs take place here throughout the year.

Harpers Ferry became a virtual ghost town. Storer College, an institute of higher learning for African-Americans, contributed a degree of vitality before it closed its doors forever in 1955.

Gradually the National Park Service began to restore and revive Harpers Ferry. Today the town's history is revealed through ranger-conducted programs, interpretive demonstrations, and museum displays. The town also contains an astonishing number of original buildings. John Brown's Fort, which was the armory's firehouse, remains much as it was at the time of the famous raid. Other residences and commercial buildings have been restored and display period furnishings and artifacts of this turbulent era.

After seeing the town, many visitors walk along the area's footpaths to enjoy the dramatic river views and explore evocative ruins that range from Civil War forts and encampments to the remnants of a once-thriving 19th-century industrial town. The view from Jefferson's Rock, above the lower town, is a favorite with travelers.

Harpers Ferry remains a part of the Old South, although it is located close to its northern edge. A short drive northward brings visitors to the rich hilly domain of southern Pennsylvania. This was the route followed by the troops of Lee's Army of Northern Virginia during the summer of 1863. Fresh from rousing victories on the battlefields of Virginia, Lee thought the time was right to take the war out of the South and score a victory in the North. Yet Lee's daring foray into Pennsylvania, inaugurated with such confidence, turned into a massive Southern setback following three days of pitched battle in early July.

The two great armies accidentally blundered into each other on July 1, 1863, at the little town of Gettysburg. Undeterred by the superior numbers of his adversary, Lee hurled his 75,000-man army at the 95,000 troops commanded by Maj. Gen. George Meade. For the first two days the battle raged on inconclusively. But on the third day, apparently convinced of the invincibility of his army, Lee approved the massive frontal assault that would be known as Pickett's Charge. It was a

DOORWAY TO ETERNITY
The peace and tranquillity of the Mount Hebron Cemetery, left, in Winchester belies the city's battle-scarred past. Among the warriors buried in the cemetery is Daniel Morgan, a legendary rifleman and hero of the Revolutionary War.

LINE OF BATTLE
Modern-day Confederate soldiers, left, prepare to confront their Union counterparts in the Battle of Gettysburg. The reenactment of this pivotal Civil War clash, held just outside the Gettysburg National Military Park in July, attracts thousands of participants and spectators.

disastrous failure for Lee. The casualties of the bloodiest battle ever fought on American soil may have totaled more than 50,000.

In acknowledgment of the importance of the engagement, commemorative efforts began almost immediately. Only four months after the battle, Abraham Lincoln arrived to make his famous address. In 1863 the Gettysburg Battlefield Memorial Association was formed. It was the precursor to the establishment in 1895 of Gettysburg National Military Park, a tract of land that today totals more than 5,000 acres. Throughout the years, some 1,300 monuments and memorial plaques have been erected to honor the units and brave individuals who fought here.

The visitor center offers a general orientation and lectures, as well as a collection of battlefield relics. The Cyclorama Center houses a famous circular mural painting depicting Pickett's Charge. Miles of roads, bicycle paths, and footpaths traverse the great battlefield, beckoning visitors to linger and contemplate this hallowed ground.

A different way of measuring the past is found at the Watch and Clock Museum in Columbia. This 200-year-old town on the east bank of the broad Susquehanna River is a fitting place for an institution dedicated to the history of timekeeping. Exhibits feature more than 8,000 objects from four centuries of horology—a timely ending to this journey through history.

THE OLD SOUTH

Historic towns, eclectic museums, and breathtaking scenery are all just a short drive off I-20.

The land invokes a host of images of lavish antebellum homes and gracious living and memories of battles won and lost. But a journey from Florence, South Carolina, to Meridian, Mississippi, along Interstate 20 offers glimpses of something new in the South as well. Here fields of cotton are returning after years of absence, and cities such as Atlanta and Birmingham are flourishing, bolstered by new industries and an influx of migrants from colder climes.

Throughout much of the South, preserving Revolutionary War sites has taken a back seat to commemorating the battlefields and shrines of the Civil War. Yet much of the Revolution was fought here, especially in South Carolina, where more than 100 known battle sites are documented. Occupied by the British for almost a year, the lovely town of Camden was the site of not one but two battles—both of them victories for the British. The second proved hollow, however, because the Redcoats suffered such heavy losses that they had to abandon the town.

GATEWAY TO THE PAST
Among the 60 historic structures that comprise Camden's historic district is the gracious porticoed mansion, above.

REGENCY BELLE
Overleaf: Although considered one of the nation's most elegant homes, Gaineswood was originally a plain log house. The transformation to a Greek Revival villa was achieved gradually over the course of almost 20 years by Gen. Nathan Bryan Whitfield, who owned the house in the mid-1800's.

That year of occupation left its marks. The paint was still drying on Joseph Kershaw's Georgian Colonial mansion when British commander Lord Cornwallis commandeered the home as his headquarters in 1780. British troops heavily fortified the town, surrounding it with a stockade wall and building six small forts around the perimeter. Now rebuilt on its original brick foundation, the Kershaw-Cornwallis House is open for public tours and is the centerpiece of a 98-acre park known as the Historic Camden Revolutionary War Site. (The colonial village should not be confused with the Revolutionary War battle sites, which are a short drive away.) Five buildings dating to the late 1700's and early 1800's have been moved here to form the small village.

What makes Historic Camden such a remarkable place is that the original town site has remained undeveloped for more than 200 years. The land was farmed, making it possible today to locate original fortifications and house foundations. A 1781 map of Camden survives, and historians and archeologists are using this and other documents to slowly reconstruct key sites. Interpretation of the site is kept simple. Guided tours, a video, and artifact displays are available. For visitors who wish to investigate on their own, brochures with maps are posted outside the office door.

The South has long been horse country. At the turn of the century a noted New York horse-

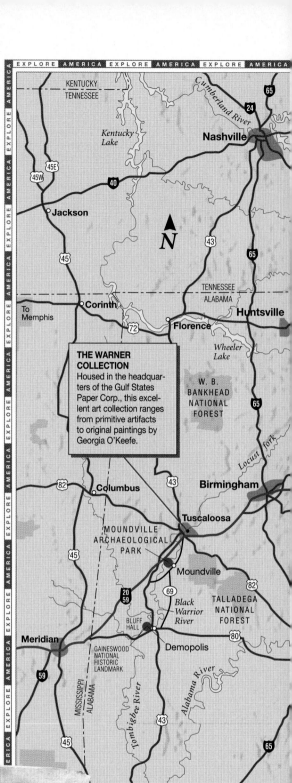

THE WARNER COLLECTION
Housed in the headquarters of the Gulf States Paper Corp., this excellent art collection ranges from primitive artifacts to original paintings by Georgia O'Keefe.

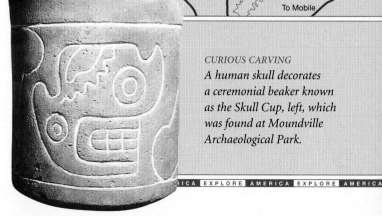

CURIOUS CARVING
A human skull decorates a ceremonial beaker known as the Skull Cup, left, which was found at Moundville Archaeological Park.

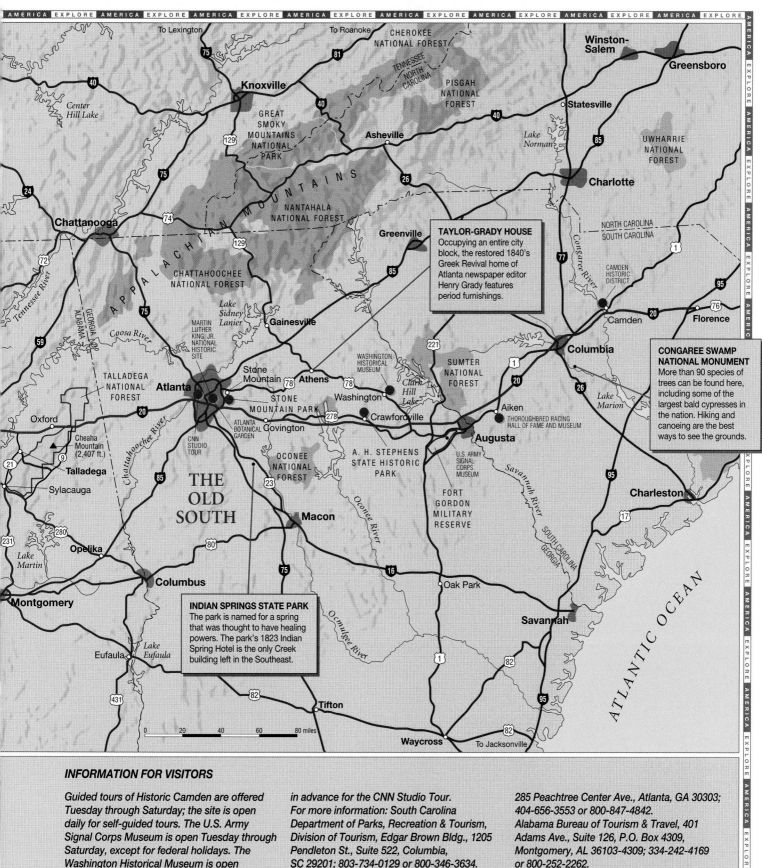

To Lexington

To Roanoke

CHEROKEE
NATIONAL FOREST

Winston-
Salem

Greensboro

Knoxville

TENNESSEE
NORTH
CAROLINA

PISGAH
NATIONAL
FOREST

Statesville

Center
Hill Lake

GREAT
SMOKY
MOUNTAINS
NATIONAL
PARK

Lake
Norman

UWHARRIE
NATIONAL
FOREST

Asheville

Charlotte

NANTAHALA
NATIONAL FOREST

Chattanooga

TAYLOR-GRADY HOUSE
Occupying an entire city
block, the restored 1840's
Greek Revival home of
Atlanta newspaper editor
Henry Grady features
period furnishings.

NORTH CAROLINA
SOUTH CAROLINA

Greenville

CHATTAHOOCHEE
NATIONAL
FOREST

Tennessee River

Coosa River

Lake
Sidney
Lanier

Gainesville

MARTIN
LUTHER
KING, JR.
NATIONAL
HISTORIC
SITE

Camden
Historic
District

Camden

Florence

Columbia

TALLADEGA
NATIONAL
FOREST

Stone
Mountain

Athens

WASHINGTON
HISTORICAL
MUSEUM

SUMTER
NATIONAL
FOREST

Atlanta

STONE
MOUNTAIN PARK

Washington

Clark
Hill
Lake

Lake
Marion

**CONGAREE SWAMP
NATIONAL MONUMENT**
More than 90 species of
trees can be found here,
including some of the
largest bald cypresses in
the nation. Hiking and
canoeing are the best
ways to see the grounds.

Oxford

ATLANTA
BOTANICAL
GARDEN

Covington

Crawfordville

Aiken

THOROUGHBRED RACING
HALL OF FAME AND MUSEUM

Cheaha
Mountain
(2,407 ft.)

CNN
STUDIO
TOUR

OCONEE
NATIONAL
FOREST

Augusta

U.S. ARMY
SIGNAL
CORPS
MUSEUM

Charleston

Talladega

THE
OLD
SOUTH

A. H. STEPHENS
STATE HISTORIC
PARK

Sylacauga

Oconee River

FORT
GORDON
MILITARY
RESERVE

Savannah River

SOUTH CAROLINA
GEORGIA

Chattahoochee River

Macon

Opelika

Lake
Martin

Columbus

INDIAN SPRINGS STATE PARK
The park is named for a spring
that was thought to have healing
powers. The park's 1823 Indian
Spring Hotel is the only Creek
building left in the Southeast.

Oak Park

ATLANTIC OCEAN

Montgomery

Ocmulgee River

Savannah

Eufaula

Lake
Eufaula

To Jacksonville

Tifton

0   20   40   60   80 miles

Waycross

INFORMATION FOR VISITORS

Guided tours of Historic Camden are offered
Tuesday through Saturday; the site is open
daily for self-guided tours. The U.S. Army
Signal Corps Museum is open Tuesday through
Saturday, except for federal holidays. The
Washington Historical Museum is open
Tuesday through Sunday. Stone Mountain Park
is open daily. Visitors are advised to reserve

in advance for the CNN Studio Tour.
For more information: South Carolina
Department of Parks, Recreation & Tourism,
Division of Tourism, Edgar Brown Bldg., 1205
Pendleton St., Suite 522, Columbia,
SC 29201; 803-734-0129 or 800-346-3634.
Georgia Department of Industry, Trade &
Tourism, 10th Floor, Marquis Tower Two,

285 Peachtree Center Ave., Atlanta, GA 30303;
404-656-3553 or 800-847-4842.
Alabama Bureau of Tourism & Travel, 401
Adams Ave., Suite 126, P.O. Box 4309,
Montgomery, AL 36103-4309; 334-242-4169
or 800-252-2262.

VINTAGE VICTORIAN
One of Aiken's finest restored period homes displays intricate gingerbread trim, above. The house was built in 1888, when the town was starting to gain a reputation as a winter resort for wealthy Northerners.

A DAY AT THE RACES
The excitement of harness racing lives on in Aiken, below. From late fall to early spring, thoroughbred horses are trained here.

carriage house. Although it is generally closed in summer, the staff will open it by appointment.

A walking or driving tour of Aiken's historic district reveals palatial homes where the Duke of Windsor and presidents Eisenhower and Kennedy once visited. A numbered brass plaque near the street identifies each historic home.

woman, Mrs. Thomas Hitchcock, fell in love with Aiken, a South Carolina town blessed with a mild climate. The Hitchcocks built a home here and brought their horses south for wintering and training. Their wealthy friends followed, bringing horses and architects, and transformed Aiken into a fashionable winter resort. Polo matches, steeplechases, drag hunts, and simple afternoon rides became a way of life. When other Southern towns were paving their roads for the first time, Aiken retained a maze of hoof-friendly unpaved streets that linked its magnificent estates to the polo fields, the training track, and Hitchcock Woods.

Throughout the years, 39 Aiken-trained horses went on to become American racing champions. Photographs and memorabilia of their victories are preserved at the Thoroughbred Racing Hall of Fame and Museum, housed in an old green-roofed

BATTLEFIELD COMMUNICATIONS

Augusta, the second-largest metropolitan area in Georgia, lies nestled among Southern pines along the banks of the Savannah River. The city hosts professional golf's famous Masters Tournament each year. Outside the city lies Fort Gordon, home of the U.S. Army Signal Corps. The corps' museum presents a fascinating look at battlefield communication, both past and present. With exhibits ranging from the red-and-white "wig-wag flags" developed shortly before the Civil War to sophisticated microwave equipment used in the Vietnam conflict and beyond, this is the most complete collection of communication devices in the nation.

The museum documents stories of individual heroism as it chronicles the development of modern communications. One of the corps' five Medal of Honor recipients earned his award for bravery in the Philippines in 1899. The museum also pays homage to the 325th Field Signal Battalion, the only African-American signal unit to serve in World War I. The unit fought in the trenches of St. Die and in the Argonne Forest, and at one point, overpowered a German machine gun position. Special note is made of the Comanche, Choctaw, and Sioux Indians who enlisted during World War II as "code talkers" and completely baffled German intelligence decoders by transmitting radio messages in their native languages.

The development of portable squad radios, or walkie-talkies, is also documented, along with ideas that turned out to be failures. An 18-ounce radio sent to South Vietnam, for instance, carried high expectations, but its batteries—strapped unprotected to the radio to minimize weight—were reduced to masses of dripping cardboard by the tropical heat and humidity.

Northeast of Augusta, the Old South is very much alive in Washington, Georgia, with leaf-shaded streets and beautifully preserved antebellum homes, the oldest of which dates from 1780. Built as a dwelling in 1835, the Washington Historical Museum is a comparative youngster in the town. This white-frame, two-story house is best known for its Civil War relics, collected for many years by the Last Cabinet Chapter of the United Daughters of the Confederacy. The museum reverently displays the camp chest used by Confederate president Jefferson Davis, who held his last cabinet meeting in Washington and was captured by Union forces six days later. Other highlights of the museum include an impressive collection of antique guns and a large, hand-crafted doll house, which is an authentic model of a real house located just a few blocks away. Native American artifacts are on display, as well as a chess set whose playing pieces are fashioned in the likenesses of Confederate and Union officers, and a Klu Klux Klan robe from the Reconstruction era. Furnishings typical of Georgia's fine homes of the mid-19th century decorate the double parlor and dining room on the main floor. Also on the ground level are a restored weaving room, kitchen, storage areas, and an early cotton gin. Another house-museum, former home of the Confederacy's secretary of state, Robert Toombs, is on the same street.

LIBERTY HALL

The Toombs home was separated by only 18 miles from that of his friend and compatriot, Alexander Stephens, vice president of the Confederacy and governor of Georgia. Each man set aside a guest room for the other. Today Stephens' Victorian mansion, appropriately named Liberty Hall, is the centerpiece of the 1,200-acre A. H. Stephens State Historic Park, the third-oldest such park in Georgia.

Located in Crawfordville, Liberty Hall is maintained as if Stephens, who died in 1883, were due to return any minute. Stephens' favorite card game—whist, a forerunner of bridge—is laid out

GRANITE SHRINE
Confederate heroes Jefferson Davis, Robert E. Lee, and Stonewall Jackson, above, tower over Georgia's Stone Mountain Park. Flame-jet torches were used to burn away the hard granite to create the immense sculpture. Begun in 1923, it was completed in 1972.

on a parlor table. So is the setting for a tea party. Some 50 bottles of Stephens' medicine, including one labeled strychnine, are arranged on a bedside table, several still containing their original preparations. Visitors are especially drawn to the Tramp's Room, a cheerful wallpapered chamber where Stephens welcomed anyone down on his luck. Robert Toombs' own room often accommodated visitors, but the guest would be asked to relocate if Toombs returned unexpectedly.

Sickly from childhood, Stephens' adult weight fluctuated between a mere 80 and 100 pounds. Nevertheless he managed to outlive seven of his siblings, was elected to 14 terms in Congress, served as second-in-command to Jefferson Davis, and died in office as governor of Georgia. A separate museum is also located in the park. Much of its collection was donated by the United Daughters of the Confederacy.

STONE MOUNTAIN Just outside Atlanta lies a massive granite dome that the Spanish explorer Juan Pardo considered his greatest discovery when he happened upon it in 1567. The lone mountain glistened in the sun, its base strewn with seemingly precious stones. Indians kept Pardo at bay, and apparently he never realized the gems were merely crystals from the world's largest exposed chunk of granite.

Formed by a surge of molten lava, Stone Mountain dominates the surrounding landscape of low red-clay hills. The mountain also dominates Georgia's tourism industry because it is now a full-fledged resort and the state's top tourist attraction. The mountain's north face boasts the largest carving in the world—a rendering of Confederate heroes Robert E. Lee, Stonewall Jackson, and Jefferson Davis. Larger than a football field, the relief is nevertheless dwarfed by the 825-foot tall mountain. It takes an aerial tram ride to gain a sense of the sculpture's proportions: the average visitor could easily stand upright in one of the sculpted horse's ears!

The trams go all the way to the summit, although seasoned climbers may opt for the challenging 1.3-mile hike. From the top, Atlanta's skyscrapers are clearly visible 16 miles away. So is the *Scarlett O'Hara*—a paddlewheeler that plies Stone Mountain Lake immediately below. The park's train makes a five-mile circuit, passing within tooting distance of the antebellum plantation—a group of authentic buildings moved here from various sites across the state. Nineteen structures, ranging from the "big house" to slave cabins, a kitchen house, and a privy, are furnished in period style.

Bustling Atlanta flies the banner for the New South. Razed by Gen. William T. Sherman during his March to the Sea in 1864, Atlanta rose again like the mythical phoenix and today stands as the undisputed economic, financial, and cultural capital of the South. The community spirit and civic pride that are strongly evident today were responsible for Atlanta's transformation during the 1960's from a segregated city to one with an enviable reputation for racial harmony. The civil rights movement's most eloquent leader is honored at Atlanta's most important heritage site—the Martin Luther King, Jr. National Historic Site.

BIRTHPLACE OF A DREAM

King was born at 501 Auburn Avenue on January 15, 1929. His father, a Baptist minister, and his musician mother were members of Atlanta's black middle class, which was centered on Auburn Avenue, a section of downtown Atlanta where black-owned and operated businesses prospered as far back as the turn of the century. The close-knit neighborhood called Sweet Auburn, which nurtured King's passion for justice, is now designated a Preservation District.

King's birthplace is a restored two-story Queen Anne–style house, originally built in 1895, which is open for guided tours. Also open to visitors is the Ebenezer Baptist Church, where King, his father, and grandfather filled the pulpit for a total of more than 80 years. King's body lay in state in this church following his assassination in 1968. Six years later, his mother was shot and killed by an assassin as she sat at the organ there. His tomb rests next to the church and bears the simple and moving

The Atlanta Botanical Garden, above, is a green oasis in the middle of the city. A variety of vegetation, ranging from roses and hardwood trees to wildflowers and carnivorous plants, makes the garden an ideal spot to get away from it all.

inscription, "Free at last, free at last, thank God Almighty I'm free at last."

Located between King's birthplace and his church is the Martin Luther King, Jr. Center for Nonviolent Social Change, founded by King's widow, Coretta Scott King. The center contains a library, archives, exhibition hall, and training center. The fallen leader's remains rest in a marble crypt surrounded by a reflecting pool—a place of pilgrimage for thousands of visitors each year.

Atlanta is also home to the nation's first round-the-clock news networks, which went on the air in 1980 and 1982. CNN and Headline News, both owned by the Turner Broadcasting System, revolutionized television journalism with their up-to-the-minute reports and analyses. Ted Turner's TV empire is headquartered in the giant CNN Center. Tours of the television studios allow visitors to look down into the newsroom, where a host of technicians, writers, editors, producers, and on-air journalists report the news as quickly as it is fed to them from around the world.

Leaving metropolitan Atlanta, I-20 runs into rolling hills that grow steadily steeper. Across the Alabama state line, mountains appear to the south. In Cheaha State Park, located within Talladega National Forest, Mount Cheaha is the highest point in Alabama, at 2,407 feet above sea level. Three trails, all within the park, lead to scenic overlooks. Dedicated backpackers can leave their vehicles in the park and set off on a full day's excursion into the Blue Mountain backcountry, where streams bump over rocky beds, and trees cling to the steep slopes. Scenic and diverse, the trails are considered moderately challenging.

Visitors with a true yen for the wild can spend several days in the Cheaha Wilderness, also accessible from the state park. Part of the wilderness

FINAL RESTING PLACE

The crypt of Martin Luther King, Jr., right, rests upon a circular platform emblematic of the global community. Directly across from the crypt, an eternal flame symbolizes the continuing effort to realize Dr. King's dream.

On a high limestone bluff overlooking the Tombigbee River sits Bluff Hall, once frequented by high-ranking Confederate officers. The house, named for its prominent location on the bluff, was the home of lawyer, planter, and statesman Francis Strother Lyon, who served in the congresses of both the United States and the Confederacy. The original Federal brick structure was built in 1832. A massive columned front portico and a large rear wing were added later, and the exterior painted white. Owned today by a local historical society, Bluff Hall has been furnished with Empire and early Victorian pieces.

covers the southern portion of the Appalachian Mountains and provides panoramic views of east-central Alabama. Motorists with less time to spare can explore portions of the 23-mile Talladega Scenic Drive. The vistas are breathtaking in any season, but the colors are spectacular during the months of October, November, March, and April.

Roughly 3,000 years ago a prehistoric farming culture established settlements along the Black Warrior River southwest of Birmingham. On a bluff overlooking the river, visitors can behold a striking vista of flat-topped earth mounds. Known today as Moundville, this was the capital of the Mississippian culture and the largest city in the Southeast between A.D. 1000 and A.D. 1500.

At least 26 mounds have been identified at Moundville Archaeological Park—the smallest about four feet high, the largest reaching 58 feet. Atop the tallest mound is a reconstructed temple, where life-size figures are depicted conducting the First Fire Ceremony. Few of the mounds contain burial sites. Instead most appear to have been sites for the houses of the nobility or centers of worship and public life.

The park's museum displays objects made from bone, stone, pottery, and copper, many adorned with images of frogs. The centerpiece is the rattlesnake disk, which measures about 13 inches in diameter and depicts what was probably the symbol for war. A boardwalk winds through the surrounding forest and beside the Black Warrior River.

The town of Demopolis sits on the rich black soil of Alabama's Black Belt. Since the soil was ideal for growing cotton, huge plantations grew up here before the Civil War. Today two of the planters' exquisite mansions—Bluff Hall and Gaineswood—invite visitors to step back into a vanished era.

Gaineswood was designed and built by Gen. Nathan Bryan Whitfield between 1842 and 1860. Now designated a national historic landmark and listed in the national register of historic places, Gaineswood is more ornate than many of its Southern counterparts. The house is noted for its lavish Greek Revival interior, imposing porticoes, and twin domes with skylights above the parlor and dining room. The house still contains its original furnishings. Of special note in the music room is the flutina, a six-foot-tall hand-cranked music box built by the general.

Among its nicknames, Alabama was formerly known as the State of Surprises. Judging from the riches and unexpected delights to be found a short drive off I-20, surprise may be a fact of life not only here, but throughout all of the Old South.

MONUMENTAL MOUND
Ominous storm clouds darken the sky above one of the mounds in Moundville Archaeological Park, above. At its apex, this ancient community was populated by approximately 3,000 people.

PIONEER ILLINOIS

The footsteps of settlers and states-men reverberate on a journey from the Great Lakes to the Mississippi.

Stretching from lakeside Chicago to riverside Cairo, Interstate 57 slices through the Prairie State, whose Midwestern landscapes are seasoned with pioneer flavor. Northern industrial areas give way to rich farmlands, followed by southern woodlands that extend to the tip of Illinois. Attractions along the way range from pioneer settlements, historic monuments, and natural areas to cultural bastions and landmarks associated with Abraham Lincoln.

Lockport, headquarters of the Illinois and Michigan Canal, is a natural starting point for exploring Illinois' pioneer past. Nestled in the valley of the Des Plaines River, just beyond Chicago, the town recalls an era when canalside hamlets were bursting at the seams with settlers and merchants who arrived on barges loaded with trade goods such as hams, whiskey, sugar, lumber, and grain. Lockport was established in 1836, and the canal opened the following year. Built to connect the Great Lakes with the Illinois River, a tributary of the Mississippi, and to unlock

TRANSPLANTED BARN
Overleaf: The log barn at Lincoln Log Cabin State Historic Site was moved here in 1981 from southern Illinois. At this living-history farm located near Charleston, the last home of Thomas and Sarah Bush Lincoln, father and stepmother of Abraham Lincoln, has been re-created for the public.

HISTORIC DEPOT
The Gaylord Building in Lockport, below, served successively as a grain warehouse, general store, lock factory, and printing plant. The building is now a visitor center for the Illinois and Michigan Canal National Heritage Corridor.

the lands of eastern Illinois for settlement, the 96-mile-long channel was the final link in a huge waterway system that connected the Atlantic Ocean, Erie Canal, Great Lakes, Mississippi River, and the Gulf of Mexico.

The canal's significance comes to life in the Illinois and Michigan Canal Museum, housed in the original 1837 canal commissioner's office. Historical documents and artifacts are on display along with tools, surgical instruments, an 1846 home sewing machine, and furniture crafted by Scandinavian settlers.

Newcomers formerly disembarked at Public Landing, now occupied by Pioneer Settlement. The complex features an 1830's log cabin, one-room schoolhouse, tinsmith's shop, smokehouse, blacksmith's shop, and jail built with hand-hewn logs and wooden pegs.

As boats on the canal were loaded and unloaded, wagons weighted with cargo entered the great arched portals of the 1838 Gaylord Building. Made of cream-colored limestone, the former warehouse has been converted into a visitor center, art gallery, and restaurant. A two-and-a-half-mile trail leads walkers along the canal as it runs through town. At Lock No. 1, the first of 15 that were built along the length of the canal, visitors can cross a bridge

and picture the stream of boats that "locked" through the passageway until the late 1850's, when railroad travel rendered the canal obsolete.

CENTER OF LEARNING

Heading south into the heart of Illinois, I-57 rolls through rural landscapes punctuated by towns such as Champaign-Urbana, two communities separated by a single street. Champaign was founded in 1852, with the coming of the railroad, to meet the commercial needs of surrounding corn farms. Urbana, settled some 30 years earlier, remained the county seat and became an important university town.

Established in 1867, the University of Illinois at Champaign-Urbana is an ideal stop for amateur anthropologists. The World Heritage Museum, located on the main campus, traces the progress of humankind from prehistory to modern times. Milestones of human achievement, such as the discovery of metal and the invention of writing, are depicted in a series of dioramas created by artist Lorado Taft and his students.

In the hushed Egyptian Gallery, a mummy sarcophagus in a re-created tomb provides a vivid glimpse of the great Nile civilization. Dynastic robes of silk and gold are showcased in the museum's

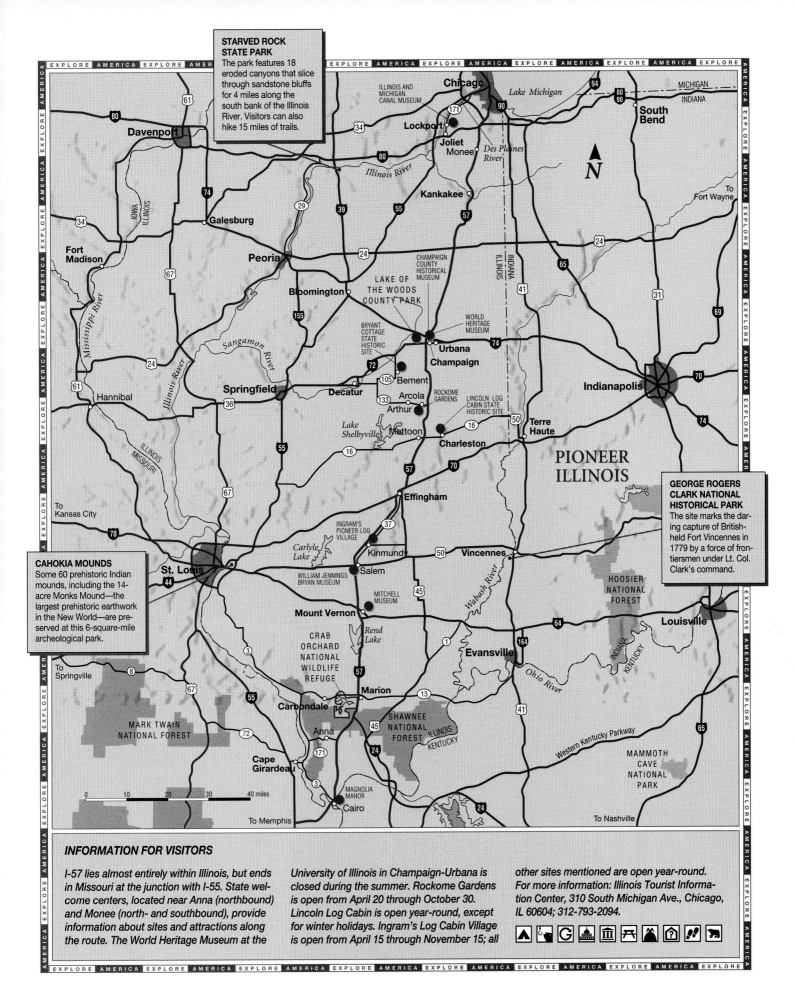

STARVED ROCK STATE PARK
The park features 18 eroded canyons that slice through sandstone bluffs for 4 miles along the south bank of the Illinois River. Visitors can also hike 15 miles of trails.

GEORGE ROGERS CLARK NATIONAL HISTORICAL PARK
The site marks the daring capture of British-held Fort Vincennes in 1779 by a force of frontiersmen under Lt. Col. Clark's command.

CAHOKIA MOUNDS
Some 60 prehistoric Indian mounds, including the 14-acre Monks Mound—the largest prehistoric earthwork in the New World—are preserved at this 6-square-mile archeological park.

PIONEER ILLINOIS

INFORMATION FOR VISITORS

I-57 lies almost entirely within Illinois, but ends in Missouri at the junction with I-55. State welcome centers, located near Anna (northbound) and Monee (north- and southbound), provide information about sites and attractions along the route. The World Heritage Museum at the University of Illinois in Champaign-Urbana is closed during the summer. Rockome Gardens is open from April 20 through October 30. Lincoln Log Cabin is open year-round, except for winter holidays. Ingram's Log Cabin Village is open from April 15 through November 15; all other sites mentioned are open year-round. For more information: Illinois Tourist Information Center, 310 South Michigan Ave., Chicago, IL 60604; 312-793-2094.

COUNTY BRIDGE

A covered bridge, below, in Lake of the Woods County Park near Champaign-Urbana keeps the roadway clear in winter. The park occupies 900 acres of rolling woodland along the Sangamon River.

Oriental exhibit. Other fascinating items include Egyptian papyrus documents, Roman glassware and wax writing tablets, medieval European armor and ship models, and African ceremonial masks.

Local history is preserved in the Champaign County Historical Museum, housed in the 1907 Wilbur Mansion. Clothing, toys, medical instruments, ornaments, and period furnishings evoke images of how the first European settlers in the area lived during the 1850's.

Tucked into the countryside a few miles west of Champaign-Urbana, Lake of the Woods County Park provides numerous picnic places, a lake surrounded by sandy beaches, and a maze of trails that weave through 900 acres of woodland. At the park's Early American Museum, costumed demonstrators make soap, stitch quilts, dip candles, and tell folktales. Exhibits on local architecture, agriculture, trades, and decorative arts interpret regional pioneer life during the period from 1820 to 1870. The vibrant Botanical Gardens round out the park's

attractions. The Heritage Garden and Roses of Yesteryear feature rare specimens, and the Prairie Sampler showcases a variety of native grasses.

HISTORIC DEBATE

Although cities and towns such as Champaign-Urbana were growing rapidly in size and number, in the mid-19th-century America was still overall a nation of small farming communities, whose voters commanded considerable political influence. In Bement, the Bryant Cottage State Historic Site is where an important meeting between the up-and-coming Springfield lawyer Abraham Lincoln and Sen. Stephen A. Douglas took place. Hoping to unseat Douglas in the 1858 Senate elections, Lincoln challenged him to a series of seven public debates on the issue of slavery. After Douglas agreed to participate, the rivals planned the agenda for the debates in the parlor of Douglas' friend Francis E. Bryant, a local politician and businessman. Although

Douglas won the race, Lincoln's arguments during the debates gained national attention, paving the way for his nomination and subsequent election as president in 1860.

In Bryant Cottage visitors can glimpse middle-class life of that era in small-town Illinois. Built near the Great Western Railroad tracks—the town's lifeline—the 1856 frame cottage was one of the town's finer residences. Decorative paper covered its walls, carpeting warmed plank floors, and several small cast-iron stoves kept the house cozy. Restored and equipped with period furnishings and original pieces, the four-room house consists of a sitting room, kitchen, bedroom, and parlor.

Approaching Douglas Valley, drivers exploring back roads may pass an Amish farmer hitched to a team of plow horses, or encounter the modestly dressed Plain People riding to town in black buggies. The region is the center of the Illinois Amish people, who eschew 20th-century gadgets, fashions, and electricity in favor of a simpler life.

THE GREAT COMMONER
A statue of William Jennings Bryan, above, in his birthplace of Salem preserves the memory of this distinguished orator, congressman, and three-time presidential candidate.

At Rockome Gardens in Arcola, visitors can tour an Amish-style home and school, browse through shops selling Amish-crafted oak furniture, or take a buggy ride through Rockome's 12 acres of rock and floral gardens. In this unique theme park, fences, arches, barns, and garden walls are made of stone set in concrete.

The Great Depression marked the beginning of the unusual rock creations. With business slow, industrialist Arthur Martin set his employees to work in the garden, constructing beautiful rock formations with stone collected from Illinois and other states. Old-time crafts and hobbies are revived during regular festivals that feature miniatures, model trains, counted cross-stitch embroidery, dolls, quilts, and bluegrass music, as well as delicious Amish specialties such as shoofly pie. The Haunted Cave, Elves' Workshop, and a petting farm populated with European fallow deer are perennial favorites with children.

BLUE FLIER
The eastern bluebird, above, favors conspicuous perches such as a fence-post, from which it can swoop down to the ground in pursuit of insects. The only bluebird found east of the Great Plains, the bird is sighted along Illinois' roadsides and in farmyards and orchards.

MEMORIES OF LINCOLN In the farmlands that surround Charleston, early 19th-century settlers coaxed a living out of the land through unending daily toil. When they purchased Goosenest Prairie in 1840, Abraham Lincoln's father and stepmother became some of the area's first settlers and farmers.

Today the Lincoln Log Cabin State Historic Site preserves the Lincoln home and re-creates early rural life in central Illinois. Abraham was already a Springfield lawyer by the time Thomas and Sarah Lincoln moved to the farm, but he visited them here periodically. Costumed interpreters portray the Lincoln family and their neighbors, welcoming visitors to their home in the lilting dialect of the Southern Upland.

The original cabin disappeared after it was sent to the 1893 World's Columbian Exposition in Chicago, but it was reconstructed in 1935 according to photographs and affidavits. The plain saddlebag cabin—two rooms with a central chimney —was home to as many as 18 family members in 1845. A smokehouse, barn, reconstructed well, and a root cellar are among the farm's outbuildings.

During the spring, workers sow 19th-century crop varieties that include bearded wheat and open-pollinated corn. Costumed farmhands feed barnyard animals that resemble the breeds of the 1840's. Horses and oxen provide draft power, sheep contribute wool, and hogs provide meat that is cured and smoked in the old-fashioned way. Visitors learn about various crafts including weaving and soap-making. In a dyeing demonstration, hand-spun wool takes on vivid colors when it is dipped in logwood, indigo, and onion skin dyes.

Near Kinmundy, travelers can take a detour off I-35 to Jacob's Well Inn, built in 1828. Once a stage-coach stop on the old Egyptian Trail between Cairo and Rockford, the large two-story tavern is one of 17 authentic log buildings comprising Ingram's Pioneer Log Village.

Thirteen pre–Civil War cabins, furnished with old-fashioned rope beds, corner cupboards, chests, and cradles, are open to the public. Dating from 1818 to 1860, the structures include a general store, cobbler's shop, preacher's home, apothecary's shop, and church. A small walnut cabin called Meadows was hastily built by a couple whose final destination was the West. Ben Doolen's Home is dominated by a generous, rough-hewn stone hearth, where cast-iron pots filled with pioneer-style meals still simmer from time to time. Extending over 74 acres, Pioneer Log Village has a small lake and numerous spots for leisurely picnicking.

Farther south, a stagecoach stop along the Vincennes Trail evolved into the booming town of Salem, incorporated in 1837. Salem's first wave of prosperity came with the arrival of the railroad in the 1850's, followed by another boom in the early 1900's with the discovery of oil in the area.

The William Jennings Bryan Museum chronicles the active life of the city's most prominent historical figure. Trained as a lawyer, Bryan served as congressman and secretary of state under Woodrow Wilson. He was also a three-time Democratic nominee for the presidency. Because Bryan championed the rights of ordinary people, he was called the Great Commoner. The museum is located in the home where he was born, a two-story Greek Revival house built in 1852.

A collection of photographs and memorabilia traces the politician's career and conveys a sense of Bryan's deeply religious nature.

Following a walking tour of historic Salem, visitors pass the stagecoach station, the Marion County Courthouse, and a statue of Bryan created by Gutzon Borglum, sculptor of Mount Rushmore.

Warm Southern-style hospitality greets everyone who stops for a visit in Jefferson County. The area is populated by the descendants of Southern families who migrated to this part of southern Illinois from Virginia, Kentucky, and Tennessee by way of the Mississippi and Ohio rivers. Mount Vernon, the county seat, is known locally as King City.

If Mount Vernon reigns over this corner of southern Illinois, then the Mitchell Museum, with its splendid white marble facade, is the jewel in its crown. Bordered with a row of arches, the museum stands on the 85-acre grounds of Cedarhurst, one of the state's most important cultural centers. On the grounds, the Cedarhurst Sculpture Park displays works of art made of everything from wood and stone to fiberglass and polystyrene. With an emphasis on both 19th- and

AMERICAN IMPRESSIONIST
Frederick Childe Hassam's The Table Garden, *left, painted in 1910, is among the collection of American art at the Mitchell Museum in Mount Vernon. The museum is part of Cedarhurst, an arts and nature complex.*

SNOWY SHELTER
Winter lends a cozy air to an 1828 log cabin, left, at Ingram's Pioneer Log Village, near Kinmundy. Life for the early settlers in this part of Illinois was often challenging.

20th-century American art, the museum hosts biannual shows that focus on southern Illinois artists. Original works by American painters such as Mary Cassatt, George Bellows, Frederick Childe Hassam, Maurice Prendergast, Thomas Eakins, and John Singer Sargent fill the main gallery.

MUSIC AND SCULPTURE

In the gardens that surround the museum, striking configurations of stone and metal are part of the outdoor sculpture program. During the summer months music lovers can spread out a blanket and listen to popular music during the center's outdoor concert series. Two walking trails wind through Cedarhurst's quiet woods. One of these is a specially designed Braille path for the visually impaired. The trails pass bright wildflowers, a bird sanctuary, and a small lake.

More and more trees appear on the side of I-57 as open farming country yields to Illinois' southern woodlands. At the edge of Shawnee National Forest, visitors can roam through tranquil grasslands, wetlands, and oak forests during a stopover in Crab Orchard National Wildlife Refuge, located near Carbondale. Created in 1947, the 43,550-acre refuge developed out of a soil conservation project. Ever since the area was first cultivated in the early 1800's, its economy was based on agriculture and hunting. By the time of the Depression, overgrazing and the cultivation of corn and cotton had severely depleted the soil. Revival began with reforestation during the 1930's, followed by the conservation of wildlife areas and the creation of Crab Orchard, Little Grassy, and Devil's Kitchen lakes.

Today Crab Orchard's woodlands look much as they did prior to the arrival of the first European settlers. Oak flats tower above flowering dogwood and sassafras shrubbery, whose thick vegetation provides a dense cover for quail, songbirds, and rabbits. On the forest floor, plants such as mayapple and poison ivy flourish in the shade.

Each year up to 120,000 Canada geese descend on the refuge. An agreement with local farmers ensures that the birds will have a steady supply of winter feed: farmers cultivate corn, milo, and clover on 5,000 acres of refuge lands, offering 25 percent of their harvest for bird fodder in lieu of rent.

Overlooking Crab Orchard Lake, Wolf Creek Causeway is an excellent vantage point from which to view Canada geese, ducks, gulls, and wading birds in the water. Keen birders may even catch glimpses of bald eagles perched in the trees across the lake. Boat ramps, picnic areas, and marinas dot the waterfronts of Crab Orchard, Little Grassy, and Devil's Kitchen lakes. Swimming, boating, and canoeing are popular activities, and campsites are available in three lakeside campgrounds. Anglers head to the waters for superb catches of largemouth bass, dandy crappie, and bluegill.

Nature trails pass log dams assembled by industrious beavers, whose lodges shelter as many as nine animals. White-tailed deer dart through the trees, and foxes, raccoons, weasels, mink, bobcats, and coyotes prowl the forest. As part of the refuge's wildlife population-management program, recreational hunters may hunt deer, wild turkey, and waterfowl in designated areas.

The journey down I-35 comes to a close in Cairo, a historic center of river traffic located at the southern tip of Illinois. Strategically positioned at the confluence of the Ohio and Mississippi rivers, Cairo's growth accelerated with the construction of the Illinois Central Railroad in 1855. The town was a supply center for Union troops during the Civil War. Wartime fortunes were amassed by local businessmen, including miller Charles Galigher. While negotiating flour sales to the government, Galigher befriended Gen. Ulysses S. Grant, who was placed in command of the Cairo military district in November 1861. Grant used Cairo as a base to mass troops and supplies for his 1862 invasion of the South. When peace returned, Galigher constructed an Italianate mansion on a leafy boulevard that was later dubbed "Millionaire's Row." The

dark green foliage of magnolia trees offsets Magnolia Manor's four stories of red brick, lacy wrought iron, and white trim.

Inside the mansion, glittering chandeliers, marble fireplaces, and grand staircases exemplify Victorian elegance. Magnolia Manor's 14 rooms are partially decorated with original furnishings, including the bed occupied by President Grant when he revisited Cairo upon his retirement. Needlework, garments, and the preserved wedding bouquets of the Galigher ladies are also on display.

A cupola atop the Magnolia Manor overlooks the meeting of the brown Mississippi currents and the blue waters of the Ohio River. After journeying the length of Illinois to this confluence of rivers, visitors may pause to admire the ambition, drive, and ingenuity of the state's early settlers, who cleared land for farms, founded settlements, and forged the transportation links that would bind a growing nation together.

RESOURCEFUL RODENT
In the same way that the early settlers tried to tame the new land, a beaver, left, tirelessly works to transform its watery environment by building dams and lodges.

MERCHANT'S MANOR
Standing amid two acres of lush gardens, Cairo's Magnolia Manor, below, preserves the memory of its builder, milling merchant Charles Galigher. The 14-room Italianate house, which is listed on the National Register of Historic Places, was completed in 1872.

THE HIGH PLAINS

*A journey across the plains holds
unexpected treasures, from a Viking
ship to a French chateau.*

Like the pioneers of old who turned their
backs to the Mississippi, left the bustling cities
of the East, and headed for the wide-open West,
Interstate 94 rolls away from metropolitan
Minneapolis and aims steadily for the high plains
country to the far northwest. Along the way, the
distinctive Minnesota countryside unfolds in a
panorama of small towns, pleasant groves, and
sprawling farmland. This is heartland country,
inhabited by the Sioux and Cheyenne Indians,
then occupied and nurtured by hardy Scandinavian immigrants who arrived here in the mid-
19th century.

These people were courageous and determined
pioneers in a new land. They came here filled
with dreams and fueled by a strong work ethic.
They cleared the land, planted crops, weathered
the winters, and celebrated the hard-won blessings
of successful harvests. They also endured wilderness isolation, grieved the deaths of the young
and the old, and survived the bloodshed of the
1862 Santee Sioux uprising. In so doing, they not

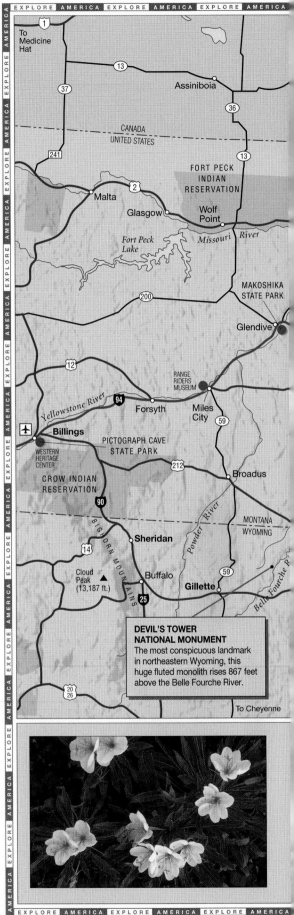

HOMESTEADING DAYS
Attired in period costume, a young girl at the Oliver H. Kelley Farm, above, goes about her daily chores.

A VISIONARY'S PARK
Overleaf: Prairie Pond, nestled amid a landscape of sagebrush, beckons visitors who travel along the 36-mile Scenic Loop Drive, which circles the South Unit of Theodore Roosevelt National Park. Gumbo evening primrose flowers, right, are one of the botanical treasures of the South Unit.

only made Minnesota their homeland, but they also bequeathed to this unique land a legacy that endures to this day.

PIONEER LEGACY That legacy is now commemorated at the Oliver H. Kelley Farm, a 189-acre living history farm located northwest of the suburban sprawl of Minneapolis on the northern bank of the Mississippi River. Oliver Kelley and his young bride, Lucy, broke ground here in 1849. It was a hard start: they lived on little more than wild rice and cranberries the first year, and soon after they set up housekeeping, Lucy and a baby girl died of childbirth complications. Resolved to succeed, Kelley worked the land, remarried, and built a model Minnesota farm. Visitors to the Kelley Farm can observe for themselves the lifestyle of a Minnesota farm family of the mid-19th century. Neatly attired in period clothing, farmers plow the fields with 19th-century implements and a team of oxen, shear sheep by hand, and operate an antique McCormick Daisy self-raking reaper. Rows of King Philip corn fill the fields, lineback cattle graze on the grounds, and plump Berkshire hogs await inspection by visitors young and old. Inside the restored home, costumed interpreters churn, cook, sew, make soap, and demonstrate other aspects of daily life on the farm. Pleasant nature trails meander along the river through 90 acres of woods and a restored prairie.

Less than 40 miles to the northwest lies the Mississippi River town of St. Cloud, home to the Stearns County Heritage Center. The museum presents a colorful glimpse of Minnesota life from the

DEVIL'S TOWER NATIONAL MONUMENT
The most conspicuous landmark in northeastern Wyoming, this huge fluted monolith rises 867 feet above the Belle Fourche River.

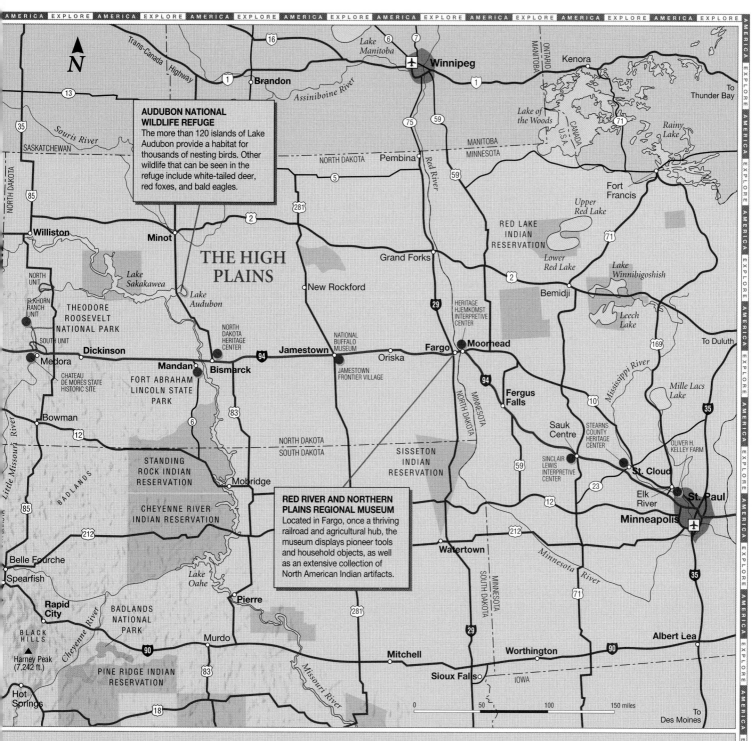

N

AUDUBON NATIONAL WILDLIFE REFUGE
The more than 120 islands of Lake Audubon provide a habitat for thousands of nesting birds. Other wildlife that can be seen in the refuge include white-tailed deer, red foxes, and bald eagles.

THE HIGH PLAINS

RED RIVER AND NORTHERN PLAINS REGIONAL MUSEUM
Located in Fargo, once a thriving railroad and agricultural hub, the museum displays pioneer tools and household objects, as well as an extensive collection of North American Indian artifacts.

INFORMATION FOR VISITORS

Visitor information centers along I-94 are located in Moorehead, MN, Oriska, ND, and at Beach, ND. The Oliver H. Kelley Farm in Elk River is open from May through October. The Stearns County Heritage Center in St. Cloud is open year-round. The Sinclair Lewis Boyhood Home in Sauk Centre, the Heritage Hjemkomst Interpretive Center in Moorhead, Jamestown Frontier Village, and Fort Abraham Lincoln State Park are open year-round.

Theodore Roosevelt National Park is open year-round, although some park roads are closed in winter. Backpacking permits are available; water should be carried in. Chateau de Mores in Medora is open from mid-May through mid-September. Makoshika State Park is open year-round; inclement weather may cause some road closings. The Range Riders Museum in Miles City is open from April through October. Pictograph Cave State Park

is open from mid-April to mid-October. For more information: Minnesota Office of Tourism, 100 Metro Sq., 121 East Seventh Pl., Saint Paul, MN 55101-2212; 800-657-3700. North Dakota Tourism, 604 East Blvd., Bismarck, ND 58505; 800-HELLOND. Travel Montana, 1424 9th Ave., Helena, MT 59620; 800-VISITMT.

AMERICA EXPLORE AMERICA EXPLORE AMERICA EXPLORE AMERICA EXPLORE AMERICA EXPLORE AMERICA EXPLORE AMERICA EXPLORE AMERICA EXPLORE AMERICA EXPLORE

THE HIGH PLAINS 53

era of the Ojibwa Indians to the present and spotlights regional industries of the 19th and early 20th centuries. Visitors can explore a life-size replica of a granite quarry, a century-old dairy barn, and Ojibwa and Dakota dwellings. Perched on the banks of the river, St. Cloud is an attractive city with a population of 60,000. Fifth Avenue is lined with late–19th-century buildings that attest to the town's early prosperity.

"To understand America," observed novelist Sinclair Lewis, "it is merely necessary to understand Minnesota." Understanding Minnesota is made easy in Sauk Centre, which Lewis memorialized as the fictional town of Gopher Prairie in the novel *Main Street*. America's first Nobel Prize–winning author, Lewis was born in Sauk Centre, grew up here, and drew from his childhood experiences in writing the 23 fictional works that earned him a place as one of the great American novelists of the 20th century.

In Sauk Centre visitors can explore the author's life and times at his boyhood home and at the Sinclair Lewis Interpretive Center. The town's Main Street still retains the flavor and friendliness of small-town America—an appeal, ironically, that Sinclair Lewis appeared never to have appreciated fully. A professional cynic as well as a novelist, Lewis died in Italy in 1951, alone and miserable by some accounts. But the townspeople of Sauk Centre, whom Sinclair caustically satirized in *Main Street*, nonetheless salute him as a favorite son.

In the town of Moorhead, on a wooded, riverside setting on the Minnesota–North Dakota state line, the spacious Heritage Hjemkomst Interpretive

Center houses a full-scale replica of a 76-foot Viking ship that proved its mettle by sailing the Atlantic from America to Norway. At the center visitors learn the story of Robert Asp, whose dream was to build and sail an authentic Viking longship. Asp began work on the vessel at his Minnesota shipyard in 1972, finished the giant replica eight years later, and christened it *Hjemkomst*, Norwegian for "homecoming." The eight-year construction consumed more than 100 white oak trees.

HOME TO NORWAY

Tragically, the shipbuilder died before his ship could make the transatlantic voyage for which it was built. In 1982, however, a crew of 13—including four of Asp's children—successfully took the *Hjemkomst* on a 6,000-mile journey from Duluth, Minnesota, to Bergen, Norway. They traveled through three of the Great Lakes, the Erie Canal, and the Hudson River to reach New York City and the Atlantic. Changing science and history exhibits are also featured at the center, and picnic grounds are set up in Viking Ship Park, located along the Red River.

Soon after crossing into North Dakota, I-94 changes character. Gone are the green summer groves of Minnesota, replaced by the treeless grasslands of the Great Plains. Exit signs beckon travelers to prairie hamlets whose names ring with the sound of the Old West—Absaraka, Buffalo, Fort Ransom, Sibley, and Spiritwood Lake. The state's Wild West heritage is well commemorated at Jamestown's Frontier Village and the National Buffalo Museum. Jamestown was the site of Fort Seward, an army post established in 1872 during the Plains Indian wars. A seasonal interpretive center

is located on the site of the old fort. At Frontier Village, a reconstructed pioneer settlement, visitors can amble through a frontier-style school, church, railroad depot, and other structures. The nearby National Buffalo Museum uses displays and exhibits to evoke the great bison herds that once covered the Great Plains like a huge dark cloud. Here visitors can view the "World's Largest Buffalo," a huge, 60-ton bison-shaped sculpture.

ANCIENT CROSSING

Sprawled on the east bank of the Missouri River is Bismarck, North Dakota's state capital. The city is known for its capitol, which dominates the skyline. The city arose on the site of an ancient ford on the Missouri, which served as a crossing for buffalo, Native Americans, mountain men, and pioneers. A windblown, river-

side settlement arose in 1871, occupied by settlers awaiting the arrival of the Northern Pacific Railroad, which made its appearance in 1873. Locals christened the village Bismarck, hoping that by their honoring German chancellor Otto von Bismarck, German railroad moguls would be flattered and lured into investing. Bismarck became the territorial capital in 1883 and the state capital in 1889. Today visitors to Bismarck won't spot any buffalo fording the Missouri, but a handsome riverside park hosts the popular Dakota Zoo, where buffalo, pronghorn antelope, bighorn sheep, and a variety of exotic animals are on display. Moored nearby and available for warm-weather cruises and historic trips to Fort Abraham Lincoln is the steamboat *Lewis & Clark*, reminiscent of a Missouri River steamer. The most popular regional attraction is the town's North Dakota Heritage Center,

PIONEERS' LEGACY
The reconstructed blockhouse at Fort Abraham Lincoln, above, is surrounded by a sea of green prairieland. The fort, located near the mouth of the Heart River, was erected to protect settlers and railroad workers. Lt. Col. George Armstrong Custer and the 7th Cavalry set out from the fort for their historic encounter with the Sioux at the Little Bighorn in 1876.

located on the capitol grounds. The massive 127,000-square-foot facility boasts a first-class collection of displays and artifacts that traces North Dakota's history and geology from prehistoric times up to the Great Depression.

On the west bank of the Missouri, four miles south of the town of Mandan, lie two historic sites: On-A-Slant Indian Village and Fort Abraham Lincoln, both located within Fort Abraham Lincoln State Park. Here, on a bluff that is within sight of the wide Missouri River, a sprawling Mandan Indian village flourished from approximately 1660 to 1780. The village was named for the slanting hillside on which the earthlodges were erected. Although virtually wiped out by a series of smallpox epidemics in the early 19th century, the Mandans were once among the most numerous and powerful tribes of the northern Plains. They abandoned the village, probably to avoid Sioux raids, shortly before Lewis and Clark camped here in 1804 on their way up the Missouri River. A marker in the park points out the campsite. Artist Karl Bodmer painted the distinctive earthlodges

of the Mandan, and Clark described the site in a diary entry: "The Countrey is fine, the high hills at a Distance with gradual assents. Great numbers of Buffalow, Elk & Deer. Our hunters killed 10 deer & a Goat today and wounded a white bear." Some of the reconstructed lodges, including a 60-foot long council lodge, are open to the public. An adjacent museum and visitor center contains displays of Mandan artifacts, as well as exhibits relating to Lewis and Clark, the fur traders of the region, and the early days of homesteading.

Nearby is the reconstructed Fort Abraham Lincoln, still standing as a monument to the culture clash between white civilization and Native American tribes of the Great Plains. Established in 1872, Fort Abraham Lincoln was one of the army's largest Western posts. It was famous as home to the U.S. 7th Cavalry in the 1870's, and for three years the post commander was Lt. Col. George Armstrong Custer. Today the reconstructed infantry blockhouses stand like lonely sentinels on a high bluff above the Missouri, offering visitors a view of wide-open spaces reminiscent of the vanished West. The fort was abandoned by the army in 1891, and its buildings eventually succumbed to the ravages of time. Some post structures have been reconstructed, including Custer House, the fort's most popular site. Original plans were used to reconstruct the home, where period furnishings and memorabilia provide a glimpse of the life of George and Libby Custer at the fort. Costumed interpreters conduct guided tours of the home. It was from this post that the 36-year-old Custer and his 7th Cavalry rode away on the campaign that ended at the Battle of the Little Bighorn, where Custer and five companies of his regiment were wiped out by Sioux and Cheyenne warriors. On Sunday, June 25, 1876, the day of the "Custer Massacre," Libby Custer and other officers' wives gathered in the parlor of Custer House to sing away their fears with gospel hymns. And it was here, too, at 7 A.M. on July 6 that Libby Custer received the news of Custer's Last Stand.

Theodore Roosevelt came to the Dakota Territory in 1883 at the age of 24 to hunt buffalo. He returned intermittently over the next three years, running 3,500 head of cattle on Elkhorn Ranch, one of his two ranches in the territory and his principal home. Although he spent less than 400 days in this area, Roosevelt always claimed that his short respites here changed him from a sickly youth to the robust man who eventually occupied the White House. He also left the West determined to save America's natural wonders, and went on to become the father of the conservation movement. During his term as the 26th president, Roosevelt established five national parks and was a founding member of the U.S. Forest Service. Referring to his experience in the badlands, Roosevelt later said, "I would not have been President had it not been for my experience in North Dakota."

A PRESIDENT'S PARK

Visitors to Theodore Roosevelt National Park can revel in the landscape so dear to its namesake. The park's North and South units surround a long, wild stretch of the Little Missouri River overlooking a section of the badlands of North Dakota. This is a rugged landscape of colorful canyons, buttes, and rock pillars surrounded by undisturbed prairie and cottonwood stands. The National Park Service offers tours of Roosevelt's Maltese Cross Cabin, now located near the South Unit Visitor Center. The South Unit

PLAINS COUNTRY
The fertile countryside near Bismarck, below, lured many settlers to North Dakota during the late 19th century, where they reaped the riches of the land by planting wheat and other crops.

takes in two-thirds of the park's 70,447 acres; the North Unit is located 50 miles north of I-94. Outdoor activities include hiking, backpacking, camping, horseback riding, wildlife viewing, and cross-country skiing. Wildlife enthusiasts may encounter pronghorn antelope, elk, and even the elusive mountain lion. About 500 bison live in the park. After a rainy spring season, wildflowers display their colors in the park's river bottomlands and prairie flats.

A WESTERN CHATEAU

Leaving the grandeur of the park's scenery behind, visitors along I-94 soon arrive in Medora. This colorful prairie town with a distinctive Western flavor is home to the Chateau de Mores State Historic Site. The chateau was once the residence of the Marquis de Mores, a French aristocrat who founded the town in 1883 and named it for his wife. De Mores came here to make his fortune in cattle ranching and meat processing, but instead he lost millions in a futile attempt to become a cattle baron. Left behind today are his 26-room chateau, now open for tours, and the ruins of his packing plant, which eventually was burned to the ground. The marquis died in Africa in 1896, while on another adventure. His life and times are depicted in the chateau's fascinating interpretive center.

When I-94 enters eastern Montana, travelers know they're in Big Sky Country. Surrounded on all sides by a treeless horizon, the land is swept by unbroken winds that can roll the prairie grass like waves. It is easy to imagine how these grasslands

appeared to hunting parties of Oglala Sioux in the mid-19th century. In prehistoric times, the region was home to the dinosaur: *Tyrannosaurus rex*, *Triceratops*, and *Edmontasaurus* once lumbered across this land. These ancient reptiles—as well as prehistoric mammals, fish, and birds—are the focus of interpretive displays housed in a year-round visitor center at Makoshika State Park, just east of the town of Glendive. Makoshika is a variant spelling of a Lakota phrase meaning "land of bad spirits." More than 65 million years ago, the region was a vast swampland. Today the landscape is dramatically different: the forces of wind and rain have sculpted it into unusual sandstone formations. The fossilized remains of more than 10 species of dinosaurs and other prehistoric creatures have been uncovered here. The big draw at the interpretive center is a *Triceratops* skull. Visitors are asked to report—but not touch—any fossils they discover in the park.

Montana's largest state park, this 8,832-acre site is crisscrossed by approximately 12 miles of roads—two-thirds of them primitive—marked by scenic overlooks. The expansive park also offers superb hiking trails, a campground, picnic grounds, an archery range, and prime spots for viewing the annual migration of turkey vultures. An annual event, which the locals call Buzzard Day, is celebrated the first weekend in May, after the vultures

have made their return flight to Montana from their winter visit to the Southwest.

From Glendive to Billings, I-94 runs along the mighty Yellowstone River. Lewis and Clark traveled this stretch of the river as they explored the upper reaches of the Louisiana Territory in 1806. At Miles City, a moderate-size Montana town of about 8,500, visitors may tour the Range Riders Museum, a complex of frontier-era structures featuring displays on eastern Montana history. Located where Col. Nelson Miles established a military post in 1877, the museum houses thousands of historical artifacts, including a collection of about 400 firearms and the works of the frontier photographers Huffman, Barthelmess, and Morrison. In addition, the museum features a frontier town with 11 period buildings, replicas of Fort Keogh and Lame Deer Indian Village, and numerous Sioux and Crow artifacts.

Upriver lies Billings, Montana's largest city, which is somewhat prosaically named for a 19th-century railroad executive. Home to more than 80,000 people, Billings is known for its livestock auction yards and railroads. The city also houses the Western Heritage Center in the Parmly Billings Library, a Romanesque-style structure built in 1901. The center features interactive interpretive exhibits on the heritage of the Yellowstone River region. Displays related to Plains Indian cultures, farming, and ranching are also presented. At the visitor center stands a large bronze sculpture of a cattle drover, erected in honor of the city's strong ties to the cattle industry. Billings also boasts several historical landmarks, including the Moss Mansion, erected in 1903. Made of brown sandstone from the Lake Superior region, the house was designed by Henry J. Hardenburgh, who also designed the Plaza and Waldorf-Astoria hotels in New York City. In the historic district, the Rex Hotel was once frequented by Buffalo Bill Cody.

| ANCIENT ARTWORK | The remains of a far older civilization are located six miles southeast of Billings at Pictograph Cave State Park. |

By studying the stone points, awls, knapping tools, pottery shards, and other artifacts found in the cave, scientists have estimated that the cave was inhabited between 6,000 and 8,000 years ago. Preserved in Pictograph Cave, largest of the three caves in the park, are depictions by prehistoric artists of buffalo, elk, turtles, and shield-bearing warriors. The pictographs were painted on the walls of the cave using paint made from clay and different vegetable substances, as well as pollen and charcoal. Though the cave paintings had been known for decades, their archeological importance was not understood until 1937. Now the site is carefully preserved. Visitors to the park, located in the Bitter Creek Valley, can wander through the gulch where the caves are found, study the local fauna, and enjoy the Western landscape.

From rustic pioneer homesteads and stately mansions to a national park fit for a president, the northern Plains offer modern-day travelers the opportunity to explore the riches of this part of the country. Route I-94 takes visitors back in time as they follow in the footsteps of the first settlers, who headed west in the hopes of finding a place they could call home.

ORNAMENTAL SCULPTURES
Hoodoos in the Cap Rock area of Makoshika State Park, above, were carved by the hand of erosion. The park is also famous for the fossilized remains of dinosaurs that once roamed the region.

CHISHOLM TRAIL

Memories of the great longhorn cattle drives of the Old West surface along this strip of I-35.

The cattle drives began as far south as the Mexican border. Immense herds of longhorn cattle—a breed brought from Spain to the Americas by Columbus—were herded up the dusty, sage-napped Texas plains toward San Antonio and north to Fort Worth, across the Red River into Indian Territory, north to Wichita, and through the Flint Hills to Abilene, Kansas, on the long march to market and the slaughterhouse. In the brief epoch of the great drives, more than 10 million longhorns were driven out of the Southwest to supply the nation's appetite for beef, leather, and tallow. In the 18-year period from 1867 to 1885, an estimated 5 million longhorns followed this path of wagon ruts and hoofprints known as the Chisholm Trail. When the railroad pushed into Texas during the 1880's, the cattle drives quickly became obsolete. But the era had already made a profound impact on America's westward expansion and the rise of major cities across the Midwest. It helped to put Texas on the path to economic recovery following the Civil

taxis, and the strains of strolling mariachis lend it a hushed ambience of another time and place. Scattered throughout town, a string of festivals and parades, street dances, fireworks, and year-round musical productions appease contemporary San Antonio's considerable appetite for a party.

GERMAN HERITAGE

Half an hour's drive up I-35 lies New Braunfels, another time-honored settlement that also knows how to let the good times roll. Founded by Prince Carl of Solms-Braunfels in 1845, following a large land grant that encouraged German immigration to the Republic of Texas, the town has retained not only German architectural influences but also the Bavarian penchant for song and dance abetted by hearty food and drink. Situated at the confluence of the Comal and Guadalupe rivers in Texas' lovely Hill Country, New Braunfels is inundated each summer by

RUSTIC HOMESTEAD
A log cabin at the Museum of Texas Handmade Furniture in New Braunfels, above, displays home furnishings and cabinetmaking tools used by early settlers in Texas.

War, encouraged railroad expansion on the frontier, provided stock for new ranches to the north, and turned Chicago and Kansas City into meatpacking centers. The trail also witnessed colorful chapters in the history of smaller centers such as Wichita and Abilene, and entered the literature and mythology of the American West.

Named for Jesse Chisholm, a Scottish-Cherokee trader who guided the earliest drives through Indian Territory, the Chisholm Trail has long since been plowed under, paved over, bypassed, subdivided, incorporated, or otherwise given the stamp of the 20th century, but echoes of it still rumble somewhere just beyond the interchanges and medians and landscaped aprons of modern roadways. Like the old cattle route, Interstate 35 between San Antonio and Kansas City runs through 734 miles of American landscape rich in lore, legend, and natural wonders, much of which can be experienced within a few miles of the egress ramps.

From a downtown San Antonio exit, it is hard to miss the city's two premier attractions: the 280-year-old Spanish mission and presidio known as the Alamo and the below-street-level Paseo del Rio, or River Walk—a promenade of hotels, outdoor restaurants, shops, and nightclubs that follows the San Antonio River on its meandering course through the heart of the city. Strung along a busy downtown thoroughfare, the Alamo and its surrounding grounds are now a state park, library, and museum of artifacts from the famous battle of 1836 and the subsequent period of colonization of the Republic of Texas. Accessible from Alamo Plaza, River Walk beckons visitors to enjoy its charms. Flagstone footpaths and bridges flanked by cypresses and palms, the leisurely drift of river

STATELY ENTRANCE
The ornate door hinges of the State Capitol Building in Austin, right, have been faithfully restored to their original beauty.

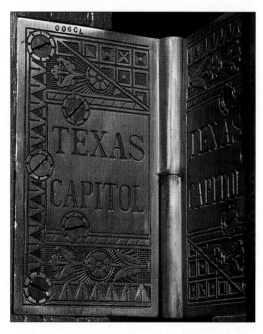

FRONTIER FARMING
Overleaf: The National Agriculture Center and Hall of Fame in Bonner Springs, Kansas, features Farm Town U.S.A., a replica of an early 1900's rural village. The streets are lined with a blacksmith's shop, general store, schoolhouse, railroad depot, and poultry hatchery.

hundreds of thousands of "tubers," who float downstream in the inner tubes of automobile tires. Many are content to float the gentle waters of the Comal, an icy, spring-fed stream that begins and ends inside the city limits. It meanders past beer gardens and stately residences and spills over low man-made falls on its way to the Guadalupe, which roils with whitecaps when large amounts of water are released from Canyon Dam. The Guadalupe is the preferred rafting channel of the adventurous. A less demanding itinerary includes a walking tour of streets lined with German *fachwerk*—half-timber, half-masonry cottages—and a visit to the Sophienburg Museum to further investigate the town's Germanic roots. The Museum of Texas

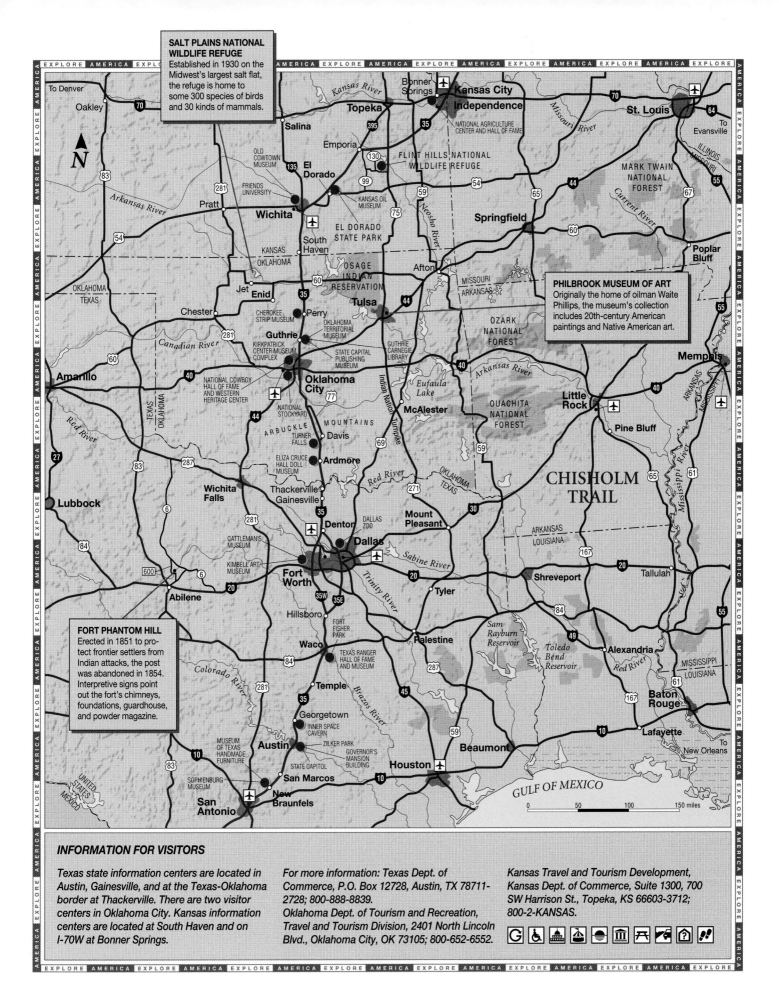

SALT PLAINS NATIONAL WILDLIFE REFUGE
Established in 1930 on the Midwest's largest salt flat, the refuge is home to some 300 species of birds and 30 kinds of mammals.

N

To Denver

Oakley

70

83

Arkansas River

54

Pratt

KANSAS
OKLAHOMA

OKLAHOMA
TEXAS

Jet

Chester

60

281

Canadian River

Amarillo

40

60

27

Red River

83

287

Lubbock

84

6

600

6

Abilene

20

FORT PHANTOM HILL
Erected in 1851 to protect frontier settlers from Indian attacks, the post was abandoned in 1854. Interpretive signs point out the fort's chimneys, foundations, guardhouse, and powder magazine.

Kansas River

Bonner
Springs

Topeka

Salina

OLD
COWTOWN
MUSEUM

El
Dorado

135

FRIENDS
UNIVERSITY

Wichita

281

South
Haven

EL DORADO
STATE PARK

Enid

35

CHEROKEE
STRIP MUSEUM

Perry

Guthrie

KIRKPATRICK
CENTER MUSEUM
COMPLEX

OKLAHOMA
TERRITORIAL
MUSEUM

STATE CAPITAL
PUBLISHING
MUSEUM

GUTHRIE
CARNEGIE
LIBRARY

Oklahoma
City

77

NATIONAL COWBOY
HALL OF FAME
AND WESTERN
HERITAGE CENTER

NATIONAL
STOCKYARD

44

MOUNTAINS

ARBUCKLE

TURNER
FALLS

Davis

ELIZA CRUCE
HALL DOLL
MUSEUM

Ardmore

69

Wichita
Falls

Thackerville

Gainesville

35

281

Red River

DALLAS
ZOO

Denton

CATTLEMAN'S
MUSEUM

KIMBELL ART
MUSEUM

Fort
Worth

35W

35E

Hillsboro

FORT
FISHER
PARK

Waco

TEXAS RANGER
HALL OF FAME
AND MUSEUM

84

Colorado River

281

Temple

35

Georgetown

INNER SPACE
CAVERN

ZILKER PARK

Austin

MUSEUM OF
TEXAS
HANDMADE
FURNITURE

GOVERNOR'S
MANSION
BUILDING

STATE CAPITOL

83

10

SOPHIENBURG
MUSEUM

San
Marcos

San
Antonio

New
Braunfels

UNITED
STATES

MEXICO

395

Emporia

130

99

KANSAS OIL
MUSEUM

75

Neosho River

60

OSAGE
INDIAN
RESERVATION

Tulsa

44

35

NATIONAL AGRICULTURE
CENTER AND HALL OF FAME

FLINT HILLS NATIONAL
WILDLIFE REFUGE

54

59

Afton

MISSOURI
ARKANSAS

Indian National Turnpike

*Eufaula
Lake*

McAlester

271

Mount
Pleasant

Sabine River

Dallas

20

Tyler

Trinity River

Palestine

287

45

Brazos River

Houston

10

GULF OF MEXICO

Kansas City

Independence

70

St. Louis

64

To
Evansville

Missouri River

44

MARK TWAIN
NATIONAL
FOREST

Current River

55

67

Springfield

65

60

Poplar
Bluff

OZARK
NATIONAL
FOREST

Arkansas River

40

55

OUACHITA
NATIONAL
FOREST

Memphis

40

Arkansas

Mississippi

Little
Rock

Pine Bluff

65

61

OKLAHOMA
TEXAS

30

**CHISHOLM
TRAIL**

ARKANSAS
LOUISIANA

167

20

Tallulah

Shreveport

84

55

49

Red River

Alexandria

MISSISSIPPI
LOUISIANA

61

167

Baton
Rouge

10

Lafayette

To
New
Orleans

*Sam
Rayburn
Reservoir*

*Toledo
Bend
Reservoir*

59

Beaumont

PHILBROOK MUSEUM OF ART
Originally the home of oilman Waite Phillips, the museum's collection includes 20th-century American paintings and Native American art.

0   50   100   150 miles

INFORMATION FOR VISITORS

Texas state information centers are located in Austin, Gainesville, and at the Texas-Oklahoma border at Thackerville. There are two visitor centers in Oklahoma City. Kansas information centers are located at South Haven and on I-70W at Bonner Springs.

For more information: Texas Dept. of Commerce, P.O. Box 12728, Austin, TX 78711-2728; 800-888-8839.
Oklahoma Dept. of Tourism and Recreation, Travel and Tourism Division, 2401 North Lincoln Blvd., Oklahoma City, OK 73105; 800-652-6552.

Kansas Travel and Tourism Development, Kansas Dept. of Commerce, Suite 1300, 700 SW Harrison St., Topeka, KS 66603-3712; 800-2-KANSAS.

Handmade Furniture celebrates the skills of the German cabinetmakers of the past century. Together with handmade tables, wardrobes, clocks, sofas, and cupboards, the museum houses a large collection of pewter and ironstone beer steins.

Four miles from New Braunfels, on the banks of the Guadalupe River, is the resurrected ghost town of Gruene, a turn-of-the-century cotton farming community. The old livery stable is now a dance hall, the gristmill a steak house, and even the town's winery has been reactivated. The narrow streets, originally designed for horse-drawn wagons, are fronted by antique shops, inns, general stores, and float-trip outfitters.

SEAT OF GOVERNMENT

Rivers and streams are an integral part of life and commerce in Hill Country towns, and nowhere more so than in the state capital of Austin. Approaching the city from the south, I-35 crosses Town Lake, a reservoir formed by the Colorado River a few blocks from the seat of the state government. This popular recreation area offers shaded jogging and bike paths, broad parks, and canoeing and sculling facilities. In Zilker Park, icy waters rise from a limestone strata to form the nearly 1,000-foot-long Barton Springs Pool. Once a gathering place for Indian tribes, it is now the city's most popular swimming hole. Fanning out from the pool are the Austin Nature Center, the Zilker Botanical Gardens, eight miles of nature trails along Barton Creek, and a limestone quarry where dinosaur tracks and 99-million-year-old turtle bones have been found.

Austin's imposing pink granite statehouse is several feet taller than the national Capitol. From its hilltop perch overlooking downtown Austin, the Renaissance Revival structure—crowned by a metal dome and Goddess of Liberty statue—is the focal point of the city's skyline. Although this stately structure is more than 100 years old, a recent two-year restoration project, based on archival photographs, newspaper articles, and other early documents, has returned much of the interior to its turn-of-the-century condition. The library is vintage 1915, complete with faithfully reproduced brass chandeliers, sections of glass block flooring, and tall bookcases. The chambers in which ses-

GOVERNMENTAL GRANDEUR
The magnificent pink granite Texas State Capitol Building, opposite page, was completed in 1888. It was the fourth capitol to be constructed in Austin; the first was a simple wooden structure.

BIG CAT
Home to some 5,000 different animals, the Fort Worth Zoo includes a successful elephant breeding ground and the nation's largest collection of reptiles. The rare white tiger, above, dwells in surroundings that mimic its native habitats.

GILDED LILIES
Flowering water lilies, left, decorate one of the ponds in the Isamu Taniguchi Oriental Garden in Austin's Zilker Botanical Garden.

ANCIENT MASTERPIECE

ANCIENT MASTERPIECE
Among the rare treasures of the Kimbell Art Museum in Fort Worth is a terra-cotta head titled Portrait of a King, *right. The sculpture, which dates from the 14th century, is from southwestern Nigeria.*

SUBTERRANEAN SCULPTURES
Lake of the Moon, below, at Inner Space Cavern, near Georgetown, displays unusual geological formations of calcite stalactites and stalagmites. Paths provide access to many chambers within the cavern.

sions of the state house and senate are held have been restored to their 1910 appearance. A flag from the battle of San Jacinto in 1836, in which Sam Houston and his Texan army put to flight a large Mexican force led by Gen. Antonio López de Santa Anna two months after the loss of the Alamo, hangs prominently behind the speaker's desk.

A few blocks from the capitol building, political history of more recent vintage reposes in the Lyndon B. Johnson Library and Museum. The colorful and controversial political career of one of Texas' favorite and most flamboyant sons is told through LBJ's private and public papers, mementos of his years in public life, and a replica of the Oval Office.

Outside the city of Austin, the Chisholm Trail leaves the hills and plunges into an expanse of fertile, rolling blackland prairie. Near Georgetown, I-35 passes over the state's most recently discovered and most easily accessible subterranean spectacle—Inner Space Cavern, found during construction of the Interstate in 1963. Skillful lighting enhances the natural beauty of the underground chambers, which are adorned with stalactites, stalagmites, and flowstones. The cavern has yielded the remains of mastodons, wolves, and other Ice Age animals.

Farther to the north, Waco is home of the Texas Ranger Hall of Fame and Museum. Along with the founders of the Republic of Texas, the Rangers are the state's most exalted cultural icons, as well as the oldest statewide law enforcement agency in the nation. Believed to have existed as early as 1823, when Texas was still a part of Mexico, the Rangers helped tame a violent frontier as scouts and Indian fighters, and they left behind as many legends as hoofprints. The Texas Rangers still exist as an investigative arm of the Department of Public Safety. Their history is preserved in the museum on the banks of the Brazos River in Waco's Fort Fisher Park. Multimedia presentations, displays of firearms, artifacts, photographs, and a library make the museum an important research facility. Relics of Wild West shows, Mexican history, and the longhorn drives are also on view.

Forty miles north of Waco, I-35 divides: one branch arcs toward Fort Worth and the other toward Dallas. The two metropolises are often referred to as Dallas–Fort Worth, but in both appearance and spirit, these two giants are vastly different municipalities.

A TALE OF TWO CITIES

Fort Worth's beginnings as a cowtown are evident in such attractions as the Amon G. Carter Museum of Western Art, the Cattleman's Museum, Cowtown Coliseum, Log Cabin Village, and the Stockyards Historic Area—a district of boardwalks and renovated frontier-style buildings on narrow streets near the old cattle exchange. A larger-than-life trail herd sculpture greets visitors to the cattle exchange. Other attractions of note in Fort Worth include the botanical gardens, which showcase 2,500 species of plants, and the Museum of Science and History, with exhibits related to the history of human physiology, medicine, computers, geology, paleontology, and space travel. Exotic animals roam the Fort Worth Zoo, and the Kimbell Art Museum displays works from antiquity to Picasso.

Dallas breathes only faint wisps of the Old West: there are longhorn sculptures beside the starkly modern City Hall, and the replica of the log cabin John Neely Byran built in 1840 to found the city is near the plaza where President Kennedy was assassinated in 1963. Dallas' downtown Arts District is anchored by a spectacular symphony hall and the Museum of Art, which exhibits pre-Columbian art, as well as paintings by Claude Monet, John Singer Sargent, Henri Matisse, and the sculptures of Auguste Rodin and Henry Moore. The West End Historic District is composed of former warehouses that have been converted into popular restaurants and nightclubs. Fair Park's cluster of Art Deco buildings houses not only the annual Texas State Fair but also a garden center, planetarium, the Southwest Museum of Science and Technology, and the Dallas Aquarium, home to more than 3,500 aquatic animals, including some that are extinct in the wild.

A few miles away, sprawling over both sides of Cedar Creek, the Dallas Zoo holds more than 1,600 species of animals, including the world's largest collection of rattlesnakes. Exotic birds occupy a walk-through tropical rain forest. A nature trail offers a close-up look at simians, hoofed animals, jungle cats, and other African wildlife. The exhibits can be viewed from an elevated monorail.

COWBOY HERITAGE
The National Cowboy Hall of Fame in Oklahoma City houses an extensive collection of fine Western art, including the legendary sculpture titled End of the Trail, *right. The work was created by James Earle Fraser in 1915.*

TURN-OF-THE-CENTURY CHARM
A stroll through Guthrie, below, Oklahoma's capital for 20 years, reveals its rich architectural heritage. Some of the commercial buildings were designed by Joseph Foucart, a French architect.

In Denton the two branches of I-35 merge once again, and the Interstate gallops across a 40-mile expanse of North Texas prairie that is known as horse country. North of Gainesville, it crosses the Red River—a rampaging challenge to the cattle drives, especially during the heavy spring rains—and begins a long climb toward the Arbuckle Mountains of southern Oklahoma.

In the town of Ardmore, the public library has a display of rare and valuable dolls amassed during the lifetime of Eliza Cruce Hall, a Kentuckian who came here with her parents in 1896, when Ardmore was still part of Indian Territory. Mrs. Hall bought her first doll in 1936, when she was in Europe to view the coronation of Great Britain's George VI. Over the years she acquired more than 300 dolls, including a group of carved wooden dolls originally owned by French queen Marie Antoinette. Before her death in 1971, Hall donated the collection to the Ardmore Library, along with a monetary bequest to build a special room in which to display them.

Farther up the highway, the Arbuckle Mountains present an abrupt departure from Ardmore's delicate collectibles. The rugged range of rounded limestone, sparsely covered with cedar and blackjack oak, is one of the oldest geological formations in the nation. The mountains have been described as one of three geological windows into America's past, the Grand Canyon and the Black Hills being the other two. In the heart of the range, myriad springs form Honey Creek, which tumbles down a 77-foot falls into a pool ringed by beaches and stone bluffs. Turner Falls has been a fashionable recreation area since the 1860's. Today the town of Davis operates a 720-acre private park area less than half a mile from the highway.

Oklahoma City, the capital of a state whose land was once envisioned as an independent Native American nation, celebrates its Western heritage with the same devotion as Fort Worth. That passion is enshrined in the National Cowboy Hall of Fame and Western Heritage Center, which boasts the finest collection of Western art and artifacts in the world. Among the exhibits are sculptures by both Frederic Remington and Charles M. Russell, as well as panoramic paintings by Albert Bierstadt and W. R. Leigh. Various rooms pay tribute to famed rodeo performers and stars of Western films. A 1,200-seat auditorium accommodates annual events such as the Cowboy Poetry Gathering and Western Heritage Awards.

For a glimpse of more recent history and per-haps of the future, the Kirkpatrick Center Museum Complex offers a host of attractions under one 10-acre roof. The complex features an air and space museum, planetarium, science museum, conservatory and botanical gardens, art galleries, the International Photography Hall of Fame, and the Red Earth Indian Center.

Like many Oklahoma towns born in the Great Land Run of 1889, Oklahoma City was conceived in a single afternoon of swirling dust and tent can-vas. It was not, however, the original seat of gov-ernment. Guthrie, 30 minutes away, was both the territorial capital and the first state capital. While Oklahoma City grew into a modern metropolis, time stood still in Victorian Guthrie: 400 blocks of the town are on the National Register of Historic Places. The Scottish Rite Masonic Temple sits on land originally chosen for the state capitol com-plex. The State Capital Publishing Museum holds one of the nation's largest collections of turn-of-the-century printing equipment. The Oklahoma Territorial Museum tells the story of the Great Land Run. Few local structures, however, possess the historic richness of the Guthrie Carnegie Library. Built in 1902, the Renaissance Revival building is a bridge between territorial days and statehood; the last territorial governor was inau-gurated on its front steps. It is as grand as a state-house and is the only Carnegie library with a dome paid for with Carnegie funds. (Andrew Carnegie, it is said, disliked domes and made a practice of not funding them.)

When this was still Indian Territory, a strip of land that extended across the northern edge of Oklahoma was known as the Cherokee Outlet. How these tenacious pioneers converted the rough prairie land to ordered farm acreage is part of the story that is preserved and interpreted in the Cherokee Strip Museum in Perry. Artifacts of the Otoe-Missouria Indians of the region, re-created offices of a doctor and a dentist, memorabilia of

Oklahoma governors Henry Bellmon and Henry Johnson, historic farm implements, photographs, and artifacts make up the permanent exhibits.

RELICS OF THE WILD WEST

From all evidence, the settlers succeeded wildly in domesti-cating the prairie: northward from Perry, I-35 unrolls across some of the most productive wheat and cotton fields in America before arriving in Wichita, Kansas. An important and once-unruly stop on the Chisholm Trail, Wichita is strewn with relics of the Old West and monuments to the colorful charac-ters—Wyatt Earp, Bat Masterson, Kit Carson, and the Kiowa war chief Santana among them—who left their mark on the city's history.

In Highland Cemetery a towering statue marks the final resting place of William Mathewson, a sharpshooting Indian fighter widely known as Buffalo Bill long before Ned Buntline gave the same moniker to William Cody in his novels. Still stand-ing near the restored Old Town district of restau-rants and boutiques is the former Carey House—now the Eaton Hotel—whose swank basement bar was trashed by ax-wielding temperance crusader Carry Nation in 1900. Pioneer history is the focus

PIONEER CATTLE TOWN
*The Arkansas Valley Elevator,
below, the only completely restored
wooden grain elevator in the
nation, is preserved in Wichita's
Old Cowtown Museum.*

at the Fellow-Reeve Museum at Friends University, and artifacts of several North American tribes are showcased at the Mid America All-Indian Center. The flora of the prairie is cultivated at the Wichita Gardens, where bluestem and buffalo grasses that once nourished the great herds of bison are displayed alongside lavender, indigo, crimson, and yellow wildflowers. Bison, grizzly bears, antelope, wolves, eagles, and prairie dogs flourished in Kansas before being hunted nearly to extinction. Today these species thrive in miniature-scale natural habitats at the Sedgwick County Zoo.

FRONTIER CITY

Perhaps Wichita's grandest tribute to the past is the Old Cowtown Museum, a reconstructed frontier community spread over 17 acres, where the Chisholm Trail crosses the Arkansas River. Many of the buildings hark back to Wichita's founding and the heyday of the cattle drives. The town's original jail is here, as are the timber-and-mud Munger House, built in 1869, and the Victorian-Gothic Murdock House, which dates to 1874.

Outside Wichita I-35 bends away from the Chisholm Trail route on a course to Kansas City. It passes through the Flint Hills, a rolling 50- by 100-mile oval that derives its name from the flint cobbles sprinkled over limestone upthrusts. The hills are shrouded in prairie grass so lush that each year more than 1 million head of cattle are fattened here before being sent to slaughter. Just a few miles off the Interstate, it is still possible to see the Flint Hills as the settlers and drovers viewed the area in its rawest state. The Teter Nature Trail in El Dorado offers a path through a wilderness area that harbors a diverse range of plants and provides sanctuary for deer, raccoons, and wild turkeys. Overnight covered-wagon trips take would-be pioneers deep into the prairies.

In El Dorado, it soon becomes apparent that, along with beef and bottomland farming, oil played a major part in shaping the region's character and economy. Although Kansas is not normally thought of as a major oil producer, in 1860 it was the site of the first oil well drilled west of the Mississippi. Subsequent finds—including the huge El Dorado field in 1915—pushed Kansas to the forefront of oil

PASTORAL SPLENDOR
*Wildflowers grace the gentle slopes
of the Arbuckle Mountains, right,
during spring and summer.*

70

production. Within 18 months of the initial strike, El Dorado's population grew from 1,000 to 7,000. Some three years later, the town had more than 20,000 residents and the field was yielding 28 million barrels a year.

The oil-boom era is recalled at the Kansas Oil Museum, where a 100-foot steel derrick, a 12-foot band wheel used for driving drill bits, a 1929 railroad tank car, a 1914 International truck, assorted tools and drilling paraphernalia, and photographs are on display. Just outside town, less than a quarter of a mile from I-35, are the ghostly remains of Oil Hill. Once a thriving community of 2,500, where such industry titans as William Skelly and Al Derby got their start, the town is now deserted. But along its forsaken streets, beside its old foundations and empty schoolyards, flowers still bloom in their neglected beds, proof of the prairie's resilience and tenacity.

Farther along the highway, however, is testimony to the land's vulnerability in the face of nature's whims. Lying in a broad, flat valley southeast of Emporia, the John Redmond Reservoir impounds the runoff from more than 3,000 acres that drain

into the Neosho River and its tributaries. Before the dam was completed in 1964, the lush valley had flooded 57 times in 34 years. In the worst of those disasters, floodwaters ran 30 feet deep at the present dam site, and 350,000 acres were inundated. Today the area is a mecca for hunting, fishing, hiking, waterskiing, swimming, camping, and picnicking. The lake backs up to a plain of marshes, hardwood lowlands, leas, and sloughs that make up the 18,500-acre Flint Hills Wildlife Refuge. At

least 291 varieties of birds—including pelicans, ospreys, geese, bald eagles, swans, herons, sandpipers, and owls—are regular visitors to the refuge.

FARMING COUNTRY

From here, I-35 rises and falls through expansive croplands as it approaches the confluence of the Kansas and Missouri rivers. The National Agriculture Center and Hall of Fame in Bonner Springs exhibits more than 30,000 artifacts from the nation's farming past. Among them are the Midwest's first mass-produced farm truck, Harry Truman's plow, and an assortment of steam engines, threshing machines, and blacksmithing tools.

This strip of blacktop between San Antonio and Kansas City refutes the often-heard argument that, in giving Americans unprecedented mobility, superhighways have bypassed the heart and soul of the country—the small towns and majestic vistas, the nuances of everyday life that connect the whole nation to its past. It's all still here—just beyond the exits off I-35.

FARMING HISTORY
A steam-powered tractor, above, is on display at the National Agriculture Center and Hall of Fame in Bonner Springs, Kansas. Honoring America's farmers, the center exhibits farm machinery and implements and houses an unusual collection of barbed wire.

Through the Rockies

A blend of mountains and desert offers an ever-changing vision of natural wonders along I-70.

From the mile-high city of Denver, Colorado, to the valley town of Richfield, Utah, Interstate 70 is surely one of the most spectacular stretches of highway in the country. Leaving the Great Plains behind, the highway rises into the splendor of the Rocky Mountains, crosses the Continental Divide, and descends into fantastic sandstone wilderness. Wonders both natural and cultural abound in this land—the heart of the American West. Dinosaurs, Indians, cowboys, miners, resorts, parks, and museums offer something for everyone. There are so many diversions that visitors may have difficulty reaching the intended destination with any great dispatch.

The first stop is Red Rocks Amphitheatre in Morrison, 15 miles west of Denver. Set amid dramatic upswept rock formations in the foothills of the Rocky Mountains, the natural amphitheater's superb acoustics have enhanced the performances of countless artists—from soprano Mary Garden, who sang "Annie Laurie" here in 1911, to Jimi Hendrix and the Beatles.

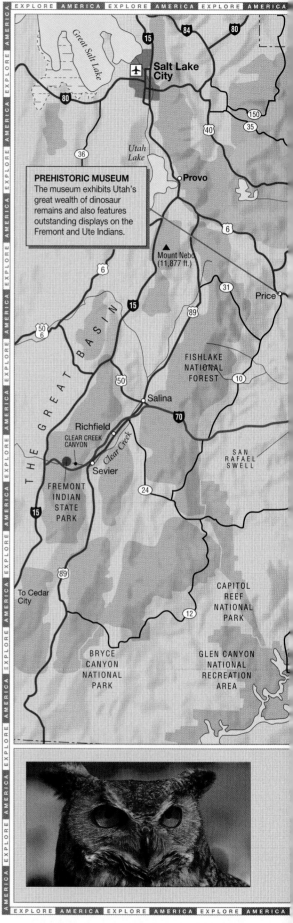

PREHISTORIC MUSEUM
The museum exhibits Utah's great wealth of dinosaur remains and also features outstanding displays on the Fremont and Ute Indians.

SPLENDOR AT SUNRISE
Early morning sun bathes an Easter service at Red Rocks Amphitheatre, above, outside Denver. The venue's main seating area is flanked by Ship Rock and Creation Rock, to the right and left, respectively, of the spectator. Each of these red sandstone massifs towers more than 400 feet in height.

LAND OF EXTREMES
Overleaf: From the Fiery Furnace Viewpoint in Arches National Park, winter's mantle softens the contours of the distant La Sal Mountains. This high desert landscape endures extremely hot summers and freezing winter temperatures.

Red Rocks was born in the early 1900's, when Denverite John Brisben Walker bought 4,000 acres of land and built a railroad to the property. In his Garden of the Angels theater, Walker hoped to host the world's greatest artists. Although his dream was never fully realized, it partly came true when the city of Denver bought the facility in 1927, and completed the theater in 1941. Red Rocks has seen many renovations in recent years: its amphitheater now seats 9,000 spectators.

MOTHER LODE

A little more than a century ago, travelers avoided the Rocky Mountains. But when John Gregory, a prospector from Georgia, struck gold in a gulch up Clear Creek in the winter of 1859, some 20,000 souls soon flocked in, eager to get rich quick.

The towns of Central City and Black Hawk were established in that year. By 1890 Central City was dubbed the "Richest Square Mile on Earth." More than $125 million in precious metals was extracted from the mines and sent down the hill to the smelter built by Nathaniel Hill at Black Hawk.

Less than a mile apart, the towns make up a single national historic district. Notable among the fine old buildings and Victorian homes that have been restored here are the Central City Opera House and the Teller House on Central City's Eureka Street. In the lobby of the Teller House stands an ornate grandfather clock, carried here by oxcart in 1865. Painted on the barroom floor is the face of a woman named Madeline, after the

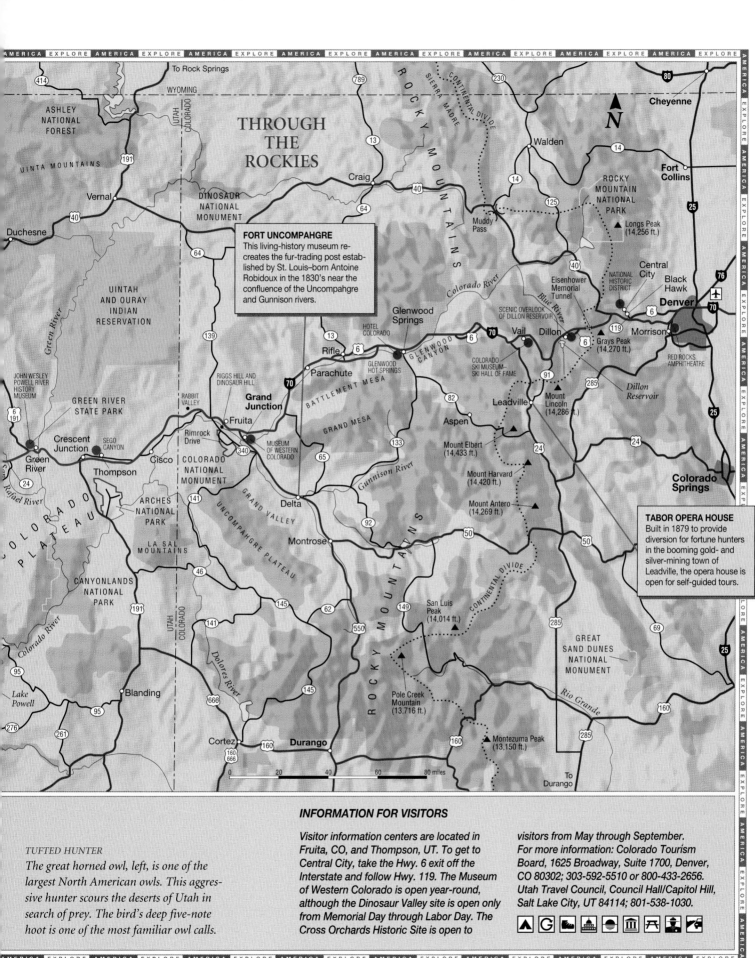

THROUGH THE ROCKIES

FORT UNCOMPAHGRE
This living-history museum re-creates the fur-trading post established by St. Louis–born Antoine Robidoux in the 1830's near the confluence of the Uncompahgre and Gunnison rivers.

TABOR OPERA HOUSE
Built in 1879 to provide diversion for fortune hunters in the booming gold- and silver-mining town of Leadville, the opera house is open for self-guided tours.

TUFTED HUNTER
The great horned owl, left, is one of the largest North American owls. This aggressive hunter scours the deserts of Utah in search of prey. The bird's deep five-note hoot is one of the most familiar owl calls.

INFORMATION FOR VISITORS

Visitor information centers are located in Fruita, CO, and Thompson, UT. To get to Central City, take the Hwy. 6 exit off the Interstate and follow Hwy. 119. The Museum of Western Colorado is open year-round, although the Dinosaur Valley site is open only from Memorial Day through Labor Day. The Cross Orchards Historic Site is open to visitors from May through September. For more information: Colorado Tourism Board, 1625 Broadway, Suite 1700, Denver, CO 80302; 303-592-5510 or 800-433-2656. Utah Travel Council, Council Hall/Capitol Hill, Salt Lake City, UT 84114; 801-538-1030.

AMERICA EXPLORE AMERICA EXPLORE AMERICA EXPLORE AMERICA EXPLORE AMERICA EXPLORE AMERICA EXPLORE AMERICA EXPLORE AMERICA EXPLORE AMERICA EXPLORE AMERICA EXPLORE

THROUGH THE ROCKIES 75

For centuries prior to the construction in 1888 of Glenwood Hot Springs Pool, right, the mineral waters at Glenwood Springs were renowned for their healing powers.

MAIN STREET

Central City, below, wears its past with pride. In gold-rush days, the community's diverse and cosmopolitan population gave it a reputation as one of Colorado's most "civilized" mining towns.

character in the poem *The Face Upon the Floor*. The portrait was painted in the 1930's, when an actor often recited the poem to the bar's patrons.

Visitors to the two towns can pan for gold or experience a modern version of gold-rush fever: legalized gambling. Jangling slot machines, blackjack tables, and other games of chance draw tourists by the busload to the more than 30 casinos in Central City and Black Hawk.

Once back on I-70, observant motorists may be treated to the sight of Rocky Mountain bighorn sheep poised on the cliffs right by the Interstate near the Dumont exit. The highway burrows under the Continental Divide by way of Eisenhower Memorial Tunnel. At more than 11,000 feet above

sea level, this is the highest point on any Interstate highway in the entire United States.

The western slope of the Rockies has long provided much of Denver's water supply. In the mid-1960's the city constructed a dam on the Blue River to form Dillon Reservoir, transferring the water to the east slope by means of a tunnel. The lake can be seen from overlooks along the highway, as can Torreys and Grays peaks—two of Colorado's "Fourteeners" (mountains over 14,000 feet high).

WINTER'S WONDERS

Vail is Colorado's most famous winter recreation destination. As downhill skiers and snowboarders clomp off toward the lifts, they pass the Colorado Ski Museum–Ski Hall of Fame. Here well-designed exhibits recount the development of skiing in the state from its beginnings in 1860, when skiers strapped homemade pine boards to their feet so that they could carry the mail or spread the gospel across snowbound mountains. By the 1930's ski clubs, winter carnivals, and ski-jumping contests had become popular, and the first downhill trails were cut into the mountains. During World War II, the U.S. Army trained ski troopers of the famed 10th Mountain Division at Camp Hale, near Vail. In the postwar years, skiing evolved into big business, with the development of Vail, Aspen, and a host of other resorts carved out of the forests, complete with condominium villages and chic restaurants.

Heading westward, I-70 begins to trace the course of the Colorado River. In Glenwood Canyon, the highway is hemmed in by the river on one side and sheer canyon walls on the other. Design, engineering, and construction of the road through the canyon was a monumental feat. For much of the 12-mile length, I-70 makes use of a tiered arrangement. Four rest areas within the canyon provide

largest outdoor mineral-springs pool. Ute Indians first discovered the healing qualities of these waters. In the 1880's British investors and mining engineer Walter Devereux developed the pool, the elegant red sandstone bathhouse, and the Hotel Colorado. Glenwood Springs soon became known as the Spa in the Rockies. Water temperatures in the pool range from 90°F to 104°F, and the facility is open year-round. The Frontier Historical Museum and Doc Holliday's grave are other notable attractions in the town.

TRANSITION ZONE From Glenwood Springs, I-70 continues along the Colorado River, where magpies, eagles, and herons perch in the cottonwoods. The wide-open spaces are classic Western ranching country. Near the towns of Rifle and Parachute rise the gray ramparts of Battlement Mesa, where entrepreneurs in the late 1970's and early 1980's tried without great success to squeeze oil from the shale rocks. This is also the transition zone between two major geologic provinces: the Rocky Mountains and the Colorado Plateau.

Grand Junction, founded in 1882, is the largest town on the west slope of the Rockies. Upon the arrival of the Denver and Rio Grande Western Railroad, Midwesterners flooded in. They planted fruit trees and alfalfa fields, irrigating them with water from the Grand (now Colorado) and

picnic places and river access for boaters, anglers, and hikers. A bicycle path parallels the Interstate, and native plants were saved to the greatest extent possible. The difficult construction of the I-70's westbound lanes was only completed in 1992, with the opening of Hanging Lake Tunnels.

The friendly mountain town of Glenwood Springs is especially inviting at Christmas, with shining lights, chestnuts roasting on open fires, and hot spring waters waiting to warm visitors. Clouds of steam wafting off the water and the faint smell of sulfur signal the presence of the world's

BALD MOUNTAIN
Snow crowns the pyramidal summit of Bald Peak, below, high above the 3,300-acre Dillon Reservoir. Created to store water for the Denver metropolitan region, the scenic reservoir is the center of a popular recreation area.

two short blocks from Grand Junction's inviting Main Street. Inside the museum, a timeline traces the history of the earlier inhabitants of the Grand Valley. The Native American hallway features fine examples of Ute beadwork and Mimbres pottery. The natural history section introduces the flora and fauna of western Colorado.

The museum's Dinosaur Valley features dinosaur skeletons and robots, a quarry where children can dig up real dinosaur bones, and a laboratory where visitors can watch paleontologists prepare bones for study. The first *Brachiosaurus* remains in the world were discovered at Riggs Hill in 1899. Riggs Hill, Dinosaur Hill, and Rabbit Valley along I-70 on the Colorado-Utah border are all managed by the Museum of Western Colorado as outdoor sites with self-guiding trails.

ONE MAN'S VISION

At Fruita, Colorado, a side trip leads to Colorado National Monument, one of the nation's lesser-known but most beautiful preserves. The 23-mile Rimrock Drive, built by the Civilian Conservation Corps and other agencies during the Great Depression, curls through the park. Along the route are spectacular views of the Grand Valley and Grand Mesa, the Colorado River, the Book Cliffs, and fanciful sandstone spires. Colorado National Monument stands on the northeastern edge of the 130,000-square-mile province known as the Colorado Plateau, a vast wilderness of slickrock sandstone and canyons.

The park owes its establishment to the efforts of many concerned citizens, particularly John Otto. He hacked out trails and did everything he could to

Gunnison rivers. The Grand Valley still produces peaches, apples, Bing cherries, grapes, and pears. The Museum of Western Colorado celebrates this agricultural heritage at its Cross Orchards Historic Site, a 24-acre living-history farm. Costumed guides demonstrate farm life of the early 1900's and offer tours of the workhouse and packing shed. Other exhibits display agricultural tools and equipment, narrow-gauge railroad cars, and antique construction equipment.

Two other museum sites are located five miles from Cross Orchards in downtown Grand Junction. The Regional History Museum stands

Scattered throughout Arches National Park are petroglyphs, below, left behind by the Fremont culture—Utah's first prehistoric people—and by the Ute Indians, who lived in the area at the time of the first European contact.

MONUMENTAL TRAILS

Eleven different trails, each bearing an evocative name such as Parade of Rock Art, Hidden Secrets Trail, and the Court of Ceremonies, take visitors through Clear Creek Canyon in Fremont Indian State Park, right. This late Stone Age culture lived in central Utah, farming and hunting in the region's deep canyons.

promote the area's preservation for future generations to enjoy. His tireless crusade succeeded when President Taft declared the area a national monument in 1911, ensuring a home for the deer, bats, lizards, and other creatures that live in this high desert land. Hikers can still follow some of Otto's trails into deep canyons with exposures of rock nearly 2 billion years old. Westward, signs along I-70 warn motorists to keep an eye open for golden eagles. These magnificent birds frequent the badlands of the Cisco Desert for its bounty of prairie dogs. At Thompson, a three-mile detour to the north leads to Sego Canyon, where prehistoric Indians and 19th-century Ute carved and painted human and animal likenesses on the rock walls. Sego was a turn-of-the-century coal-mining town, and Thompson was an important watering stop along the railroad.

At Crescent Junction, Highway 191 goes south to Arches National Park, a bewitching region of sandstone. The park protects more than 2,000 rock arches. Among the most famous are Delicate Arch, framing the La Sal Mountains; Landscape Arch, at 306 feet wide and 100 feet high the largest in the park; and the Windows section, where three major arches and many smaller ones look out onto a beckoning expanse of southern Utah desert.

Arches are creations of erosion. Here they are carved out of narrow fins of 150-million-year-old Entrada sandstone. The extraordinary number of arches in the region results from a fortunate combination of a core of domed salt and overlying sedimentary rock, with breaks or joints along which water etches the openings.

The best places to see the arches are in the Fiery Furnace and Devils Garden areas. The Windows section is easily accessible from the main park road; other arches can be reached by trail.

GREEN RIVER INTERLUDE

The small town of Green River, Utah, is named for one of the West's greatest rivers, upon whose banks the town sits. As the only river crossing for 300 miles, Green River has been a strategic place for Native Americans moving to hunting grounds, trappers and traders on the Old Spanish Trail, and daring river explorers such as Maj. John Wesley Powell.

The river burbles softly by at Green River State Park. Tall cottonwoods line the shore, shading campers and sheltering kingfishers, herons, and flickers. Every Memorial Day weekend, the park's boat ramp is the launch spot for the Friendship Cruise, during which hundreds of motorboats go down 200 miles of the Green to its confluence with the Colorado. In late spring and early summer, rafters, canoeists, and kayakers put in here for scenic trips through Labyrinth Canyon to Mineral Bottom, or even farther down into the wildness of Cataract Canyon.

This river-running legacy is recounted at the John Wesley Powell River History Museum, north of the main road in Green River. In an epic 1869 journey, Major Powell and his crew of nine men became the first to navigate the unknown reaches of the Green and Colorado rivers.

Visitors to the area in September may be the luckiest of all: they get the chance to sample Elberta peaches in Grand Junction and also to try Green River melons. A taste of either one of these sweet delicacies is one of life's unforgettable experiences.

West out of Green River, I-70 passes through a rawboned wilderness known as the San Rafael Reef and San Rafael Swell. In this part of the world, a reef is a land feature that has often proved a barrier to east-west travel. But the San Rafael Reef did not stop the builders of I-70. When this segment of

highway was opened in November 1970, Salt Lake City's *Deseret News* declared it "the gate to what is acclaimed to be the most scenic 70 miles of Interstate Highway in the country."

The Interstate penetrates the reef through Spotted Wolf Canyon, which rises into sawtoothed formations of rock. Ghost Rock, Black Dragon, Eagle Canyon, and other rest areas offer breathtaking views of the scenery, where the lonely cry of a raven is often the only sign of life. Ranchers have traditionally run cattle here, and outlaw Robert Leroy Parker, better known as Butch Cassidy, had no trouble hiding in this maze of canyon country.

From this stark desert terrain, I-70 enters Fishlake National Forest. Rock outcrops are banded in orange and gray and studded with piñon and ponderosa pines. These high plateaus of Utah mark a transition from the Colorado Plateau to the basin and range country around Salina and Richfield.

South of Richfield the Interstate runs through the largest prehistoric Indian village excavated in the state, with more than 100 structures. From about A.D. 400 to 1300, the Fremont Indians lived in hilltop villages and grew corn, beans, and squash along Clear Creek. They hunted deer and waterfowl and gathered cactus fruits and piñon nuts.

Although the village was destroyed during road construction, Fremont Indian State Park was established here in 1987 to preserve many other prehistoric and later features. The park is set amid the high volcanic cliffs of Clear Creek Canyon. In winter bald eagles soar over the creek searching for fish. The visitor center's museum contains Fremont artifacts unearthed at the village on nearby Five Finger Knolls. Among them are hide moccasins, carefully crafted clay figurines, fine obsidian arrowpoints, and a set of perfectly preserved deer legs—tanned, bundled, and placed in a jar.

Along several of the park trails are outdoor galleries that display the Fremonts' petroglyphs and pictographs, some of which have been interpreted as hunting scenes and creation stories. The park also exhibits an important collection of Fremont artifacts unearthed during the construction of I-70.

Long after the Fremont Indians had disappeared, Paiute Indians and Mormon homesteaders passed through or lived along the flowing waters of Clear Creek. Today I-70 whisks visitors through the region at speeds unimaginable in pioneer days. But just over the horizon, amid the slickrock canyons and majestic desert scenery, hidden worlds beckon those with time to linger.

DELICATE MONUMENT
The most famous landmark at Arches National Park is the 45-foot-high Delicate Arch, above. The park contains innumerable stone arches, created through the erosion of layers of sandstone and underlying salt domes.

DESERT DISCOVERY

*The arid Southwest offers glimpses
of nature's richness and the
triumph of human ingenuity.*

The summer sun rises over jagged blue mountains. As it ascends, heat shimmers off the pallid basins. By midday nothing stirs: it is the hour of the dust devil and the mirage. Hot gusts rattle the ocotillo cacti as towering clouds sail in, like galleons bulging with treasure. Lightning laces the blackening skies and thunder shudders through the arroyos. Rain splashes down in doubloon-size drops, swelling the washes and unleashing the aroma of creosote. Gradually the clouds disperse and the air groans with the song of spadefoot toads. At sunset the tips of cactus quills sparkle ruby red as the day bows out in a vermilion blaze.

The Southwestern desert is the stage for some of nature's grandest dramas, but it also presents a human pageant filled with visionaries and vanished civilizations, masterworks of art and amazing feats of technology. As Interstate 10 rolls through this land of splendor and intrigue between Tucson and Los Angeles, every bend in the highway seems to yield a new adventure.

SOARING CACTUS
In the Cactus Garden of the
Arizona-Sonora Desert Museum,
outside Tucson, the saguaro cactus,
above, reigns supreme. The largest
member of the cactus family, the
saguaro can reach heights of more
than 50 feet. The brightly colored
blossoms of the squat, cylindrical
barrel cactus, below right, conceal
some of the plant's fearsome spines.

ROOTED IN THE ROCK
Overleaf: The spiky top of a Joshua
tree offers a striking contrast to the
rounded forms of Jumbo Rocks, an
outcrop of eroded monzogranite in
Joshua Tree National Park.

Desert vistas are clear and endless, but the desert character can be as elusive as a roadrunner. It takes time to feel at ease with its peculiar blend of grit, wit, and grandeur. The newcomer may see only sand and weeds, but in fact the desert is full of life. Tucson's Arizona-Sonora Desert Museum is a good place to get acquainted with this unique environment. Nestled between cactus-clad Gates Pass and Saguaro National Monument's western section, this unusual zoo and botanical garden is a vital part of the land it interprets.

The Sonora Desert sprawls across southern Arizona and spills deep into northern Mexico. It is usually hot and dry, shielded from ocean moisture by coastal mountains. Yet it is also a lively place, home to thousands of fascinating creatures. How these plants and animals cope with heat and aridity is a tale that is told by a myriad of intriguing adaptations and relationships.

Most animals simply avoid the sun, hiding underground during the day and foraging for food at dusk or during the night. The kangaroo rat does not drink at all; other thirsty predators get moisture from their prey. Birds fly in the heat, but they too seek refuge. Some live in air-conditioned apartments: the gila woodpecker excavates a nest in the moist flesh of the saguaro cactus.

For plants there is no escape from the heat, and those seedlings that take root usually do so by growing in the shade of others. All plants have adapted to minimize water loss. The creosote has done this by coating its little leaves with waxy resins. The cactus has abandoned leaves, and stores water in the spongy flesh of its trunk and arms.

Finding a mate can be difficult too. The Sonoran whiptail lizard has given up on mating altogether, and survives by cloning itself. The same goes for some plants: the amazing creosote, for example, replicates itself as older parts die off. Some have survived in this lonely way for 10,000 years.

WHEN RAIN COMES

Many species have become opportunists, waiting for the arrival of rain to sprout or mate. Some desert seeds are coated with hard waterproof shells that can sit on the scorched ground for years like time-release capsules before they germinate. The spadefoot toad may spend a year underground until the rains create puddles large enough for its energetic mating.

The Arizona-Sonora Desert Museum tells the region's epic story by highlighting the vital interrelationships of water, plants, animals, and the parched land. Its fascinating exhibits re-create communities that range from the underground nests of burrowing owls to rugged mountaintop habitats where sleek pumas prowl.

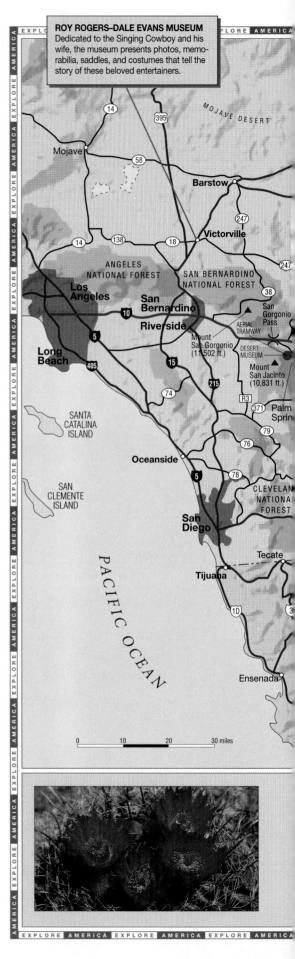

ROY ROGERS–DALE EVANS MUSEUM
Dedicated to the Singing Cowboy and his wife, the museum presents photos, memorabilia, saddles, and costumes that tell the story of these beloved entertainers.

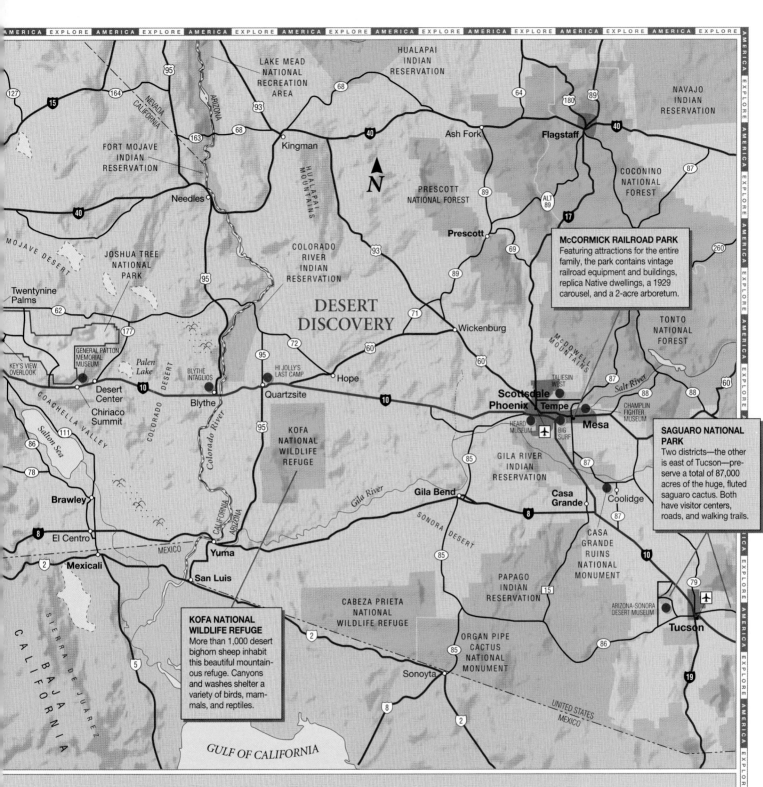

LAKE MEAD
NATIONAL
RECREATION
AREA

HUALAPAI
INDIAN
RESERVATION

NAVAJO
INDIAN
RESERVATION

NEVADA
CALIFORNIA

ARIZONA

FORT MOJAVE
INDIAN
RESERVATION

Kingman

Ash Fork

Flagstaff

COCONINO
NATIONAL
FOREST

Needles

MOJAVE DESERT

JOSHUA TREE
NATIONAL
PARK

HUALAPAI MOUNTAINS

PRESCOTT
NATIONAL FOREST

Prescott

Twentynine
Palms

COLORADO
RIVER
INDIAN
RESERVATION

McCORMICK RAILROAD PARK
Featuring attractions for the entire
family, the park contains vintage
railroad equipment and buildings,
replica Native dwellings, a 1929
carousel, and a 2-acre arboretum.

KEY'S VIEW
OVERLOOK

GENERAL PATTON
MEMORIAL
MUSEUM

DESERT
DISCOVERY

TONTO
NATIONAL
FOREST

Palen
Lake

COLORADO DESERT

BLYTHE
INTAGLIOS

HI JOLLY'S
LAST CAMP

Wickenburg

McDOWELL MOUNTAINS

Salt River

Desert
Center

Blythe

Hope

TALIESIN
WEST

CHAMPLIN
FIGHTER
MUSEUM

Chiriaco
Summit

COACHELLA VALLEY

Quartzsite

Scottsdale
Phoenix   Tempe

Mesa

**SAGUARO NATIONAL
PARK**
Two districts—the other
is east of Tucson—pre-
serve a total of 87,000
acres of the huge, fluted
saguaro cactus. Both
have visitor centers,
roads, and walking trails.

Salton Sea

KOFA
NATIONAL
WILDLIFE
REFUGE

HEARD
MUSEUM

BIG
SURF

GILA RIVER
INDIAN
RESERVATION

Colorado River

Colorado River

Gila River

Gila Bend

Casa
Grande

Coolidge

Brawley

CALIFORNIA
ARIZONA

Gila River

SONORA DESERT

CASA
GRANDE
RUINS
NATIONAL
MONUMENT

El Centro

MEXICO

Yuma

ARIZONA-SONORA
DESERT MUSEUM

Mexicali

San Luis

PAPAGO
INDIAN
RESERVATION

CABEZA PRIETA
NATIONAL
WILDLIFE REFUGE

Tucson

**KOFA NATIONAL
WILDLIFE REFUGE**
More than 1,000 desert
bighorn sheep inhabit
this beautiful mountain-
ous refuge. Canyons
and washes shelter a
variety of birds, mam-
mals, and reptiles.

SIERRA DE JUAREZ

BAJA CALIFORNIA

ORGAN PIPE
CACTUS
NATIONAL
MONUMENT

Sonoyta

UNITED STATES
MEXICO

GULF OF CALIFORNIA

INFORMATION FOR VISITORS

I-10 crosses the nation from Jacksonville, FL, to Los Angeles, CA. Between Tucson and Los Angeles, there are state information centers at Tempe, Scottsdale, and Phoenix, AZ, and a state welcome center near Blythe, CA. Summer temperatures in the desert regularly reach more than 100°F; spring and autumn are the best seasons to visit many of the outdoor sites. Big Surf is open

from Memorial Day weekend through Labor Day; all other sites are open year-round. Call ahead to check on the opening times and seasonal hours. The entrances for Joshua Tree National Park are located at Twentynine Palms and the town of Joshua Tree; the Cottonwood Visitor Center, at the north entrance, is accessible from I-10. There are nine campgrounds within the national park.

For more information: Arizona Office of Tourism, 1100 West Washington St., Phoenix, AZ 85007; 602-542-8687.
California Office of Tourism, 801 K St., Suite 1600, Sacramento, CA 95814; 916-322-2881 or 800-862-2543.

AMERICA EXPLORE AMERICA EXPLORE AMERICA EXPLORE AMERICA EXPLORE AMERICA EXPLORE AMERICA EXPLORE AMERICA EXPLORE AMERICA EXPLORE AMERICA EXPLORE AMERICA EXPLORE

DESERT DISCOVERY 85

A North American P-51D fighter, better known as the Mustang, right, shares hangar space with other restored vintage warbirds at the Champlin Fighter Museum in Mesa. The high-performance Mustang escorted bombers on daylight raids over Germany during World War II.

DESERT SAMPLER

A long-nosed bat, below, feasts on the succulent red fruit of an organ pipe cactus in the Arizona-Sonora Desert Museum. Pollen adheres to the bat's fur and fertilizes other plants the animal touches.

The museum's Desert Grasslands exhibit area features fauna native to a grassland habitat, from the termites burrowing underground to the wolf spiders and box turtles that lurk in the exhibit's 36 species of grass. Planned to replicate conditions along an arroyo, or seasonal watercourse, the exhibit even includes a re-created prehistoric mammoth kill site. Visitors who enter the hummingbird aviary shouldn't be startled if one of the tiny residents darts over and plucks a loose thread from a sweater or jacket to use for its delicate nest.

More animals than most visitors would probably imagine are at home in the harsh climate of the desert. Among the denizens that thrive in the museum's naturalistic habitats are coatis, Mexican wolves, bats, prehistoric-looking Gila monsters, ocelots, rattlesnakes, lumbering black bears, and tiny pupfish.

Some of the animals living here were injured and could never have survived in the wild. For others, like the river otters in the Desert Riparian Habitat, man's encroachment has destroyed much of their habitat. The museum returns injured animals to the wild whenever possible, and tries to draw public attention not only to the incredible vitality and complexity of the Sonora Desert but also to its extreme fragility.

Special events impart much of the traditional wisdom of the desert, such as where to look for Orion in the night sky and when to pick the fruit of the prickly pear. Such knowledge has enabled Native desert peoples to survive in a seemingly inhospitable land. Their ancestors were the first people to understand what the museum makes evident—that the desert is a bounteous place for those who know where to look and what to look for.

ECHOES ON A DESERT SEA

Heading northwest, I-10 traces the rich history of the Sonora's tribal past. The ancestors of today's Pima and Papago were a people known as the Hohokam (from a Pima word meaning "all used up" or "those who have gone"), who moved into this region more than 2,000 years ago. Their culture spread across much of Arizona and into northern Mexico before disappearing mysteriously about A.D. 1450.

At Casa Grande Ruins National Monument near Coolidge, the legacy of the Hohokam is preserved in the massive earthen walls of a giant building that is nearly 700 years old. It's hard to imagine an ancient culture thriving here, but the Hohokam had brought with them the secret of irrigation. They dug canals throughout the valley, cultivated large areas of the Gila and Salt rivers' bottomlands, and supported a sizable population on bumper crops of corn, squash, amaranth, and tepary beans.

The Hohokam were so successful for so long that their sudden decline baffles experts. At the center of the enigma stands Casa Grande, a multistory block built of caliche that was erected by hand. Fitted with massive floor and roof beams, the ruin contradicts everything known about the Hohokam, who lived not in pueblos but in scattered villages of mud-and-twig huts. The shadows of Casa Grande are mute, guarding its secrets. One theory holds that it was a primitive observatory from which the vanished people were able to observe and unlock the secrets of the heavens. But what caused their sudden disappearance? Was it overpopulation, a change in climate, or the influx of salt, the eternal foe of irrigation?

Scholars believe it was some combination of these factors. Whatever the cause, many of the people migrated elsewhere. It is possible that those who remained became known as the Pimas and Papagos, who continue to farm cotton in the area.

The Casa Grande Ruins Visitor Center boasts reconstructions of Hohokam dwellings. It also features displays of unique tools, weapons, and artifacts, such as distinctive Hohokam red-on-buff pottery and the etched shell jewelry for which they were justly renowned.

INTO THE SKIES

Farther up the Interstate, in nearby Mesa, a very different museum pays homage to aeronautical history. The Champlin Fighter Museum houses an unrivaled collection of restored vintage aircraft from World War I through the Vietnam War.

The museum traces the evolution of the fighter plane from handcrafted contraptions seemingly too flimsy to fly—much less fight—to the sleek, streaking demons of the jet age. Period music, uniforms, and posters conjure up bygone eras. World War I Fokkers mingle with Sopwith Camels; the Spitfire, plucky hero of the Battle of Britain, is wing-to-wing with its German counterpart, the deadly Messerschmitt 109.

At nearby Tempe, visitors can fly above the superheated desert floor, spin around in circles, and loop up again before zooming out of an enormous tubeslide to splash down in the middle of a gigantic wave pool. The slides are one attraction in Big Surf water park, which offers wet relief from the dog days of summer. Anyone looking for something wilder can rent a boogie board and rip up the big waves that surge across the main basin. Visitors can also work on a tan by playing volleyball on several sandy courts. The park features children's pools and shallow-water areas, as well as gentler slides for smaller thrill seekers.

Across the Valley of the Sun in Scottsdale, it appears as if an ark is ready to set sail. With bright white sails pitched and a redwood prow pointed out over the sea of sand, Taliesin West seems to

GREAT HOUSE
Protected from erosion by a modern steel shelter, the ruins of the four-story Casa Grande, below, present an enduring enigma. Archeologists remain uncertain as to its function or its significance to the people who erected it. Located in the Gila River valley, the structure towers above the ruined Hohokam Indian village that surrounds it.

rise out of the cactus and rock like a magnificent clipper slicing through the waves. The longtime winter residence and studio of famed American architect Frank Lloyd Wright and now a national historic landmark, Taliesin West is home to the Frank Lloyd Wright School of Architecture, and is open to the public year-round.

Wright was in his seventies when he purchased land here in 1937, but settling down was the last thing on his mind. Instead he and his wife and a group of apprentices constructed Taliesin West.

The name means "shining brow" in Welsh, the language of Wright's ancestors, and refers to Wright's Midwestern residence, Taliesin, which perches on the brow of a ridge overlooking the Wisconsin River just south of Spring Green. In similar fashion, Taliesin West rides the crest of a gentle mesa, looking out into the future as well as the desert.

For the last two decades of his life, Wright spent winters here with the students, "planning, playing, working, singing, dreaming," as he said, "all to pretty good purpose." Indeed, it was the most productive period in his life, and the work on Taliesin West became an embodiment of Wright's principles of architecture and his vision of human community.

Wright loved the desert. He marveled at the endless reach of its vistas and the stark geometry of its hills. He wanted to design a building that would enhance the natural beauty of a site, not diminish it. Taliesin West is the embodiment of Wright's principle of "organic architecture."

With roof beams that jut at angles into the sky, the structure is an architectural echo of the nearby McDowell Mountains. Despite the massiveness of its components, Taliesin West is an intimate place. The rooms themselves are not the square or rectangular boxes that we are accustomed to living in, but spaces that blur the distinction between indoors and outdoors, animating the home with the freedom of nature. Open to the sky at all angles, the building exults in the gorgeous vistas all around. The walls, which are made of stones selected from the surrounding desert that Wright loved so much, take on the spontaneous forms of local geology. Smooth lines contrast with rough surfaces; light with shadow; reds and mauves mingle subtly.

Today students at Taliesin exemplify Wright's belief that architects should be well-rounded individuals. They supplement their studies with training in construction, gardening, landscaping, and the arts, and also lead tours that give visitors a deeper understanding of Wright and his work.

Whether in the play of shadows on a rock wall or the shimmer of clouds in a sunken pond, Taliesin West invites personal reflection on the ancient harmony of mountains, sky, and desert. Perhaps this is what Wright built best: spaces for the spirit.

NATIVE SPIRIT

Situated on an elbow along I-10, the city of Phoenix has sprung up on the ruins of Hohokam waterways. A city in a constant state of change, Phoenix has grown from an oasis in the middle of an arid and unforgiving land to become the nation's ninth-largest metropolis, with a future as bright as the desert sun. But although the new has replaced the old, the past is never forgotten.

Recognized as one of the the world's major repositories of Native American artifacts, the Heard Museum in Phoenix spotlights Southwestern Native cultures. Colorful Navajo weavings, shining silver Zuni jewelry, and Pima baskets celebrate Native creativity and evoke a way of life based on the harmony of humanity and nature. From the Hopi pueblos in the north to the White Mountains of the Apaches and from the Navajo shepherds of Monument Valley to the Papago dry farmers of the Sonora, the Heard Museum documents the diversity of tribal groups while illuminating the relationships between them.

Among the museum's most important exhibits is a collection of more than 800 Hopi kachina dolls. For centuries the richly carved and decorated dolls representing kachinas, or spirit messengers, have been given to young girls on ceremonial days. During kachina ceremonies, which serve to assist in the prayers for rain, the pueblo squares reverberate with the low, rhythmic chanting of the kachina dancers wearing fantastic costumes and masks. The kachina dolls themselves are an important part of a child's religious education, teaching the unity of the physical and spirit worlds. The museum's extensive collection follows the evolution of kachina styles from the rigid figurines crafted along traditional lines to the brightly colored and lavishly clothed dolls of today.

Like the cultures it celebrates, the Heard is alive with the voices of elders and the laughter of children. Changing exhibitions, whose themes range from Native American women artists to the cul-

tural significance of rain, complement special events such as the acrobatic Hoop Dance Competition, held each February. Native artists-in-residence demonstrate weaving, pottery, and jewelry-making techniques that have been perfected over millennia; Native musicians and dancers fill the halls with song. Old Ways, New Ways, a hands-on exhibit, enables children to tap into their own natural creativity by building miniature tepees or adding traditional designs to Zuni pottery. The museum's gift shop is an outgrowth of its support for Native culture, featuring original works by Southwestern artists working in every genre.

From thriving plant communities to the ancient civilizations of the Hohokam and Hopi, survival

in the desert has always meant cooperation. But out on the sand-scoured rhyolite barrens of western Arizona, the hot winds tell strange tales of individualists and eccentrics. A case in point is the unusual story of Hadji Ali of Quartzsite.

SHIPS OF THE DESERT

To secure its newly annexed Western territories, the U.S. government planned to build a series of forts in the region during the 1850's. The army imported several dozen camels and drivers from Syria to explore the rugged country. Among the drivers was Hadji Ali, a boy who would come to coax and cajole his camels into legend as Hi Jolly.

With the fearless Hi Jolly at the helm, the camels were a triumph. They overcame blinding snows, raging rivers, and parched wastes. But their cantankerous temperament vexed man and beast alike. To make matters worse, their rolling gait left even veteran cavalrymen green around the gills. The U.S. Army chose to revert to the more familiar donkey, and cashiered its remaining camels. But for years, many of the descendants of these hump-backed beasts roamed the desert, dumbfounding the region's settlers and spooking their livestock.

Hi Jolly endured: for a time the intrepid adventurer continued to haul cargo across the Colorado Desert with his beloved camels before trying his hand at prospecting. When he died in 1902, friends erected in his honor a unique pyramidal tomb with the familiar figure of a camel perched on top. Located in Quartzsite, it still attracts many visitors. Today the Quartzsite Chamber of Commerce keeps his colorful memory alive with Hi Jolly Daze, a popular fall parade that kicks off several months of bazaars and swap meets. A gem and mineral

AN ARCHITECT'S VISION
Originally conceived as the winter home, studio, and laboratory of its designer, the great American architect Frank Lloyd Wright, Taliesin West, above, sits on a mesa in the foothills of the McDowell Mountains outside Scottsdale.

SUN SEEKER
The collared lizard, left, raises its body temperature by basking in the sun. When it becomes too hot, the animal simply scuttles into the shade. The reptile's dry, scaly skin protects it from dehydration.

show, held every February, attracts numerous dealers from all over the world.

At dawn the Colorado River gleams like mother-of-pearl as on either bank low mesas rise from the cool desert floor. Egrets and herons patrol the bulrushes. Here, where I-10 now runs, Chemehuevi farmers tilled the floodplains in the early 1800's and encountered fortune-seeking prospectors. The lower Colorado is both bringer of life and barrier to it, marking the end of the Sonora Desert and the beginning of the more barren Colorado Desert.

DESERT ART

Today's Colorado River is a well-managed system of dams, power stations, and reservoirs, but a hint of mystery remains on a riverside bluff north of Blythe: huge figures of humans and animals are etched into its dark mesa-top surface. Known as the Blythe Intaglios, the etchings are fenced off but can be viewed from an elevated platform. Named after an Italian technique of carving, intaglios are also found in Australia, New Caledonia, and parts of South America. These geometric shapes and animal and human forms beguile visitors with their simplicity and challenge them to solve the mystery of who made them and why.

Viewed from the air the intaglios leap to the eye, leading some to speculate that the figures must be religious icons created to communicate with the heavens. At ground level they are harder to see at first, but details such as the little piles of rocks that form eyes and noses soon become distinct.

Some early writers attributed the intaglios to the ancestors of nearby Native tribes. They identified one figure as a horse, which would date the intaglios from the arrival of mounted Spanish explorers in the 1450's. But some anthropologists believe the animal is a mountain lion that may represent the god Hatakulya from Mohave creation stories. Hopi legends tell of distant tribal wanderings during which clans marked their routes with sacred insignias, or fetishes. Some believe a human figure at Blythe resembles the fetish of the Hopi fire clan. Tantalizing questions remain: Were these religious sites or sacred meeting places? Were they political

boundaries or route signs? For now, the intaglios continue to guard their mysterious secrets.

West of Blythe, more curious patterns emerge from the desert: a long straight axis, a series of squares, and a line of white stones among the gray burro weed. These are the remains of the Desert Training Center, the world's largest wartime maneuver area. The General Patton Memorial Museum at Chiriaco Summit commemorates this mass experiment in desert survival, and the gritty, sometimes controversial soldier who created it.

In March 1942, the United States had just entered World War II. In North Africa, German armies advancing on the vital Suez Canal were threatening to sever Allied sea lanes. Pres. Franklin D. Roosevelt decided that American forces must stop the Nazis in the Sahara, and selected Maj. Gen. George S. Patton to establish a facility for training soldiers in a desert environment. Patton, an expert in the new science of tank warfare, toured the area and set up camp. Almost immediately recruits and equipment from across the country began to arrive by truck and train. Within a few months, the first graduates shipped out to the battlefield.

Two unyielding natures—Patton and the desert—combined to forge a force that helped to turn the tide of war. Patton directly oversaw all operations, camping with his men and personally testing food, supplies, and clothing. He enforced a relentless regimen of physical training, in which troops were required to run a mile in 10 minutes daily while carrying a fully loaded pack. The desert did the rest: temperatures inside the tanks reached 150°F, cold water was unknown, and troops battled waves of heat prostration, scorpions, and dust.

The museum portrays the struggle and triumph of the more than 1 million men who trained here. Memorabilia and photographs document daily life in the camps, and displays of vintage tanks echo with the roar of distant battles.

A PROPHET'S TREE

A short march farther down I-10, the creosote and barrel cactus thin out, the light reddens slightly, and strange erect figures rise from the mirage. Moving closer, visitors cross an imperceptible border and enter a new desert—the Mojave, land of the Joshua tree.

Straddling this biological divide is Joshua Tree National Park, known until 1995 as Joshua Tree National Monument. Half of it takes in the low Colorado Desert and the other half the higher, cooler, and wetter Mojave. In the transition zone, ocotillos grow beside yuccas, and creosote bushes share soil with the park's trademark Joshua trees. Mormon trailblazers named these members of the yucca family after the prophet Joshua, who wel-

comed the Israelites to the Promised Land. For settlers traveling to the fertile basins of Southern California, the upraised arms of these trees must have seemed welcoming indeed. For the visitor to Joshua Tree National Park, they are whimsical guides to a wonderland of colors and shapes.

The park's grandest Joshua trees are found at Upper Covington Flat. Thirty feet tall and up to 1,000 years old, the trees play a key role in a complex ecosystem, providing a habitat for woodpeckers and orioles. Once fallen, their decaying wood benefits insects.

Near the transition zone, a garden of Bigelow cholla clusters at the mouth of a canyon, patiently waiting for water. Nicknamed "teddy bear cholla," these are the spiniest of all cacti, protecting themselves with a wicked array of barbed needles. More than 10 different species of cacti live in the Mojave, with names and shapes ranging from "cushions" to "grizzly bears."

At Jumbo Rocks, climbers cling to giant granite boulders and spires, and artists soak up the subtle peach-and-bronze hues. Spring brings the colors

ARABIAN SANDS
One of the most visited landmarks in the Southwest, Hi Jolly's Last Camp in Quartzsite, above, is an affectionate tribute to the transplanted Syrian camel driver who worked as a guide and prospector in this corner of western Arizona.

The Palm Springs Aerial Tramway, right, whisks visitors on a dizzying 2.5-mile journey from Valley Station in Chino Canyon to the summit of Mount San Jacinto. At the top, visitors have access to the San Jacinto Wilderness.

ARMORED MUSCLE
Gilded by a desert sunset, an M-47 tank at the General Patton Memorial Museum at Chiriaco Summit, above, appears ready for combat. The museum commemorates the more than 1 million soldiers who trained for duty in North Africa in the harsh Colorado Desert during World War II.

of pink verbena, lilac Mojave aster, orange mariposa, and radiant yellow cassia—a mere sample of some of the 700 species of flowering plants that bloom in the desert.

About 80 million years ago, volcanic magma pushed up near the earth's surface, which was covered by soft gneiss. During that epoch, inland seas covered much of the Mojave. As water percolated along stress joints and fissures in the rock, the gneiss eroded away, leaving the fanciful, rounded monzogranite sculptures. In Hidden Valley, a nature trail winds among these bizarre rock formations. Rustlers once stashed whole herds of cattle in these shadowy desert draws. Key's View Overlook brings grander aspects of the national park's geology into view: the twin sentinels of Mount San Gorgonio and Mount San Jacinto above, and the San Andreas Fault—an ominous wrinkle in the Coachella Valley—below.

Strolling among the rocks, visitors can hear the echo of primeval seas, reminders of which are preserved in the trickle of a fan-palm oasis. Five of these treasures grace the park. More than 9,000 years ago, prehistoric Pinto Man stalked giant ground sloths through marshlands that once covered the region, and which eventually shrank to oases. For years, the region provided sustenance for the Chemehuevi, Serrano, and Cahuilla peoples. Prospectors and ranchers have slaked their thirst here. Today the oases support a rich community of plant life, including unexpected groves of maidenhair ferns. Biologists are still uncertain whether the ferns represent a remnant of ancient swamps or are wanderers from the coast.

Joshua Tree National Park is a lesson in time and space. Desert time ticks in eons with the slow but steady drip of water through layers of porous rock. To stop here and listen is to discover the patience of ageless processes and touch the mortal span of earth itself.

PALM SPRINGS

At the base of majestic Mount San Jacinto luxuriates the resort city of Palm Springs, playground of movie stars and home to the Palm Springs Desert Museum. Once devoted entirely to the Native and natural heritage of the Coachella Valley, the museum still contains a natural history interpretive center, which offers excursions, lectures, and a host of interactive dis-

plays. Having evolved over time, the Palm Springs Desert Museum now embraces a much broader range of subjects.

With a three-pronged approach, the museum focuses on art, natural science, and the performing arts. The natural science section includes interpretive dioramas that show how wild creatures survive in the region's harsh surroundings. The wondrous landscape is also celebrated in the museum's spacious art wings, where 19th-century paintings hang near contemporary works. In the Annenberg Theater, world-class dance, theater, and music turn the spotlight from the natural world to the works of those people creative enough to have bold visions and determined enough to achieve their goals.

One such man was Francis F. Crocker. As a young engineer working in the intense heat at the base of Mount San Jacinto in 1935, Crocker dreamed of being transported to the cool alpine glades of the summit. The more he sweated, the more determined he became to build a tramway leading from the desert floor to an observation area more than a mile up the sheer slot of Chino Canyon. The project's audacity earned it the nickname Crocker's Folly. Yet by opening day in 1963, the Palm Springs Aerial Tramway had silenced all doubters with its technical daring. Four of the five massive towers needed to support the tramway cables were inaccessible by road, so all workers and materials had to be airlifted by helicopters that flew more than 23,000 missions without a single mishap.

Today tramcars take passengers to an 8,500-foot elevation in just 15 minutes. Along the way, the trams pass through five climatic zones, from prickly pear cacti to aromatic juniper and pine forests. From this imposing island in the sky, an ocean of desert unfurls below. At the summit, Mount San Jacinto Wilderness State Park beckons with 54 miles of trails amid the pines. For the less adventurous,

a mile-long nature trail starts near the station. During winter, a spirited snowball fight or a brisk loop around a cross-country ski trail at the summit is proof that Crocker's dream has come true.

Rolling through the San Gorgonio Pass, I-10 leaves the desert, bound for a rendezvous with Los Angeles and the Pacific Ocean. For travelers there is time for one last glance over the shoulder as the arms of Joshua trees hoist a silver harvest moon skyward, and the purple trance of dusk engulfs the desert in magic. It really is more than just a big, hot, dry place after all.

VERTICAL VENTURE
Eroded rock formations in Joshua Tree National Park, left, are popular with climbers, who can scale faces that range in difficulty from easy to expert.

Panoramic Northwest

Natural wonders, both subtle and sublime, greet travelers along this stretch of I-84.

From the fern gorges of Oregon to the plateaus of Idaho, Interstate 84 traces the turbulent movement of elements and peoples. It is a region graced with natural riches and humming with enterprise and invention, where an abiding remembrance of the past fuels expansive dreams for the future. The wind of infinite possibilities courses across the grand open spaces, tantalizing each new visitor to this region of wide basins and thrusting mountain ranges.

From the glaciers of the Canadian Rockies, the Columbia River descends across the barren plateau of eastern Washington. It carves its way westward through the Cascades and pours into the Pacific Ocean along a rugged coastline hewn at the dawn of time. Nowhere is this grandeur more apparent than in the Columbia Gorge. Here a series of ice-age floods sliced through basalt lava flows that had taken more than 40 million years to form, creating a sea-level channel through the Cascades and bequeathing a 60-mile wonderland of sculpted bluffs, waterfalls, and forests.

LAKE VIEW

Overleaf: Basalt cliffs line the shores of 24-mile-long Lake Celilo. The lake, hemmed in by the powerhouse and spillway of The Dalles Dam, is fed by the Deschutes River and other smaller streams.

MAGIC CHASM

Mysterious Oneonta Gorge, right, lies within the Columbia River Gorge National Scenic Area. Water seeps from lichen-clad canyon walls and clubmoss drapes decaying trees. Wild ginger and mist maidens bloom in profusion within the gorge, and butterflies and nuthatches are often spotted darting through shafts of sunlight.

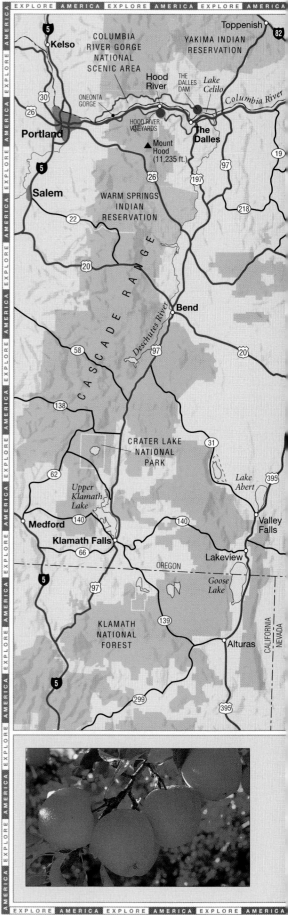

In 1986, after decades of conservation efforts by dedicated citizens, Congress designated the gorge the Columbia River Gorge National Scenic Area.

From Troutdale, historic Highway 30 winds beneath a sun-speckled canopy of alders and maples to Vista House at Crown Point, a promontory 700 feet above the river that affords spectacular views in all directions. It is an ideal place to begin a tour of the many waterfalls of the Oregon shore. At Latourell, Shepherds Dell, and Bridal Veil, short walks follow the misty whisper of falling water to sanctuaries of polished black rock and crystal pools. A few miles farther on, Wahkeena Falls tumbles down a rocky cliff in a series of rambunctious segments, and Multnomah Falls, Oregon's foremost tourist attraction, plunges 620 feet into an enormous basin scoured out of dark basalt. A paved pathway leads to a thrilling lookout atop the falls.

Oneonta Gorge lies just two miles away, but seems a world apart. A Botanical Special Interest Area, this hushed and mossy crevasse is home to many plants found nowhere else. Trails lead up Oneonta Creek to secluded waterfalls and climb through lush, fern-filled forests to glacier-carved subalpine basins. The gorge shelters a miniature rain forest in a primeval state.

HARVEST TIME

Golden Delicious apples ripen in the glorious fall sun, right. The Northwest is dotted with some of the most productive apple, pear, and cherry orchards in the nation.

96

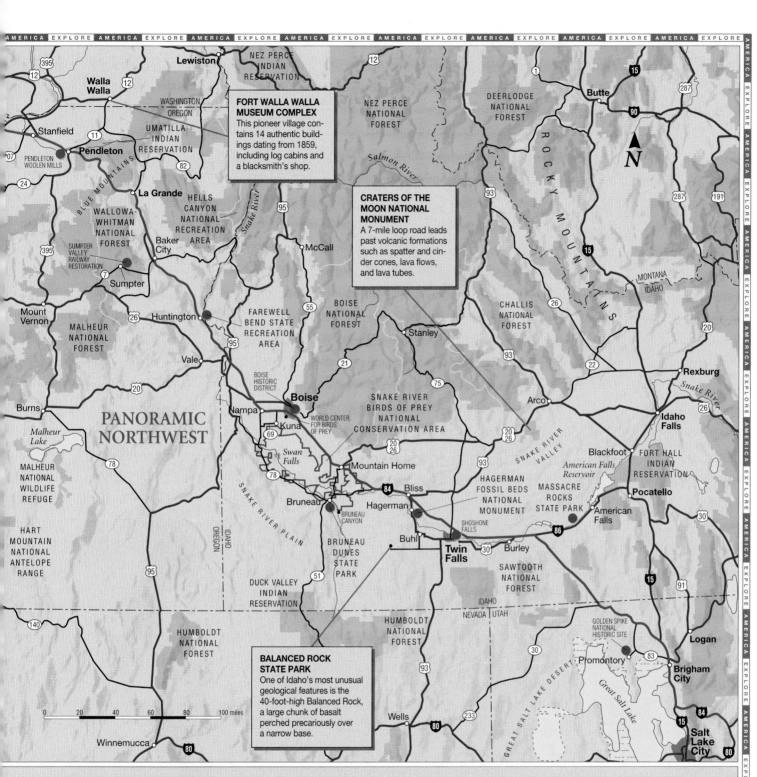

FORT WALLA WALLA MUSEUM COMPLEX
This pioneer village contains 14 authentic buildings dating from 1859, including log cabins and a blacksmith's shop.

CRATERS OF THE MOON NATIONAL MONUMENT
A 7-mile loop road leads past volcanic formations such as spatter and cinder cones, lava flows, and lava tubes.

PANORAMIC NORTHWEST

BALANCED ROCK STATE PARK
One of Idaho's most unusual geological features is the 40-foot-high Balanced Rock, a large chunk of basalt perched precariously over a narrow base.

0   20   40   60   80   100 miles

INFORMATION FOR VISITORS

State information centers along I-84 are located in Portland, OR, Fruitland, ID, and in Logan and Salt Lake City, UT. The Hood River Vineyards are open daily from March through November. The Dalles Dam and Lake Celilo are open from mid-June through Labor Day. Pendleton Woolen Mills is open Monday through Friday year-round except Christmas and New Year's Day. The Sumpter Valley Railroad Restoration is open from Memorial Day weekend through September; all other locations mentioned are open year-round. Weather varies in this region. Summers can be hot, with temperatures soaring regularly over 100°F in certain areas. From November to March icy road conditions can make driving extremely treacherous.

For more information: Oregon Tourism Division, Oregon Economic Development Dept.,

775 Summer St. NE, Salem, OR 97310; 800-547-7842.
Idaho Division of Travel Promotion, Idaho Dept. of Commerce, 700 West State St., Boise, ID 83720-0093; 208-334-2470.
Utah Travel Council, Council Mall, Salt Lake City, UT 84114; 800-200-1160.

ORCHARD RICHES
A pear orchard in the Hood River Valley, above, blossoms in the spring. Snowcapped Mount Hood dominates the skyline.

LIFE IN THE DUNES
Cheatgrass and bunch are among the desert plants that thrive in the arid environment of Bruneau Dunes State Park, right. The park is also home to coyotes, jackrabbits, lizards, and squirrels.

VALLEY VINEYARDS

Whitecaps and sail boarders skip across the river surface as I-84 reaches the Hood River. This is the fulcrum of northern Oregon's climate—a wind channel that serves as a conduit for summer warmth and winter cold. To the east the climate begins to dry out, and to the south rolling hills blanketed with apple, pear, and cherry orchards reach the foot of Mount Hood. During the 1980's Oregon's Pinot Noirs began to achieve superior quality, and some of the best are produced at Hood River Vineyards. The charming family-owned winery is open from March to November for tours, tastings, and sales.

The Dalles region has a long history of enterprise. For more than 10,000 years, this dogleg in the Columbia was a major meeting place for Native cultures from the coast and the high plains. The tribes came to fish at a spot known as Celilo Falls, where the Columbia tumbled over miles of rocky islands. Each spring millions of spawning salmon lunged through the bruising rapids to reach the upper river. The salmon caught at Celilo Falls were dried and then traded as far away as the Great Lakes and the desert Southwest.

In 1915 a series of locks bypassed Celilo Falls and permitted ships to navigate the upper Columbia. In

1957 The Dalles Dam went into operation, submerging the churning cataract altogether. From the visitor center, a small train takes tours to the cavernous powerhouse. In the control room, engineers monitor a complex system that generates electricity for much of eastern Oregon. Salmon still migrate through here, although in smaller numbers. By means of underwater viewing portals, visitors can watch them pass along fish ladders.

Along with the falls, rising waters submerged many ancient petroglyphs. Fortunately, several were relocated to the visitor center, where they preserve a sense of the past alongside exhibits charting the challenges, triumphs, and sacrifices of Columbia River navigation. The most famous petroglyph of the Columbia River Gorge is Tsagaglalal—"She Who Watches"—located across The Dalles Bridge in Horsethief Lake State Park. Perched above Celilo Falls, Tsagaglalal has witnessed the passage of many waves of humanity, and like the mighty Columbia River, her gaze is stoical, part of time itself.

Beyond the Cascades, the gorge widens and the thick forests give way to outcrops of basalt covered in cheatgrass and sage. As it leaves the Columbia behind, I-84 emerges onto a plateau of golden rangeland. Pendleton occupies a vale on the Umatilla River, a tributary of the

Columbia. The city arose as a major supply center for eastern Oregon's cattle industry and provided amusements for ranch hands. This lusty tradition lives on in the form of the Pendleton Roundup, held every September since 1910.

Pendleton is best known for its magnificent wool. Oregon pioneers found the cool, misty climate perfect for raising sheep, and the first mills went up in the 1840's. Among the experienced millers drawn west was Yorkshireman Thomas Kay, whose grandsons Clarence and Roy Bishop purchased the Pendleton mill in 1909. Here they began making their trademark Indian blankets, shirts, and coats, processing wool from sheep to shelf under one roof. Pendleton Woolen Mills, located in the town's historic center, is a world-renowned producer of quality clothing. Today a fifth-generation family business, the Pendleton facility is the heart of a manufacturing empire that includes 14 mills and factories. Weekday tours of these busy mills give visitors the opportunity to view the process of modern wool production.

RAILROAD RESTORATION

Forging east, I-84 climbs into the Blue Mountains, where fragrant ponderosa pines add spice to the crisp mountain air and the sun chases the mist through the hollows. Soon the Grande Ronde River joins the verdant valley that bears its name. Overwhelmed by its bounty, many settlers bound for the coast stopped here, and some of those who pressed ahead later returned. At the valley's southern end, historic Baker City features broad avenues, ornate facades, and sumptuous Victorian homes that attest to the prosperity that flowed from field and forest.

The town of Sumpter was founded in 1862 by five Southerners celebrating the birth of the Confederacy. For decades it remained a woebegone hamlet six miles from the nearest stagecoach stop. All that changed when gold was discovered, transforming Sumpter seemingly overnight into a roaring boomtown complete with paved streets, electric lighting, and long-distance telephone service. Today Sumpter is a quaint town with rustic restaurants, charming shops, and a historic train.

Beginning in 1890, the Sumpter Valley Railroad (SVRR) hauled timber to Baker City sawmills, but soon expanded its service to include passengers, gold, and cattle. Pieced together from narrow gauges across the West, the SVRR was a riot of styles and pedigrees, rods and gears. Regular service was discontinued in 1947, but valley residents rallied to save their beloved railroad. Through much perseverance, they established the Sumpter Valley Railroad Restoration and brought the line back to life. Pulled by a wood-burning locomotive, the train runs along the river from the old stage stop to a restored dredging ship that once mined the riverbed for gold. It is now the centerpiece of a historical park and a wildlife viewing area. Nature trails are posted with signs describing the beavers, cranes, and other wildlife that inhabit the valley.

PIONEER MEMORIAL
Located along the old Columbia River Highway, the octagonal Crown Point Vista House, below, was built in 1918. Each of the dome's eight sides is inscribed with the name of a prominent pioneer.

South of Baker City, I-84 navigates the plunging Burnt River Canyon and sails out onto rolling hills beside the Snake River. At Farewell Bend State Recreation Area, a weathered wagon commemorates the site where emigrants on the Oregon Trail bade farewell to the Snake and headed across northeastern Oregon. Engulfed in the gentle rustle of cottonwoods and willows, the grassy arc of parkland is a restful spot for a picnic, as the lustrous Snake River slithers silently past.

Boise, the capital of Idaho, is a modern political and economic center that retains a healthy measure of frontier spirit. Its historical center adds to its Western flavor. By attracting new technologies and offering a wealth of recreational opportunities, Boise ranks high in recent surveys of livable cities.

As early as the 1830's, French trappers were drawn to the dense woods, or *bois*, near the confluence of the Boise and Snake rivers, roughly 50 miles from today's city. Permanent settlement of the Boise area began in the 1860's during a gold rush in the nearby mountains. Farmers cultivated the fertile Boise River bottomlands to supply the bustling mining camps with food. After the arrival of the railroad, the territory became a state in 1890.

The U.S. Assay Office, opened in 1872, provided the important function of valuing the gold and silver brought to town by fortune-seeking prospectors. Set among prominent period residences on nearby Grove Street, the Basque Museum celebrates the contribution of an important immigrant group that brought agricultural and shepherding

acumen to southwestern Idaho. The new century found Boise brimming with a confidence that is best exemplified by the Idanha Hotel. Built in a French chateau style in 1901, the state's tallest and most glamorous edifice featured a novelty—Idaho's first elevator. On Warm Springs Avenue, successful entrepreneurs erected elegant mansions in every conceivable style, from Queen Anne to Georgian Revival. The homes were heated by local geothermal springs. Today the Warm Springs district is a pleasant neighborhood of broad streets and towering shade trees, whose new residents have

SOMBER REMNANTS
Brick rubble clings to the carved doorway of Sumpter's bank, right, ravaged by a horrific fire that destroyed many of the town's buildings in 1917.

BUSTLING BOISE
A mural in Boise, right, highlights the town's gracious past. The painting depicts horse-drawn carriages rolling down streets that are now used by automobiles.

lovingly restored their landmark dwellings. The final resting spots of the town's earliest settlers are also found off this tranquil street in the Pioneer Cemetery. Here, travelers can visit the grave of Thomas Jefferson Davis, the man who helped found Boise in 1863.

The Old Idaho Territorial Prison offers a glimpse of frontier history through the lives of local rogues and renegades. In use from 1870 until 1973, the stone-walled prison has been transformed into a museum that offers self-guided tours of the rough-and-tumble justice of the Old West. The gatehouses, officers' quarters, and cavalry barns of Old Fort Boise have survived up to the present on the bucolic grounds behind the state capitol. Some say the best view of the city is from these spacious lawns, as the summer sun begins its descent across the Owyhee Mountains.

| LAVA COUNTRY | The idyllic orchard dales fall behind and the fertile earth turns black and crusty as I-84 heads southeast from Boise. |

Great fissures tear open the plateaus to reveal the craggy canyons and rocky dells of lava country.

The Snake River Plain is one of the world's most fascinating volcanic regions. Like a gigantic treadmill, this section of the earth's crust has rolled westward across a stationary hot spot located deep within the molten mantle. Periodically the hot spot has erupted, producing a chain of craters, cones, and lava flows that extends all the way from Oregon to Wyoming. Over the eons, the Snake River has carved a rugged channel through this volcanic slab. About 15,000 years ago, a vast inland sea in Utah, called Lake Bonneville, broke through its containment and gushed across southern Idaho, gouging out the bed of the Snake on its shortcut to the sea. On one 80-mile stretch of river, the Snake's distinctive combination of rocky escarpments and sage-covered plains provides a perfect nesting and hunting ground for many species of birds of prey. In August 1993, nearly half a million acres were set aside to form the Snake River Birds of Prey National Conservation Area, which supports the most concentrated assemblage of nesting raptors on the continent.

A 50-mile loop drive leads from Kuna to Swan Falls Dam to Celebration Park. Golden eagles, peregrine falcons, ospreys, and kestrels dive toward the bushy river banks for ground squirrels or ride updrafts across the plains in search of black-tailed jackrabbits. During spring and early summer, the canyon is filled with resident and migratory birds

NATURAL TREASURES
Cirrus clouds accent the landscape of Bruneau Dunes State Park, top. A juvenile long-eared owl, above, is one of the inhabitants of the Snake River Birds of Prey National Conservation Area.

IRON HORSE

The steam locomotive Jupiter, *above, is on display at the Golden Spike National Historic Site, where East first joined West on the transcontinental railroad. This powerful engine, along with* No. 119, *are detailed replicas of the original locomotives at that historic event. Costumed interpreters re-enact the Golden Spike Ceremony every May 10 and on the second Saturday in August.*

busily courting, mating, and nesting. The area is open year-round, and other seasons bring their own wonders. Few sights can rival the majesty of a bald eagle soaring in the steely winter sky.

While not a part of the NCA, the World Center for Birds of Prey is located just south of Boise. With its informative exhibits and live bird presentations, the visitor center is a good place to learn about the region's feathered inhabitants. The center not only provides an introduction to avian biology but also explains the challenging work of conserving these species and their unique habitat.

DUNES AND CANYONS

Visitors are awarded a bird's-eye view of the Snake River Plain from the top of Bruneau Dunes, south of Mountain Home on Highway 51. Stretching for some 600 acres, this dune range is located in the center of a massive semicircular basin carved from the surrounding mesa. Here prevailing winds have converged to erect the largest freestanding sand dune on the continent. The 470-foot mound is made up of quartz and basalt grains weathered off the surrounding volcanic landscape. A pair of lakes at the base of the dunes is an important stopover for migratory birds and a popular fishing spot for bass and bluegill anglers. A five-mile nature trail leads through lakeside marshlands to the sandy summit,

where solitude reigns across an endless sea of lava and sage. In spring the subtle grays and greens of the plain are splashed with the pinks of primroses, and the air resounds with the calls of blackbirds and mallards. Aside from being a refuge for a wide variety of wildlife, the dunes also attract people looking for unique activities. As children scamper through the fine gray sand, creative adults wearing old skis can be seen racing down the slopes. Sand boarders and parasailers also use this gritty landscape to satisfy their appetite for adventure.

Twenty miles south, a seasonal road brings travelers to the brink of Bruneau Canyon, a yawning gash in the earth that is more than 800 feet deep. Its sheer walls record millions of years of eruptions and lava flows from the ancient Bruneau-Jarbidge volcano. Over the course of eons the Bruneau River has cut through countless crustal layers—evidence of repeated coolings and sedimentations—that descend in a series of precipitous steps to the bottom of this hauntingly remote and virtually untouched chasm.

A drive through Hagerman Valley on Highway 30 sweeps past meadows and meandering streams. In 1928 a valley resident discovered a few fossils in a hillside above the Snake River—a find that led to a major excavation that was sponsored by the Smithsonian Institution. Containing the remains of more than 100 species, the Hagerman area is

their sides polished smooth. One scattering of such boulders has become Massacre Rocks State Park. In the 1920's a local promoter gave this gulch its ghoulish name, calling to mind an Indian raid on five wagon trains some 60 years earlier during which 10 Oregon Trail emigrants were killed. The raw violence of the frontier seems remote today as pelicans and majestic herons glide gracefully along the river's edge, and waving grasses flash glimpses of colorful wildflower bouquets. But access to the past is close at hand: Displays in the visitor center detail the natural history of the area, and nearby wagon ruts and Register Rock—a boulder whose slick surface bears the graffiti of westbound pioneers—are relics of the Oregon Trail.

MAJESTIC UTAH

Endless sunny skies and sloping panoramas usher visitors into Utah. Windy passes and lonesome clusters of piñon pine gradually give way to tidy townships, well-tended fields, and marshlands pulsing with the flutter of migrating birds. The Wasatch Range, the spine of the state, arches majestically in the east, and antelope gambol across grassy basins sparkling with spring runoff. To the south, gulls wheel over the placid Great Salt Lake, a remnant of prehistoric Lake Bonneville.

Atop breezy Promontory Summit on May 10, 1869, Leland Stanford of the Central Pacific and Thomas Durant of the Union Pacific tapped ceremonial gold and silver spikes into a laurelwood tie, symbolically completing the country's first transcontinental railroad. The railway overcame every conceivable topographic challenge, as tireless crews bored through mountains, filled valleys, bridged rivers, and traversed wide-open plains, laying 1,776 miles of track in six years. It was a human epic that involved some 20,000 laborers, many of them Irish and Chinese immigrants who made decisive contributions to the settlement of a new land.

At the Golden Spike National Historic Site, a nine-mile auto tour commemorates the stirring events that attended the arrival of the railroad. The road allows travelers to drive along the grades, cuts, and fills of the original track. Special festivals feature guides in period clothing and handcar races, evoking the romance of the rails.

From the hunting trails of Native Americans to the wagon ruts left by emigrants; from the steel ribbons of railway to the Interstate's gentle curves, the paths of many peoples have crossed the basins and ranges of this region. Each generation blazes a new trail, and the thrill of the earliest explorers reverberates within each traveler who sets eyes upon this marvelous land for the very first time.

WATER POWER
Shoshone Falls, left, is located on the Snake River. By the 1920's a dam had marshaled the force of the torrent of water, and the falls were providing electricity for most of the region.

THE DALLES DAM
Inside the powerhouse of The Dalles Dam, above, multicolored generators hum in unison as millions of gallons of water pour through the turbines. The force of water rotates the turbines, producing electricity.

now widely recognized as one of North America's most significant fossil deposits. The rich fossil beds give paleontologists a crucial glimpse into life during the Pliocene era. In the town of Hagerman, the headquarters of the Hagerman Fossil Beds National Monument provides an overview of the finds and a few tantalizing reconstructions. At the site itself, an interpretive boardwalk leads visitors through the landscape. Among the creatures that once roamed southern Idaho were mastodons, hyenalike dogs, camels, and horses—including the 3.5-million-year-old *Equus simplicidens*, a close relative of today's zebra.

Shoshone Falls, five miles east of the city of Twin Falls, is often referred to as the Niagara of the West. At 212 feet high, this roaring cataract is actually 40 feet taller than its famed eastern cousin. Since the establishment of a railhead in nearby Shoshone in the 1880's, the thundering falls have attracted a gush of adventurers with dreams of exploiting the powerful flow for their own mercenary ends. They built hotels along the bluffs, operated ferries through the mist, and even ran battery-powered railroads from Twin Falls.

As it tracks the Snake River, I-84 offers more evidence of ice-age inundations. Sandbars a hundred feet high and flood-scoured lava buttes rim the river valley, where trailer-size boulders were tumbled along like dice, their edges rounded and

GOLDEN STATE DRIVE

From San Diego to Sacramento, I-5 offers a glimpse of California's glorious past and present.

Like a blacktopped backbone, Interstate 5 runs the length of California, from the Mexican border in the south to the wild forested splendor of the Sierra Nevada and the Cascade Range in the north. The stretch of highway from San Diego to Sacramento offers a study in contrasts; the bucolic pleasures of San Diego County give way to the frenetic sprawl of the Los Angeles basin; the Central Valley's agricultural splendor fades into memories of the Gold Rush and the 49ers in Old Sacramento.

With a population of roughly 30 million, the Golden State is almost a nation in itself. In countless fields of endeavor, California has set the pace for the rest of the country. But this Western giant began modestly enough, as an outpost of Spain's New World empire and the focus of the missionary efforts of the Franciscan order. With Mexico gaining independence from Spain in 1821, California became a distant province of the new Mexican Republic. Its benign climate, expansive cattle ranches, and bounteous orchards soon

GOLDEN GLOW
Overleaf: Sunrise transforms an eroded hillock into a fluted fantasy at Broken Hill Overlook, located in Torrey Pines State Reserve near San Diego. Silhouetted against the Pacific Ocean is a group of rare Torrey pines.

attracted attention from the young American republic to the east. After Mexico's defeat in the Mexican War of 1846, California came under American control. Settlers, gold seekers, dreamers, and fugitives began to flood into the new territory, initiating a population dynamic that continues to this day.

SAVING A SPECIES

The city of San Diego has strong ties to the past. Its bay was visited by Spanish explorer Juan Rodríguez in 1542 and by Sebastián Vizcaíno in 1602, who named it San Diego de Alcalá. The first Spanish mission founded in upper California was built here by Father Junípero Serra in 1769. The journey northward on I-5 leaves this historic city behind and soon brings visitors to one of the state's natural treasures: Torrey Pines State Reserve, located one mile south of Del Mar. The park preserves the endangered Torrey pine (*Pinus torreyana*), North America's rarest native pine. After fighting a 10,000-year struggle against a warming climate, which reduced its range, the tree also suffered the human onslaught of the last 200 years. Some 5,000 of these trees remain in the reserve and at Santa Rosa Island, about 90 miles off Los Angeles, where the trees are actually a subspecies of the Torrey pine.

A meditative walk along the Guy Fleming Trail at the reserve might reveal some of the numerous bird species that nest here, or even a distant view of dolphins and gray whales offshore. All around are the Torrey pines, stunted by wind near the coast, taller and straighter in sheltered areas. Small fires and arid conditions are actually friends of the Torrey pine. The tree's tightly sealed cones need to be heated before they open and the seeds inside

FLYING HIGH
The coast near the Torrey Pines State Reserve offers a range of outdoor activities, including the thrill of hang gliding, below.

WILD KINGDOM
Rare white rhinos, above, and other endangered animals from Africa and Asia thrive at the San Diego Wild Animal Park, located near Escondido.

INFORMATION FOR VISITORS

I-5 is the most heavily traveled route between Northern and Southern California. Although Southern California enjoys a mild subtropical climate and plenty of sun, the Central Valley can be extremely hot in summer. All attractions, parks, and sites are open year-round. There are admission fees for certain sites, including the San Diego Wild Animal Park, Universal Studios Hollywood, and the California State Railroad Museum.
For more information: California Office of Tourism, 801 K St., Suite 1600, Sacramento, CA 95814; 916-322-2881 or 800-862-2543.

OAKLAND MUSEUM OF CALIFORNIA
Devoted to the environment, history, and art of California, this acclaimed museum's three gallery levels are complemented by terraces, patios, gardens, and a koi pond.

KERN NATIONAL WILDLIFE REFUGE
A remnant of once-massive Tulare Lake, this wetland habitat is a prime viewing spot—especially in fall and winter—for migrating shorebirds and waterfowl.

LAWRENCE WELK RESORT
The lobby of the Resort Theater displays the baton, accordion, piano, bandstand, and huge champagne glass that endeared Lawrence Welk to millions of fans.

To Carson City

Sacramento
CROCKER ART GALLERY
49
16
CALIFORNIA STATE RAILROAD MUSEUM
SUTTER'S FORT STATE HISTORIC PARK
80
5
4
Bridgeport

95
TOIYABE NATIONAL FOREST
6
Coaldale
Tonopah

Oakland
680
Stockton
Ripon
Modesto
CASWELL MEMORIAL STATE PARK
SAN JOAQUIN VALLEY
99
120
YOSEMITE NATIONAL PARK
120
Mono Lake
395
6
INYO NATIONAL FOREST
Bishop
NEVADA
CALIFORNIA
95

01
280
San Jose
101
SAN LUIS RESERVOIR STATE RECREATION AREA
140
Merced
Red Hill (2,059 ft.)
Los Banos
San Luis Reservoir
UPPER AND LOWER COTTONWOOD CREEK
152
San Joaquin River
41
SIERRA NATIONAL FOREST
SIERRA NEVADA
KINGS CANYON NATIONAL PARK
SEQUOIA NATIONAL PARK
DEATH VALLEY NATIONAL PARK
To Las Vegas

1
Monterey
LOS PADRES NATIONAL FOREST
COAST RANGES
33
5
33
R. C. BAKER MEMORIAL MUSEUM
Coalinga
California Aqueduct
CENTRAL VALLEY
Fresno
Lemoore
Tulare
99
SEQUOIA NATIONAL FOREST
Lone Pine
136
Death Valley Junction
190

Big Sur
1
41
46
Lost Hills
TULE ELK STATE RESERVE
395
GOLDEN STATE DRIVE
127

Cambria
Atascadero
San Luis Obispo
58
119
Buena Vista Lake
BAKERSFIELD-KERN COUNTY MUSEUM
Bakersfield
58
14
MOJAVE DESERT
Soda Lake
15

Santa Maria
166
Mount Pinos (8,831 ft.)
FORT TEJON STATE HISTORIC PARK
Mojave
Barstow
40

Lompoc
1
101
LOS PADRES NATIONAL FOREST
TEHACHAPI MOUNTAINS
Tejon Pass
5
Santa Barbara

Santa Barbara Channel
UNIVERSAL STUDIOS HOLLYWOOD
Santa Clarita
ANGELES NATIONAL FOREST
San Bernardino
JOSHUA TREE NATIONAL PARK

PACIFIC OCEAN
SANTA ROSA ISLAND
SANTA CRUZ ISLAND
Los Angeles
1
CRYSTAL CATHEDRAL
Garden Grove
215
Coachella Canal
10

Long Beach
San Pedro Channel
SANTA CATALINA ISLAND
MISSION SAN JUAN CAPISTRANO
San Juan Capistrano
5
15
Salton Sea

SAN NICOLAS ISLAND
Del Mar
78
Escondido
SAN DIEGO WILD ANIMAL PARK

SAN CLEMENTE ISLAND
TORREY PINES STATE RESERVE
8
To Yuma

0   20   40   60   80 miles

San Diego

AMERICA EXPLORE AMERICA EXPLORE AMERICA EXPLORE AMERICA EXPLORE AMERICA EXPLORE AMERICA EXPLORE AMERICA EXPLORE AMERICA EXPLORE

GOLDEN STATE DRIVE 107

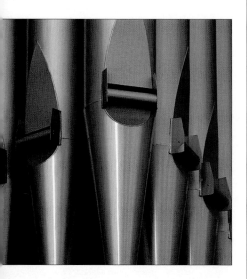

HOUSE OF WORSHIP
Its interior bathed in light, Orange County's enormous Crystal Cathedral, right, can seat almost 3,000 people in the sanctuary. The towering 16,000-pipe organ, above, situated behind the altar is the world's largest.

germinate. Fire also clears out competing plants and kills off some of the ground squirrels that would normally feast on the seeds. The state park service now arranges prescribed burns to help manage this unique tree.

Amid the developed coastal strip of Southern California, there are some areas where life is relaxed and slower paced. One of these is the city of Escondido, set amid sprawling avocado ranches and wineries. The surroundings are pastoral, with plenty of golf courses and country drives to explore. East of town is the San Diego Wild Animal Park, where 121 species of mammals and 285 species of birds gathered from Africa and Asia roam freely within the 2,200-acre grounds. Operated by the Zoological Society of San Diego, which also runs the world-famous San Diego Zoo, the Wild Animal Park was established in 1972 to provide animals with spacious surroundings similar to their natural habitats. The park's re-created environments range from the steppes of Mongolia and the East African savanna to the eucalyptus forests of Queensland, Australia. The park is a sanctuary for 41 endangered species, 30 of which have successfully reproduced here. The park's California Condor Recovery Project is responsible for breeding nearly half the condors alive today. An elevated monorail allows visitors to view the animals—except for the condors—with minimal disturbance. Most visitor facilities are located in the 17-acre Nairobi Village, where educational demonstrations on animal behavior take place in an amphitheater.

SAVING SOULS

California's first white settlers were the Franciscan missionaries, who came north from Mexico in the late 1700's with Father Junípero Serra. Visitors can explore this history at the Mission San Juan Capistrano, located in the coastal town of the same name. The mission was seventh among the 21 missions that the Franciscans founded in California between 1769 and 1830. It is one of the few California missions that still retains a large Native American congregation. Today costumed interpreters present programs that re-create mission life in earlier times, and on the grounds are the ruins of the Great Stone Church, built from 1796 to 1806. The 180-by-40-foot structure was a marvel of its time, and its 120-foot-high bell tower was visible from 10 miles away. The church collapsed during a major earthquake in 1812, killing many of the worshipers inside.

Shady arcades, above, surround the cloister at Mission San Juan Capistrano. The spacious courtyard was often the site of community events such as rodeos.

The mission prospered, with rich farmlands, more than 20,000 head of cattle, and an average of a thousand Native American converts, under the direction of the Franciscans. All the missions, including Capistrano, went into decline in the 1830's when the Mexican government replaced the system of Franciscan control with secular authority. Beginning in the 1890's, restoration work saved many of the mission buildings from decay.

Perhaps the most remarkable sight at Capistrano is the annual return of the cliff swallows, which arrive in the area about March 19. According to local lore, the birds seek out nesting places in the walls and arches of the mission, although in fact they nest throughout the Capistrano Valley.

The early missions find a modern counterpoint in Orange County at the Crystal Cathedral, a shimmering place of worship in Garden Grove. Sunlight creates an otherworldly effect in this masterpiece of modern ecclesiastical architecture. More than 10,000 windows of tempered, silver-colored glass are mounted on white-steel frames, enclosing a huge interior space 415 feet long and 297 feet wide. Designed by noted modern architect Philip

Johnson, the Crystal Cathedral serves as the home base for a nationwide televised evangelical mission that emphasizes positive thinking and holds the belief that human beings can improve themselves and the world.

Leaving the serenity of the Crystal Cathedral, I-5 enters the sprawling metropolis of Los Angeles—the hub of the nation's movie and TV industry. One of the best places to sample the magic of the movies is at Universal Studios Hollywood, located in Universal City on the northern side of the Los Angeles basin. The studio got its start in 1915, when film pioneer Carl Laemmle purchased a tract of land in the Hollywood Hills on which to make motion pictures. Public tours of the studio began in 1964, and today Universal Studios Hollywood ranks as the nation's fourth most popular man-made attraction. Tours take visitors backstage to see how movies and TV shows are created. Spectacular multimedia shows reproduce famous special effects, such as the parting of the Red Sea, the rampages of King Kong, the emergence of the great white shark from *Jaws*, and the wanderings of ET the Extraterrestrial. Each year Universal Studios adds new attractions taken from its latest block-buster releases.

THE BIG VALLEY

As I-5 pushes northward from Los Angeles, the road snakes its way through the Tehachapi Mountains and penetrates the Central Valley. Within the mountains lies Fort Tejon State Historic Park, a military post that flourished during the early years of Anglo-American settlement in California. Built in 1854 to provide regional security and protect the Native Americans of the Sebastian Reserve, the fort was abandoned in 1864. Three of the fort's original 27 adobe structures have been reconstructed and house exhibits that reveal life at a frontier outpost. This fort, whose name comes from the Spanish word for badger, witnessed one of the more unusual episodes in military history when camels were stabled near here in the 1850's, while the army considered their use as beasts of burden in the arid Southwest. Survey parties used the camels to haul supplies and freight, but the experiment ended when officers concluded that camels offered no advantage over the two-mule buckboards then in use.

As the highway passes Bakersfield, the full panorama of California's agriculture becomes apparent. Although the dream of wealth lured people from all over the world to California during the Gold Rush of 1848-50, it was the 20th-century agricultural boom that put an enduring luster on the Golden State. When California engineered a dependable water supply for agriculture in the

READY FOR INSPECTION
Uniforms and guns hang on the pegs in the spartan enlisted men's barracks, above, at Fort Tejon State Historic Park, preserving the memory of daily life at this frontier post. The fort was garrisoned by mounted troops of the 1st U.S. Dragoons, whose mission was to ensure peace and security in the southern San Joaquin Valley.

1920's, Kern County blossomed and it continues to prosper as an agricultural powerhouse today. An extensive series of dams ensures a year-round supply of fresh water for a thirsty land that would otherwise be semidesert.

The story of the Central Valley's agricultural transformation is told at the Kern County Museum. The complex spreads over 14 acres, with some 50 structures that bring to life the story of the agriculture, oil, mining, and railroad development that made Kern County prosper. Some of the buildings are historic, others are replicas. A Moorish-style clocktower is a replica of a revered Bakersfield landmark. The humble Barnes Log Cabin was the home of the first farmer to grow peach trees in the valley. The Kern City French Bakery was established in 1887 to supply a large French community in East Bakersfield. Displays recount the travails of immigrant groups such as the Chinese laborers who helped to build the Southern Pacific Railroad's Tehachapi Loop; the Basques of northern Spain, who settled in the region in the 1890's; and the strugglers who migrated here from Oklahoma during the Great Depression.

Agricultural development and the increasing human population of the Central Valley had

WOODED BOWER
Fort Tejon's tranquil grounds, left, are dotted with oak, willow, cotton-wood, and juniper trees. Woods and meadows are home to black-tailed deer, black-tailed hares, cottontail and brush rabbits, and a variety of other mammal and bird species.

TEHACHAPI TELEGRAPH
The Bena Depot, given to the Kern County Museum in 1961, houses an 1884 telegraph office, below. Operators used the telegraph to route trains through the Tehachapi Loop, a marvel of engineering that allowed engineers to complete the railroad route between San Francisco and Los Angeles.

a dramatic effect on the region's indigenous wildlife, as witnessed by the Tule Elk State Reserve, located 17 miles west of Bakersfield. The Central Valley was once home to huge herds of this large buff-colored mammal, which was hunted initially for its hide. With the Gold Rush, however, demand grew for the elk as a food supply. Both here and in the Sacramento Valley to the north, hunters slaugh-tered the magnificent animal in huge numbers to feed the growing population of San Francisco. By the 1860's it was thought that the Tule elk had been wiped out, but in 1874 a single pair was discovered in a remote part of Kern County. The owners of the Miller-Lux cattle empire took the lead in pro-tecting the remaining elk, and gradually rebuilt the herd. Eventually the state of California assumed responsibility for providing a suitable habitat. The 956-acre Tule Elk State Reserve protects a small herd of the animals. The reserve's shady viewing area is a perfect spot to catch a glimpse of the herd, and offers picnic areas and interpretive exhibits.

Agricultural wealth was the initial economic stim-ulus for the Central Valley, but the massive oil fields found in Fresno County in the early days of oil exploration helped to launch California's love affair with the internal combustion engine. Just west of I-5, in the town of Coalinga, the R. C. Baker Memorial Museum explains how oil is formed, describes the exploits of the industry's lucky heroes and notorious villains, and displays the equipment used to extract the black gold.

The geologic basis of oil in this district was the rich organic life that flourished here millions of years ago, when the area was an ancient lake bed.

The area surrounding Coalinga is rich in invertebrate fossils. Before European settlement, the Yokut people gathered oil from seepages on the surface and used it to make their baskets waterproof. Oil was one of the region's trade items that could be swapped for fish and shells with tribes from the coastal regions.

In 1896 the firm of Chanslor and Canfield drilled a well that struck oil at 890 feet down and yielded 300 barrels a day. Other discoveries soon followed, but Coalinga did not boom until 1900, when the discovery of a massive new field brought fortune hunters racing to the newly rich town. On the way into town, the nodding oil pumps at work are a reminder that oil still flows, although much more sparingly. The name Coalinga comes from Coaling Station A, a facility built by the Southern Pacific Railroad in 1887 to supply trains with coal from a mine on the western side of Pleasant Valley.

As route I-5 shoots arrow-straight northward along the Central Valley's western side, it travels through an area that once boasted endless wetlands and meandering rivers. The San Luis Reservoir State Recreation Area, near Santa Nella, lies nestled in the hills of the western San Joaquin Valley. San Luis is a major inland wetland, just as the entire northern Central Valley was once a wetland each winter when the seasonal rains turned the land into a marsh. By summer the land had dried out and became a sprawling grassland. The reservoir was created to store runoff water for irrigation. The recreation area offers boating, swimming, camping, and fishing for striped bass, catfish, crappies, perch, and trout in the unit's three lakes. The nature reserves surrounding the reservoir make it a special place. The Upper and Lower Cottonwood Creek wildlife areas host golden eagles in winter. Other birds of prey, such as hawks and

owls, hover over the grasslands, where they feed on ground squirrels, mice, and rabbits. Sections of the reserve are intended for bird-watchers; other areas are set aside for hunters. More than 200 species of birds can be seen, including the white-faced ibis, sandhill crane, and American avocet. During the fall months, dense flocks of geese and ducks arrive in the area.

Caswell Memorial State Park, near Ripon, is another special nature area, preserving 138 acres of primeval hardwood forest. Oaks were once the major hardwood tree in the Central Valley. Native Americans used to grind their acorns into meal, which was then leached of tannin in streams, before being baked in cakes or eaten as a soup gruel.

The final stop on this leg of I-5 is the state capital, Sacramento, a city that embodies the California dream as few other places in the state. Sacramento's treasures begin with Old Sacramento, a redeveloped historic district that preserves the memory of the days when this was a raw boomtown flooded with hopeful fortune hunters on their way to the mother lode. In 1848 the little village at the junction of the American and Sacramento rivers grew almost overnight into the main supply point for the goldfields. Old Sacramento's 53 historic buildings include the terminus of the Pony Express, the pioneer chambers of the California Supreme Court, the offices of the West's oldest continuously published newspaper, and the re-created passenger terminal of the Central Pacific Railroad.

SUTTER'S FORT

In 1839 John Augustus Sutter, a Swiss merchant, arrived in California and set up a trading empire called New Helvetica. Sutter became a Mexican citizen in 1840, which enabled him to receive a land grant of 48,839 acres. His settlement soon grew into Sutter's Fort—an adobe brick structure surrounded by 18-foot-high walls that is located on the eastern side of Sacramento. Sutter was soon growing crops on his land and operating a brandy distillery. With the discovery of gold in the nearby foothills, hordes of men headed to California from the East by way of Cape Horn and San Francisco.

The Gold Rush was fueled by James Marshall's discovery of gold at Sutter's Mill in Coloma, located about 50 miles east of the fort. Businessman Sam Brannan had already established a store near the Sacramento River, which was ideally situated to serve the prospectors. Brannan called his settlement Sacramento, which became a boomtown just as Sutter's empire went into decline as gold seekers and squatters gradually took over his land. The original 1840 fort is preserved within Sutter's Fort State Historic Park. Costumed interpreters bring

GOLDEN MEMORIES
Costumed interpreters at Sutter's Fort State Historic Park, left, recall the era of the Gold Rush in California's future capital city of Sacramento.

history to life as they go about their daily chores of baking bread and making candles. A blacksmith and cooper are also on hand to display their tricks of the trade to interested visitors.

In the 1860's, at the northern end of the Central Valley, Leland Stanford and his cronies Charles Crocker, Mark Hopkins, and Collis P. Huntington financed the Central Pacific Railroad. The ribbon of steel stretching east from Sacramento and over the mountains succeeded in finally tying the entire country together. Old Sacramento's California State Railroad Museum, the largest museum of its kind in North America, tells the story of the Central Pacific Railroad. The mechanical and engineering achievements of the railroad builders are celebrated here, and the museum also relates how the iron horse opened up the West. Among the displays are the *Governor Stanford*—the first locomotive purchased by the Central Pacific—along with 20 other steam and diesel locomotives and cars.

Before the coming of the railroads, visitors reached Sacramento by riverboat from San Francisco. The salvaged and refurbished riverboat *Delta King*, now anchored as a hotel at Old Sacramento's Embarcadero, or waterfront, serves as a poignant reminder of that era.

Today I-5 whisks visitors from San Diego to Sacramento at a much faster pace. But along the way, they can stop and glean fascinating insights into California—past and present.

Merritt Island National Wildlife Refuge, Florida.

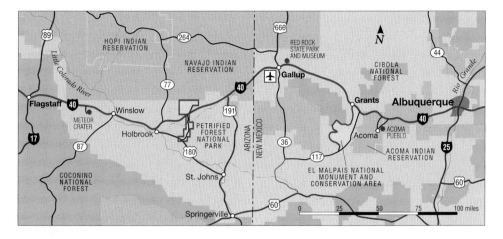

Driving across the high desert segment of Interstate 40 from eastern Arizona into New Mexico, it is easy to be mesmerized by the sublime beauty of the landscape. Here, where cobalt-blue sky meets arid desert hardpan, the full scope of nature's power is on permanent display.

Some 40 miles east of Flagstaff, Arizona's Meteor Crater is a spectacular reminder of that force. Seen from afar, the crater looks like nothing more than a thin, raised scar on the plateau's dusty surface. But visitors standing on the rim are awed by the massive chasm that yawns before them.

More than three miles in circumference and 570 feet deep, the crater could swallow the Washington Monument. The haunting stillness of the site belies the cataclysmic scene that must have taken place more than 49,000 years ago, when a meteoric chunk of iron traveling faster than 40,000 miles an hour plowed into the earth, killing every living creature for miles around.

In recent years, this strange lunar landscape has attracted everyone from miners digging for nickel to Apollo astronauts training for walks on the moon.

Scattered sections of a petrified tree trunk at Petrified Forest National Park, below, reveal multicolored quartz formations.

But some of nature's alchemy, like that found in Petrified Forest National Park, takes millions of years to complete. Divided into two sections, the park is framed by the Painted Desert in the north and one of the world's largest and best preserved collections of fossilized wood in the south.

Once a lush prehistoric forest, the park is named for the massive petrified conifer logs that glisten in the desert sun. Four brilliant concentrations of logs and a restored Anasazi pueblo made entirely of the rainbow-hued wood are found along the park's 27-mile scenic drive. One of the most spectacular sites is Blue Mesa, where erosion's patient work has left petrified logs perched atop sandstone columns. At the northernmost tip of the road shimmer the colorful bands of the Painted Desert.

LAND OF RED ROCK

The region's Native peoples have always embraced the high desert. Nowhere is this more evident than at New Mexico's Red Rock State Park. In the shadows of sheer red cliffs, Native people from over 50 North American tribes gather for the annual Inter-Tribal Ceremonial. Held in August, this major festival showcases everything from tribal dances to professional rodeo contests.

The Red Rock Museum offers a fascinating look at the rich history of the Ancestral Pueblo (or Anasazi), Navajo, Hopi, and Zuni peoples. Local Native American art is on display here, as well as an exhibit on the traditional uses of indigenous plants. Outdoor plots blaze with desert wildflowers or brim with corn, beans, and squash in a traditional Pueblo garden.

New Mexico's earliest Spanish explorers came upon a valley encrusted by jagged lava fields. They dubbed it El Malpais—the Badlands—and detoured around the undulating terrain. Today's visitors flock here to scramble among the bizarre landscape of El Malpais National Monument and

Conservation Area. Trails wind among spatter and cinder cones, an extensive lava tube system, and La Ventana, a 125-foot-high natural arch carved by the desert wind out of the relatively soft sandstone. Nestled in the crater of one of the many dormant volcanoes is a desert anomaly—a natural ice cave. Covered in thick slabs of greenish ice, the grotto's temperature never exceeds 31°F.

It is only fitting that the journey should end high above the desert floor in Sky City. Acoma Pueblo, perched atop a mesa almost 400 feet above the surrounding plains, is the oldest continuously inhabited village in the nation. The San Estevan del Rey Mission, with its 60-foot whitewashed walls, dominates the skyline. As imposing as the massive rock on which it sits, the mission is proof that man, too, is capable of the most sublime creations.

FOR MORE INFORMATION:
Arizona Office of Tourism, 110 West Washington St., Phoenix, AZ 85007; 800-842-8257.
New Mexico Tourism Dept., 491 Old Santa Fe Trail, Santa Fe, NM 87503; 800-733-6396.

The twin belfries of the mission church of San Estevan del Rey, above, watch over the simple adobe dwellings of Acoma Pueblo.

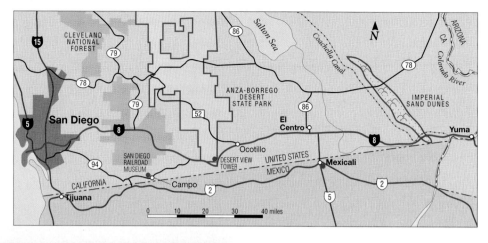

Seen from Font's Point, the badlands of Anza-Borrego Desert State Park present a stark vista.

Although the stretch of Interstate 8 that runs from San Diego to Yuma is one of the region's more modern thoroughfares, it boasts primitive parks, desolate deserts, and barely explored canyons. Traveling along this byway, it's still possible to feel like an early explorer.

Just 60 miles from the coast, the San Diego Railroad Museum evokes nostalgia for the vanished age of steam trains. Every Saturday and Sunday visitors can take a 16-mile round trip on vintage railroad equipment. The museum also offers walking tours that reveal ongoing restorations of historic cars and locomotives.

For pioneers traveling between San Diego and Yuma, the Desert View Tower was an important stop. For those traveling west, it gave a glimpse of the bountiful lands toward the Pacific coast; for those traveling east, the view of the distant mountains hid the harsh desert yet to be traversed. A museum at the site displays old firearms, swords, lamps, war trophies, antiques, and relics of the region's Native American peoples and early pioneers.

DESERT PARK

From the top of Desert View Tower, Anza-Borrego Desert State Park can be seen to the north. The view hardly prepares visitors for the realities of California's first desert state park, established in 1933. Spanish explorer Juan Bautista de Anza traveled this way in 1774 in search of a land route from Sonora, Mexico, to the California coast. Amazingly, the park's 600,000 acres of desert terrain remain as primitive today as in Anza's day.

The park's unique setting—between the Peninsular ranges and the bone-dry Salton Trough—combines bleak desert flats with mountains that plunge into secluded canyons. Plant life is diverse and abundant: willows and ferns grow side by side with cactus, yucca, and desert apricot. Native bighorn sheep wander freely, protected in state wilderness areas. Other points of interest include the Borrego Palm Canyon, with its famous groves of California fan palms, and the Carrizo Badlands, an area strewn with marine and mammal fossils.

After leaving the wild beauty of Anza-Borrego, visitors can enjoy a border-town experience in Mexicali, the booming capital of the Mexican state of Baja California. Located in the Mexicali Valley, one of Mexico's most important agricultural

The canyons of the desert yield up surprising natural treasures, such as flowering beavertail and common phacelia, above.

regions, the area is acclaimed for its game hunting. The city's thriving Galería de la Ciudad features the work of Mexican painters, sculptors, and photographers; and the Teatro del Estado promotes music, dance, and theater. Families enjoy the spacious shopping centers and a forestlike city park and zoo.

The Imperial Sand Dunes offer another kind of desert—the largest mass of sand dunes in California. Roughly 40 miles in length and 5 miles wide, the wind-created dunes reach heights of up to 300 feet. They provide outstanding opportunities for off-highway vehicle recreation. However, the dunes are home to many fragile plants and wildlife species. In order to protect the delicate ecosystem, portions of the park have been designated as wilderness study areas.

FOR MORE INFORMATION:
California Division of Tourism, P.O. Box 1499, Sacramento, CA 95812-1499; 800-462-2543.

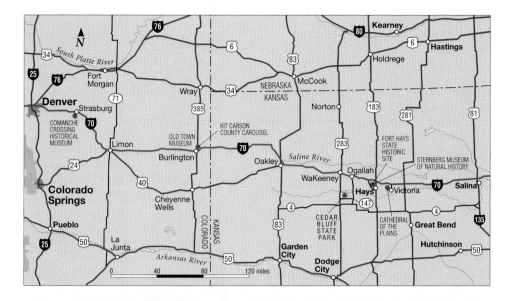

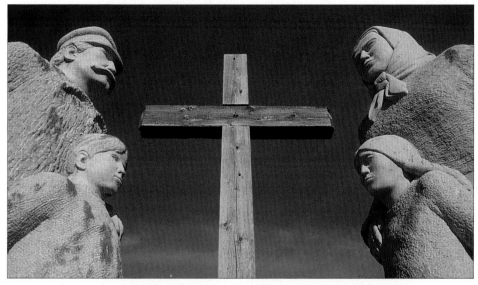

Flanked by statues commemorating the region's Volga German settlers, a simple wooden cross, above, in the town of Victoria, Kansas, is a monument to the Roman Catholic faith of the town's founders.

Despite the endless horizon and the lack of dramatic scenery, the Great Plains of Colorado and Kansas conceal innumerable surprises. Just a short drive off Interstate 70 lie attractions as diverse as an old-time carousel, dinosaur bones, and a majestic stone cathedral.

Some 25 miles from Denver, just outside Strasburg, the Comanche Crossing Historical Museum commemorates the completion of the New York to San Francisco railroad line in 1870. Located not far from where the last spike was driven, the museum's seven historic buildings include a homesteader's cottage, a one-room schoolhouse, a 19th-century windmill, and a railroad depot. Fossils and Indian artifacts, period furnishings, old farm vehicles,

fire trucks, and a Union Pacific caboose give visitors a rare look at what life was like when this region was still untamed.

For a different taste of the Wild West, the Old Town Museum in Burlington fits the bill. Horse-drawn wagon rides, melodramas, staged gunfights, and spirited cancan dances are just some of the colorful daily activities that help bring this bygone era back to life. Complete with an old-time saloon, a 2,000-square-foot Emporium, and a blacksmith shop, the museum boasts a collection of 40 vintage wagons and numerous turn-of-the-century artifacts in 19 fully restored buildings.

Hitching a short ride on a horse-drawn wagon to the Kit Carson County Carousel, travelers will delight in taking a spin on this

magical merry-go-round. Built in 1905, the carousel features 46 hand-carved, brightly painted creatures that range from a proud, medieval charger to an elegant giraffe with a snake slithering sinuously up its neck. The carousel turns to the sounds of a 1909 Wurlitzer Monster Military Band Organ.

The animals in Cedar Bluff State Park are less cooperative than their carousel cousins, but just as thrilling to watch. Deer, turkeys, raccoons, Canada geese, and pelicans are among the many creatures that make the park their home. The park's diversity is also reflected in the variety of outdoor activities it offers. Whether driving to the top of a 150-foot limestone bluff to soak in the view, or enjoying an 18-hole Frisbee golf course, visitors can unwind in a multitude of ways.

FRONTIER FORT

Life was less relaxed for the soldiers who were stationed at Fort Hays in the late 1800's. A major supply depot for forts in the South and West, Fort Hays was also the base for the troops who defended railroad crews and white settlements from Indian raids. Uniforms, firearms, and military artifacts are on permanent display in the fort's four remaining original buildings.

Turn-of-the-century history gives way to prehistory at the Sternberg Museum of Natural History. Life-size models of ancient plants and dinosaurs allow visitors to step back in time to the Late Cretaceous period, some 63 to 88 million years ago. In the Discovery Room, budding paleontologists can handle specimens and participate in a simulated excavation. An extensive fossil collection includes the famous "Fish-Within-A-Fish"—the remains of a 14-foot predatory fish with a smaller fish in its belly.

The flat terrain around the town of Victoria is dominated by the twin 141-foot bell towers of St. Fidelis Church. Erected in 1911, the huge church is made of Vermont granite, Indiana Bedford stone, and great slabs of Kansas limestone carted in from seven miles away. Supported by 18 pillars weighing up to 15 tons each, the majestic 220-foot-long structure well deserves its nickname of the "Cathedral of the Plains."

FOR MORE INFORMATION:

Colorado Tourism Board, Suite 1700, 1675 Broadway Ave., Denver, CO 80202; 303-592-5510.
Kansas Travel & Tourism Development, Kansas Dept. of Commerce, Suite 1300, 700 SW Harrison St., Topeka, KS 66603-3712; 800-252-6727.

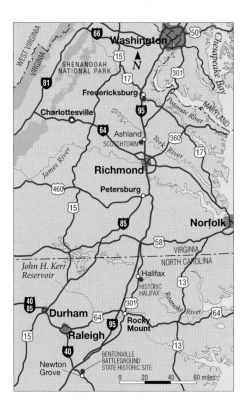

C ast a stone almost anywhere in the District of Columbia, Virginia, or North Carolina, and chances are it will land on a spot where history was made. Starting in the nation's capital in Washington, D.C., a trip along Interstate 95 through this fascinating region—where presidents were born, revolutions planned, and epic battles fought—is like going back in time to the very birth of our nation.

Few towns in the country are as rich in history as Fredericksburg, Virginia. George Washington grew up here, a young James Monroe practiced law in the town, and Thomas Jefferson drafted the Statute of Religious Freedom. Founded in 1728 as a tobacco trading post, Fredericksburg enjoyed a strategic position on the banks of the Rappahannock River that made it a coveted prize during the Civil War. Union and Confederate forces clashed four times in a bloody tug-of-war for the town.

A Confederate cemetery honors the Southern dead and the walls of some of the city's historic buildings still bear the pockmarks of cannonballs. Fredericksburg's magnolia- and honeysuckle-lined streets hold everything from stately brick Federal buildings to charming Queen Anne–period homes. Some of the most intriguing sites

Halifax's red-brick Clerk's Office, right, was built in 1833 to provide a fireproof repository for the town's court records.

include an 18th-century apothecary shop fitted with medical instruments from colonial times, an elegant plantation mansion where George Washington's sister lived, and the quaint tavern built by his youngest brother. The Fredericksburg Museum and Cultural Center outlines the region's evolution from prehistoric times to the present.

"Give me liberty or give me death!" were the fiery words with which Patrick Henry established himself as the impassioned voice of the American Revolution. Henry penned his immortal call to arms in his sprawling plantation home called Scotchtown in Fredericksburg. Built in 1719, the mansion was auctioned off to Henry in 1771. Although he owned Scotchtown for barely seven years, it was the backdrop for his election as the first governor of the independent Commonwealth of Virginia. Restoration of the mansion began in 1958, and today the house is appointed with period furnishings, including Henry's original mahogany desk. Visitors can stroll through the re-created 18th-century garden, law office, kitchen, and guest house.

HISTORIC HALIFAX
The American Revolution gained much of its early impetus in Halifax. It was here, at North Carolina's Fourth Provincial Congress in 1776, that the Halifax Resolves calling for independence were drafted. When the war broke out, the city became a recruitment center, military depot, and weapons factory. Today the town's rich heritage has been preserved in its Historic Halifax district. Replete with buildings dat-

ing from the colonial and early statehood periods, this important site permits visitors to tread the same floorboards as their forefathers. The Owens House, furnished with period pieces, is an accurate replica of a merchant's home and office, complete with a counting room and family parlor.

Many of the nation's most significant sites are the fields, forests, or farms where brother clashed with brother in the Civil War. Bentonville was the location of the biggest land engagement in North Carolina and the last major Confederate offensive of the war. Here Gen. William T. Sherman's 60,000 Union troops were surprised by 17,000 Confederate soldiers under the command of Gen. Joseph E. Johnston. After several days of fighting, Union reinforcements repulsed the outnumbered Southerners. Visitors can learn about the battle by means of plaques placed throughout the site. At the two-story Harper House, used as a Union field hospital, doctors worked to save the lives of the wounded on both sides. History is sometimes just a stone's throw away in a region that claims such a rich past.

FOR MORE INFORMATION
Virginia Division of Tourism, 19th Fl., 901 East Byrd St., Richmond, VA 23219; 800-847-4882.
North Carolina Division of Travel & Tourism, 430 North Salisbury St., Raleigh, NC 27603; 800-847-4862.

Interpreters in period costume, above, recall Spanish colonial days at Castillo de San Marcos.

The same stretch of stunning Florida shoreline that beckoned Juan Ponce de Leon to the New World in 1513 today serves as the launching pad for America's forays into space. Instead of the fountain of youth, Ponce de Leon found an enchanting landscape of woodlands, marshes, mangroves, and miles of sandy beach, nurtured by a benign climate and teeming with wildlife—the same landscape that marks a journey on Interstate 95 today.

South of Jacksonville, the city of St. Augustine sits on the shores of Matanzas Bay. Founded in 1565 by the Spanish, it is the oldest permanent European settlement in the nation. The most prominent site on the bay is Castillo de San Marcos National Monument, a masonry fortress completed in 1695 to guard Spain's lucrative trade

routes. Within the fort's 10-foot-thick stone walls lies a virtual time-capsule of Spanish colonial rule. From its chapel and sacristy to the bombproof storerooms surrounding the central courtyard, the Castillo brings to life 300 years of Florida history.

At Kennedy Space Center, the past yields to the future. An elbow of land that juts into the Gulf Stream, Cape Canaveral and the Kennedy Space Center have been the hub of America's space program since 1964. The visitor center, Spaceport USA, offers a spectacular look at space exploration. In addition to an IMAX theater and countless exhibits, Spaceport offers bus tours that take visitors to the Mercury and Gemini launch pads, NASA headquarters, and other facilities. Surrounding the Space Center are the more than 140,000 acres of fertile wetlands set aside as Merritt Island National Wildlife Refuge. More than 500 bird and animal species inhabit the refuge, which is home to more endangered species than any other site in the country.

Situated on a barrier island just 40 miles south of the Cape, the Sebastian Inlet State Recreation Area encompasses pristine beaches, dunes, and coastal hammocks

Massive rocket modules, left, stand outside the giant Vehicle Assembly Building at Cape Canaveral's Kennedy Space Center.

along the Atlantic Ocean, and groves and maritime forests lining the Indian River to the west. Besides world-class snorkeling, scuba diving, and surfing, this maritime paradise offers excellent fishing, shrimping, and clamming opportunities. Gentle manatees are visible from either shore, along with rare wading birds and sea turtles that nest in the seagrass beds of the Indian River. Within the recreation area, the McLarty Treasure Museum recounts the 1715 sinking of a homeward-bound Spanish fleet laden with gold and silver. This unique museum is situated on the site of the survivors' camp and documents the many attempts to salvage the sunken treasure.

On Hutchinson Island, the Elliott Museum pays tribute to American inventor Sterling Elliott. Creator of the quadricycle, the forerunner to the automobile, Elliott epitomized the early American spirit of ingenuity. The museum also preserves a slice of turn-of-the-century Americana, with its period ice cream parlor, blacksmith forge, and apothecary.

FOR MORE INFORMATION:
Florida Division of Tourism, Rm. 505, 558 W. Gains St., Tallahassee, FL 32399-200; 904-487-1462.

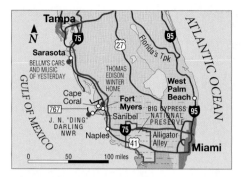

A yellow-crowned night heron, above, stands at attention at Florida's J. N. "Ding" Darling National Wildlife Refuge.

S outhwest Florida's lush, steamy, subtropical terrain alerts the senses with its colorful migratory birds, fresh, tangy scent of salty swampland, and the hushed but stirring noises of nature. Interstate 75 meanders through this wonderland, passing nature preserves and museums, and taking visitors on a voyage through time and beauty.

Some 50 miles west of Miami, the Big Cypress National Preserve in Ochopee comprises more than 2,400 square miles of sandy islands, marshes, wet and dry prairies, and estuarine mangrove forests. A third of the preserve is covered with dwarf pond cypress trees. Because of logging activity during the 1950's, the preserve's remaining giant or great bald cypresses are quite small.

Big Cypress' original inhabitants were the Miccosukee and Seminole Indians. Groups of these Native peoples still live here on small parcels of land. The completion of the Tamiami Trail in 1928 raised the possibility that this watery wilderness might be drained and the sawgrass prairies turned into sugarcane and citrus plantations. In 1974, however, Congress set aside 45 percent of the Big Cypress Swamp as a national

Thomas Edison's flasks, retorts, and beakers, above, are preserved just as the inventor left them in his Fort Myers laboratory.

preserve. Although this magnificent wild country enjoys federal protection, many commercial activities have been allowed to continue, including oil exploration.

The rainy season here begins in May, so most visitors arrive during the dry winter season. The preserve is home to alligators, red-cockaded woodpeckers, wild turkeys, deer, minks, and even bald eagles. For hikers, there is the 31-mile Florida National Scenic Trail.

For more of nature's beauty, the J. N. "Ding" Darling National Wildlife Refuge is hard to beat. The refuge was established in 1945 to help protect the numerous species that inhabit this 6,350-acre coastal site. The refuge aims to protect and enhance the unique subtropical ecosystems for wildlife, including a wide diversity of shorebirds, waterfowl, raptors, and other migratory birds. The refuge also protects subtropical barrier island habitats such as mangroves, and beach and interior freshwater marshes, which support a rich mosaic of animal life.

Originally called the Sanibel National Wildlife Refuge, it was renamed in 1967 to honor Jay Norwood "Ding" Darling, a Pulitzer Prize–winning political cartoonist and avid conservationist. Darling was a winter resident of nearby Captiva, and championed the establishment of this important refuge. Nearly 750,000 people visit the refuge each year. Some cycle, kayak, canoe, fish, or simply observe and photograph the wildlife. Some of the magnificent birds to be spotted here include bald eagles, hawks, pelicans, doves, cardinals, herons, woodpeckers, and ducks. The refuge is also home to several endangered and threatened species, including the American crocodile, Arctic peregrine falcon, wood stork, osprey, and Atlantic loggerhead turtle. Since the refuge is located in one of the nation's fastest-growing areas, the habitat exists in a delicate balance with human development.

HISTORICAL SITES

To delve into the mind of one of the world's great inventors, visit the Thomas Edison Winter Home, near Fort Myers. It boasts original furnishings, Edison's laboratory, and abundant botanical gardens. The home is really two houses connected by a breezeway, and was prefabricated in Maine, then shipped by schooner to Fort Myers, where the pieces were assembled. The house and lab have been preserved much as Edison left them when he died at 84, after spending 33 winters in Florida.

It was at Fort Myers that Edison pioneered the search for synthetic rubber; the specimens of local and exotic plants he

assembled in his search have now grown into a lush garden. The estate also features one of Florida's first swimming pools, one that is still filled today. The 7,500-square-foot museum contains the largest collection of Edison memorabilia in the world, including his car—a prototype Model T given to him by his friend and Fort Myers neighbor, Henry Ford—and a huge collection of phonographs.

In Sarasota, Bellm's Cars and Music of Yesterday claims one of the world's largest and most complete collections of musical instruments. It boasts a 16-foot Belgian dance organ, disc and cylinder music boxes, calliopes and hurdy-gurdies. There are more than 1,200 different instruments, some of them featuring beautiful cabinetwork hand-made by European and American craftsmen. More than 50 antique cars are on display, including such immortal makes as Rolls Royce, Pierce Arrow, Auburn, and Stutz.

FOR MORE INFORMATION:
Florida Division of Tourism, Rm. 505, 558 W. Gains St., Tallahassee, FL 32399-200; 904-487-1462.

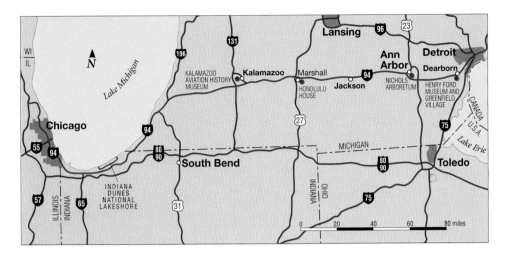

Dissecting America's heartland, Interstate 94 is the major route between two of the nation's busiest industrial centers—Chicago and Detroit. But for curious motorists, this busy highway is also the road to many sightseeing gems, both natural and man-made.

Just east of Chicago lies a preserve that poet Carl Sandburg called "a signature of time and eternity." Indiana Dunes National Lakeshore is a living monument to nature's work. Carved by the massive ice-age glacier that would eventually become Lake Michigan, this area contains a startling diversity of ecosystems. Here Arctic bearberry grows beside prickly pear cactus, and hiking trails pass through oak savannas, bird-filled marshes, ancient prairie land, and spongy bogs that are home to carnivorous plants. Towering sand dunes that constantly shift position and huge expanses of unspoiled beaches paint the southern rim of Lake Michigan with a grainy, golden brush. Along the water's edge, visitors are serenaded by the soft musical tones emitted by the famous "singing sands." The clear ringing sound is produced by the combination of quartz crystals, moisture, pressure, and friction from walkers' feet. Often greeted by the excited yips of coyotes at dusk, lucky visitors can spot deer, opossums, red foxes, and cottontail rabbits.

Wildlife of a different kind reside at the Kalamazoo Aviation History Museum. The Curtiss Warhawk, Grumman Hellcat, and Bell Aircobra are just some of the winged predators belonging to this unique collection. The museum displays fighting planes from World War II, as well as the Korean, Vietnam, and Persian Gulf wars. One of the vintage aircraft is flown every day in the spring and summer months. When visitors are done perusing the permanent exhibits of engines and authentic uniforms, they can work the throttle in mock-up cockpits and flight simulators. From May to October those who want to try the real thing can hitch a ride aboard a vintage Ford Tri-Motor airplane. Also on the premises, the Guadalcanal Veteran's Museum commemorates one of the longest and bloodiest campaigns of World War II.

Although Abner Pratt wasn't a pilot, some of his neighbors in Marshall, Michigan, must have thought he had his head in the clouds. Pratt served as U.S. consul to Hawaii in the 1850's and was so smitten with the tropical paradise that, upon his return stateside, he built a replica of Honolulu's executive mansion. With its 15-foot ceilings, spacious porch, and majestic spiral staircase that winds its way to a pagodalike tower, the Honolulu House brings the tropics to small-town Michigan. Pratt decorated the interior of the sandstone mansion with coral, seashells, and murals of tropical plants and animals. Pratt's abode is not the only exotic building in town, however. Marshall is renowned for its eclectic architecture, ranging from the Greek Revival style of the Governor's Mansion to the Gothic flavor of Capitol Hill School.

BOTANICAL BEAUTY

Just minutes from downtown Ann Arbor, the University of Michigan's 123-acre Nichols Arboretum contains more than 1,000 herbaceous and woody plant species representative of the world's temperate zone. From a 10-acre restored prairie to historic collections of peonies, lilacs, and rhododendrons, the grounds offer visitors visual delights all year round.

Human ingenuity is celebrated at the Henry Ford Museum and Greenfield Village, outside Detroit. Exhibits ranging from the simple beauty of a Revere teapot to a 600-ton locomotive span 300 years of American innovation. Founded by the great auto maker in 1929, the facility houses more than 100 historically significant cars, including a 1896 Duryea Motor Wagon and the limousine in which John F. Kennedy was assassinated. More than 80 relocated historic structures grace the Greenfield Village site, including Thomas Edison's Menlo Park Lab, the Wright Brothers' cycle shop, and the courthouse where Abraham Lincoln's career began.

FOR MORE INFORMATION:

Indiana State Tourism, 101 North Governor, Evansville, IN 47711; 800-289-6646. Michigan Travel Bureau, Michigan JABS Commission, P.O. Box 30226, Lansing, MI 48909; 800-543-2937.

Strands of wind-whipped marram grass anchor the beaches, left, on Lake Michigan in Indiana Dunes National Lakeshore.

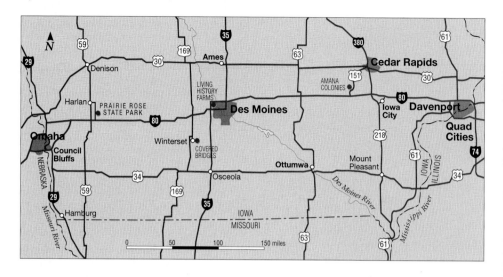

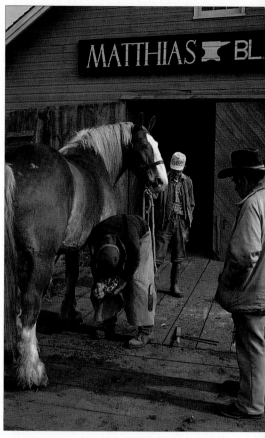

I owans describe their state with pride as "Places of Quiet Beauty." Nestled in the heartland of the nation, the Hawkeye State provides visitors with an array of sightseeing options that act as a soothing balm to the stresses of modern life. Interstate 80 runs straight and true through the state, offering many wonderful opportunities to sample Iowa's quiet beauty.

The Amana Colonies, one of the most popular tourist attractions in the state, can be found by traveling east from the Quad Cities. First settled in 1855 by German Pietists, the colony was the refuge of a sect that had fled religious intolerance in Germany. They settled on 26,000 acres of rolling land along the Iowa River, and called their new settlement Amana, which means "to remain faithful." Over the years the original colony expanded into seven villages: Amana; East, Middle, High, West, and South Amana; and Homestead.

The early settlers practiced a communal lifestyle, sharing all goods and services. In 1932, during a period called the Great Change, the people of the Amana colonies voted to abolish their communal system, but the move, which led to more commerce, didn't change the essence of life in the villages. Through the years, the descendants of the original settlers have preserved the colonies' unique architecture, communal lifestyle, and beautiful crafts with such success that the Amana Colonies are designated a National Historic Landmark.

Taking a step back in time, visitors can shop for finely crafted woolens at the Amana Woolen Mill. Artisan studios feature unique quilts and rag rugs; baskets and brooms are woven from the cultivated willow of the original settlers at the Broom and Basket Shop. Traditional custom wood furniture and clocks are available in shops throughout the villages.

Outside Des Moines, in the town of Urbandale, the Living History Farms offers a realistic recreation of Midwestern agriculture and farm life. Founder Dr. William Murray felt that the heart of farming consisted of living things, and that the history of farming could not be truly represented in a static museum setting. As a result of his vision, and much hard work, the Living History Farms opened to the public in 1975. The 600-acre open-air museum allows visitors to savor the amazing changes in farming by traveling through five time periods: the bark lodges of the 1700 Ioway Indian Village; the 1850 Pioneer Farm, with its log cabin and oxen; the 1875 Town of Walnut Hill, which demonstrates the growing interdependence between farmers and townspeople; the 1900 Farm site, featuring horses, cast-iron implements, and frame buildings; and the modern Crop Center, with displays of new and experimental farming techniques.

THE CHARMS OF MADISON COUNTY

Thanks to Hollywood and a bestselling novel, there is a place in the heart of Iowa that is fast becoming one of the most popular tourist destinations in the state. Located southeast of Des Moines, Madison County has always been well publicized as the birthplace of actor John Wayne (born Marion Roger Morrison in 1907). But nothing in recent years has caught the imagination of the public as much as Robert James Waller's novel *The Bridges of Madison County* and the 1995 movie of the same name. Madison County is delightfully picturesque. The main attractions, especially for visitors wanting to re-create romantic moments, are the six historic wooden covered bridges—Cedar, Cutler-Donahoe, Hogback, Holliwell, Imes, and Roseman— all located around the county seat of

A farrier replaces a shoe on a Belgian work horse, above, at the 1875 Town of Walnut Hill part of Living History Farms.

Winterset, founded in 1849. Winterset also hosts the Madison County Covered Bridge Festival, held every year on the second full weekend in October.

Embracing a 218-acre lake northeast of Council Bluffs, Prairie Rose State Park is a fine example of Iowa's commitment to preserving its natural beauty. Opened in 1962, the park offers many picnic areas and excellent camping facilities. As well, the Prairie Rose beach is an excellent spot for sunbathing and has a play area located beside it. The lake offers ideal conditions for swimming, fishing, and boating— including canoeing, sailing, and motor boating. There is also a Nature Trail for hikers. For winter sports enthusiasts, there is ice boating and a snowmobile trail in the eastern portion of the park.

FOR MORE INFORMATION:
Iowa Tourism, Department of Economic Development, 200 East Grand Ave., Des Moines, IA 50309; 800-345-4692.

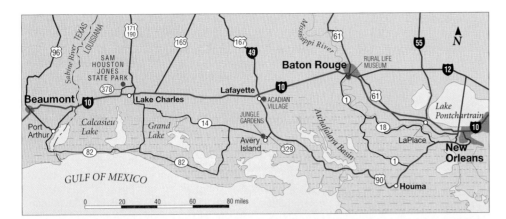

white-tailed deer, and geese can be spotted from the winding nature trails.

After being expelled from Nova Scotia and New Brunswick by the British in 1755, a large group of Acadians chose to settle in the bayous of southern Louisiana. Bringing their language and customs, these French Catholic exiles, whose descendants are called Cajuns, added another swatch to Louisiana's colorful cultural quilt.

Lafayette's Acadian Village offers an authentic look into the lives of these fascinating people. Set in 10 acres of subtropical gardens and woodlands on the banks of a man-made bayou, this re-creation of a 19th-century village comes complete with schoolhouse, chapel, blacksmith shop, and general store. The whitewashed cabins are furnished with moss-filled mattresses and colorful hand-woven blankets.

JUNGLE ISLAND

Perched atop a huge salt dome, Avery Island is home to one of the continent's most spectacular horticultural gems. A labor of love for Edward Avery McIlhenny, the Jungle Gardens display an array of flora and fauna that was collected from around the globe. Lotus and papyrus from the upper Nile, towering 60-foot canes of Chinese timber bamboo, and majestic purple water lilies native to Africa are just some of the imported beauties that fill this 250-acre paradise. Each spring, the gardens come alive with the elegant forms of herons soaring overhead. Once on the brink of extinction, some 20,000 of these brilliantly plumed birds return each year to hatch and raise their downy chicks.

Beneficiaries of the rich bounty of the land, plantations were a main component of Southern economy and culture. Comprised of 20 different reconstructed or replicated buildings, the Rural Life Museum in Baton Rouge gives visitors insight into the daily life of 19th-century agricultural workers. Everything from farming implements and period furniture to antique woodcrafts and Civil War memorabilia are housed inside the large barn. The Working Plantation includes the overseer's house, slave cabins, and gristmills. Strolling past the magnificent blooming azaleas, camellias, and crape myrtles in the gardens, visitors get a feel for the horticultural tastes of the 1800's.

Each year, thousands of herons return to nest at Bird City, above, in Jungle Gardens.

R aucous Mardi Gras celebrations, mouth-watering gumbo, zydeco-fueled two-stepping, and alligator-filled bayous are just some of the exotic treats to be sampled in Louisiana's Cajun Country. With unique sights lurking at every turn, Interstate 10 from the Texas border to New Orleans invites visitors to stop and sample its off-ramp diversions.

Of all the picturesque spots in this wondrous region, few are as beautiful as Sam Houston Jones State Park. Nestled at the confluence of a river and a bayou near the city of Lake Charles, the park boasts 1,068 acres of unblemished natural splendor. Dense woodlands, pristine lakes and streams, and a lagoon hemmed with massive cypress trees are home to a wide variety of wildlife. The white perch, bream, and bass that inhabit the crystal waters in and around the park make it an obvious destination for recreational fishermen. Nutrias,

The College Grove Baptist Church, above, in the Rural Life Museum was built in 1870.

FOR MORE INFORMATION:

Louisiana Office of Tourism, P.O. Box 94291, Baton Rouge, LA 70804-9291; 800-633-6970.

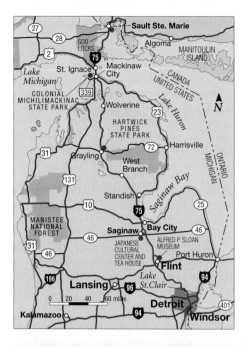

Tugboats are the real workhorses of Michigan's Soo Locks. A jaunty red-and-green tug, below, idles at its mooring between Lake Huron and Lake Superior.

Wearing the uniform of a soldier in the British 8th Regiment of the 1770's, a costumed interpreter, above, fires a cannon at Colonial Michilimackinac State Park.

It was not until 1957, when the the five-mile-long Mackinac Bridge—dubbed "Mighty Mac"—joined the Upper and Lower peninsulas, that Michigan became truly united. Today the state is connected by Interstate 75, a wonderful stretch of highway from which visitors can discover much of the region's colorful history.

Named for the man who was president of General Motors in the 1920's and 1930's, the Alfred P. Sloan Museum is situated just off I-75 in Flint. The museum celebrates the historical links between Michigan and the automotive industry. Its collection includes the Pierson Automotive Gallery, which displays a unique collection of cars. An exhibit titled "Flint and the American Dream" traces the development of GM. Among the gleaming four-wheeled works of art are a 1903 Flint Roadster and a 1905 first-year-production Buick. Each June the museum hosts one of the largest antique car shows

in the state. Not all of its 100,000 artifacts, photographs, and documents are related to shifting transmissions and steering wheels, however. The eclectic exhibits include everything from prehistoric stone tools and a 10,000-year-old mastodon skeleton to two Victorian period rooms and a collection of neon signs from the 1950's and 1960's.

After taking a nostalgic journey into America's past, travelers along I-75 can enjoy a short visit to the Far East at the Japanese Cultural Center and Tea House. The center is the joint effort of Saginaw, Michigan, and its sister city of Tokushima, Japan. Visitors stroll along a quaint stone path that leads through clusters of pine and cherry trees. The Awa Saginaw An tea house was built without nails; the exquisite structure is held together instead by intricate Japanese joinery, a technique it has taken hundred of years to perfect. Inside, hostesses demonstrate the ancient art of preparing and drinking tea, which, when done correctly, is considered a profound and meditative experience.

LOGGING COUNTRY

Traveling north on the Interstate, visitors soon come to Hartwick Pines State Park. The park pays tribute to the rugged loggers who helped make Michigan a center of the industry. Nestled among 9,000 acres of woodland, the park's museum outlines the development of logging in the region. A mess hall, bunkhouse, and blacksmith shop are part of this reconstructed camp. The park is named after one of the last stands of virgin white pine trees in the state.

Located in Mackinaw City, Colonial Michilimackinac State Park is a reconstruction of a French fur-trading village and military outpost built in 1715. The fort was occupied by the British in the 1770's. Costumed interpreters and reenactments bring colonial times to life.

At the northern limit of I-75 lies the port of Sault Ste. Marie, affectionately known to seafarers as the Soo. Soo Locks was constructed to allow ships to travel from Lake Huron to Lake Superior. A visitor center displays a model of a lock, as well as charts and photographs. A 22-story observation tower provides a birds's-eye view of the locks. Visitors can also take a two-hour cruise through the waterway.

FOR MORE INFORMATION:
Michigan Travel Bureau, Dept. of Commerce, P.O. Box 30226, Lansing, MI 48909; 800-543-2937.

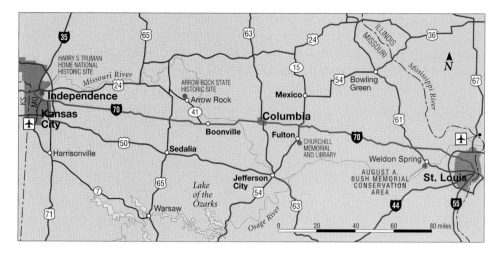

A journey across central Missouri evokes a time when pioneers trekked across this land, seeking to settle the American West. As they traveled up the Missouri River they found vast expanses of green grasses and high bluffs crowned with giant oaks and hickories. When Missouri entered the Union in 1821, the state was nicknamed the "Mother of the West" because of its position at the western frontier of the United States. In the early 19th century, many of the settlers who opened up the region between Missouri and the Pacific Ocean used Independence and St. Louis as their starting points, traveling at a slow pace in cumbersome horse-drawn covered wagons. Today Interstate 70 follows the same route that the wagon trains once took.

Reminders of the pioneer past are to be found in the quiet town of Independence. In the early 19th century, goods from Mexico and the Southwest poured into the town, which was also the starting point for settlers heading west on the Oregon Trail. A mural of these early trailblazing days is found at the Harry S Truman Library. The facility was the brainchild of Truman, who took a keen interest in preserving some 3.5 million papers from his personal and presidential years. Although Truman was born in Lamar, Missouri, he always claimed Independence as his hometown, and boasted that he had read all the books in the Independence Public Library by his 14th birthday. Visitors can catch a glimpse of his life by touring the Truman family home, a 14-room, Victorian mansion on 219 North Delaware Street. It was from his living room here that Truman addressed the nation by radio on the eve of the 1948 election. Designated a national historic site, the house contains many family heirlooms, including the hat and coat Truman donned for his early morning walks.

PIONEER PAST

Farther along I-70, near Boonville, lies historic Arrow Rock, a 167-year-old pioneer village perched on a high bluff overlooking the Missouri River. The first permanent settlers arrived here in 1815 and by the mid-1800's Arrow Rock had more than 1,000 inhabitants. Today the village has only 70 residents. Designated a national historic landmark, the village preserves more than a dozen buildings dating from the 19th century, including an old brick tavern and the gun shop of John P. Sites, who made highly prized pistols and rifles.

History of another kind was recorded in the town of Fulton. It was here that Winston Churchill delivered his famous Iron Curtain speech at Westminster College in 1946, warning of Soviet expansion into Eastern Europe. To commemorate the British statesman, the 17th-century Church of St. Mary the Virgin, Aldermanbury, was shipped, stone by stone, from London in 1966 and reconstructed on the college grounds. Today the Churchill Memorial and Library houses a complete collection of Churchill's writings and speeches, as well as North America's most extensive collection of World War II microfilm from the British Public Records Office.

A detour through the August A. Bush Memorial Conservation Area rounds out the trip before I-70 heads into the metropolis of St. Louis. Several hiking trails wind through the 6,987-acre wildlife area, leading visitors past forests of oak and hickory, gurgling creeks, and lakes known for largemouth bass, bluegill, and channel catfish. Visitors who walk quietly may well end their trip on a high note, serenaded by the songs of nesting birds.

FOR MORE INFORMATION:

Missouri Division of Tourism, Truman State Office Bldg., 310 West High St., Rm. 290, Jefferson, MO 65101; 573-751-4133 or 800-877-1234.

After they married in 1919, Harry and Bess Truman lived in a house, below, built by her grandfather in 1867.

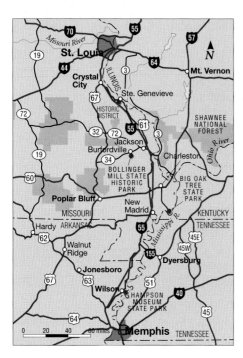

Located on the Whitewater River, the Bollinger Mill, left, is a picture of tranquillity. During the Civil War, Union troops torched part of the mill because they believed that the Confederate Army was obtaining supplies from it.

Moved to its present site in 1784, the Bolduc House, below, is a popular stop for architectural historians. This view of the front porch shows just some of the 18th-century colonial furniture and tools that are on display.

When Mark Twain wrote his world-famous *Huckleberry Finn,* he captured the spirit of "Old Man River," as the Mississippi is affectionately called, and secured it a place in American lore. The river courses through broad plains, and tells tales of pioneers, riverboats, and prehistoric Native cultures.

Visitors should explore the river valley one segment at a time, and a trip along Interstate 55 from St. Louis, Missouri, to Memphis, Tennessee, offers a particularly tempting slice. The highway passes through quiet towns, gentle hills, and sun-dappled stands of hickory, maple, and oak.

The historic village of Ste. Genevieve, which was established by French settlers in 1735, is located about 55 miles from St. Louis. Missouri's oldest permanently inhabited community still preserves a look of yesteryear. Designated a historic district in 1976, its downtown streets are lined with gracious homes dating from the late 18th and early 19th centuries that represent the greatest concentration of French colonial architecture in the nation. The town's farmers and fur traders built many homes using a unique method of construction in which vertical cedar logs formed walls. Homes built in this way include the Bequette-Ribault home, dating back to 1778, and the Amoureux House, with its steeply pitched roof. Particularly notable are the walnut-trimmed Green Tree Inn, which set up commerce in 1789 as the first tavern, inn, and tobacco shop west of the Mississippi; Felix Valle House, a well-stocked mercantile store; and the Bolduc House. The last,

built in 1770, was the nation's first authentically restored Creole-style house and is now a national historic landmark.

A short detour off I-55 into the town of Burfordville takes travelers to a four-story stone-and-brick gristmill that has been grinding corn for more than 180 years. Next to the Bollinger Mill is the 140-foot Burfordville Covered Bridge, completed about 1867 and built almost entirely of yellow poplar. It is the oldest of four such spans left in Missouri.

Approaching the southeastern tip of Missouri—a bulge known as the Boot Heel—motorists encounter the remnants of a vast swamp forest that once covered the area. At Big Oak Tree State Park, a boardwalk leads into the delta past towering trees, many of them the largest of their species.

North of Memphis, outside the town of Wilson, is Hampson Museum State Park, which began as a pet project of Dr. James K. Hampson. In 1927 he discovered the remains of a Native American farming

community on his property that had inhabited the area from A.D. 1400 to A.D. 1650. The excavated 15-acre village includes ceremonial mounds, family cemeteries, and a plaza for religious ceremonies.

I-55 then heads into Memphis, home of the Mississippi River Museum and Graceland, the ornate mansion that was once the residence of Elvis Presley.

FOR MORE INFORMATION:
Missouri Division of Tourism, Truman State Office Bldg., 302 West High St., Rm. 290, Jefferson MO 65101; 573-751-4133 or 800-877-1234.
Arkansas Division of Parks & Tourism, One Capitol Mall, Little Rock, AR 72201; 501-682-7777.
Tennessee Dept. of Tourist Development, P.O. Box 231170, Nashville, TN 37202-3170; 615-741-2258.

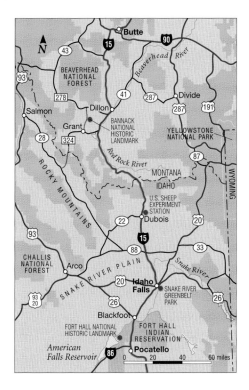

It's a big sky that greets motorists on the stretch of Interstate 15 running from Butte, Montana, to Pocatello, Idaho. Fringed by forests of green pine and Douglas fir, the road traverses a rugged terrain of snowcapped mountains, valleys and meadows, white-water rivers, and creeks filled with blue-ribbon trout. In this wild and pristine pocket of the Rockies, civilization is sparse. Except for a smattering of backwater towns colored with pioneer history, much of the countryside is populated by fewer than one person per square mile. Along the route, travelers may spot elk, moose, mountain goats, and bighorn sheep.

The vast tract of land in southwestern Montana remained virtually untouched by settlement until gold, silver, and copper were found in the region. Towns grew up overnight to meet the needs of the prospectors. In 1880, the discovery of a rich vein of copper put Butte on the map.

About 60 miles from Butte, motorists come to another boomtown. Bannack sprang into being when gold was discovered in 1862 near Grasshopper Creek. Within a year, Bannack's population swelled to more than 3,000 pioneers hoping to strike it rich. The town became the site of Montana's first territorial capital, school, hotel, and commercial sawmill. Bannack also claims the first two jails ever built in Montana, where troublesome outlaws were chained to rings bolted into the floor. Today visitors can walk the dusty streets of this 19th-century ghost town, now listed as a national historic landmark. The streets are lined with miners' cabins and some 90 other buildings, including Skinner's Saloon, and the Goodrich Hotel.

The majesty of the scenery intensifies as I-15 cuts across and then hugs the banks of the Beaverhead River. If visitors keep a sharp lookout, they may spot deer and marmots sheltered among the conifers of Beaverhead National Forest.

ALONG THE SNAKE RIVER

Heading past the sparkling waters of the Red Rock River into eastern Idaho, the highway enters a transitional zone known as the Snake River Plain. Here the jutting peaks of the Rockies slowly give way to a flat, fertile plateau at the foothills of the Continental Divide. In 1915 Dubois was selected as the location for the U.S. Sheep Experiment Station—an 87,000-acre research center whose mission is to produce technology to increase the efficiency of livestock production. The facility has developed three major sheep breeds. Visitors can glimpse the fenced-off pastures where sheep graze under the watchful eyes of a herder.

The mighty Snake River is the major attraction of this region. Now federally protected as a wild and scenic river, the Snake courses for 1,038 miles, its waters teeming with whitefish, trout, and kokanee salmon, while ospreys, bald eagles, and falcons soar overhead. In the heart of downtown Idaho Falls, the state's third-largest city, visitors can stroll the pathways of the Snake River Greenbelt Park, following the turbulent river as it narrows and plunges over a scenic rock cascade.

I-15 continues along the Snake River until it reaches the replica of Fort Hall, on the outskirts of Pocatello. A part of Idaho's frontier history was played out here in the 19th century, when a young New England businessman named Nathaniel Wyeth chose it as the location for his new fur-trading enterprise. In July 1834 Wyeth constructed a log fort on a sheltered bend of the Snake River, in a spot where Shoshone and Bannock Indians were known to have camped for thousands of years. Wyeth named Fort Hall in honor of the oldest member of the New England company that had provided the financing for his enterprise.

Fort Hall, located between Fort Laramie and Fort Boise, became a major stopping place for pioneer wagon trains along the Oregon Trail and the California Trail. A replica of Fort Hall, located on the Fort Hall Indian Reservation, was constructed from the original plans. On display are exhibits on the early days of the fort, as well as Indian artifacts. This journey ends in Pocatello, which sprang up in 1822 as a small tent camp at a railway crossroads, and went on to become one of the largest railroad centers west of the Mississippi River.

FOR MORE INFORMATION:
Travel Montana, 1424 9th Ave., Helena, MT 59620; 406-444-2654 or 800-VISITMT. Idaho Division of Travel Promotion, Idaho Dept. of Commerce, 700 West State St., Boise, ID 83720-0093; 208-334-2470.

The weathered sign of Butte's Old Bootshop, left, is part of the rugged charm here. The starting point of this trip down I-15, Butte was once a major copper-mining town.

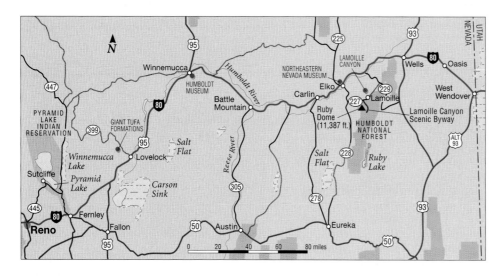

The last Western territory to be settled, Nevada encompasses large chunks of the Great Basin and the Mojave Desert, as well as some 200 mountain ranges. Interstate 80 crosses the state's northern tier, offering visitors an unusually wide range of geological wonders.

About 80 miles from Reno, a short detour off I-80 brings visitors to the Giant Tufa Formations near Lovelock. Resembling a landscape from another planet, these geological oddities are among the most bizarre natural formations in the state. Jutting up from what was once an ancient seabed, the clumps and columns of porous limestone stand like eerie sentinels. Formed some 10,000 years ago, these stone pillars have been sculpted into their present shape by the relentless action of wind and water. But visitors who wander through the 100-acre site soon realize that the region is very far from a barren moonscape. Splashed with colorful patches of lichen, the tallest formations of tufa often serve as perches for hawks and owls as they stalk the small rodents that scurry below them among the cracks and crevices.

Continuing along I-80, motorists arrive at the town of Winnemucca. Named for a Paiute chief, this former fur-trading outpost was the site of a 1900 bank robbery allegedly masterminded by the notorious outlaw Butch Cassidy. Much of the region's fascinating history is chronicled here in the Humboldt Museum. Housed partially in the old St. Mary's Episcopal Church, this eclectic collection contains everything from

Among Nevada's fascinating geological oddities, few are as striking as the pyramid-shaped rock, right, that gave Pyramid Lake its name. Today the lake is the only place in the world where the rare cui-ui sucker fish can be found.

Native American projectile points and cowboy memorabilia to a hand-inked 1867 survey map and a talking machine invented by Thomas Edison. Winnemucca's first piano and the county's first car—a 1901 Merry Oldsmobile—are two of the museum's most popular objects. The "Remembering the 20's" display celebrates the Hollywood success of locally born actress Edna Purviance, and includes the beaded dress she wore in the 1917 film *The Adventurer*—just one of the 35 silent movies in which she costarred with Charlie Chaplin.

The next stop along the route is in Elko, home to the Northeastern Nevada Museum. One of the most comprehensive regional museums in the state, it is renowned for its highly informative and artistic displays. Reflecting Nevada's rich history of ranching, mining, and railroading, the museum contains pioneer period rooms, antique vehicles, and even the old bar from the Halleck Saloon. Another exhibit celebrates the rich heritage of the region's Basque settlers, who came here

in the mid-1800's to work as miners and shepherds. The museum also houses an art gallery that exhibits the work of talented local artists. Ranch life, desert landscapes, and indigenous wildlife are all depicted in this ever-changing collection.

CANYON COUNTRY

Museums notwithstanding, the state's true beauty has always been found in the land. Nowhere is this more evident than in Lamoille Canyon, located just outside the town of Lamoille. Nestled in the heart of the majestic Ruby Mountains, this sheer-walled, U-shaped valley is called the Yosemite of Nevada. Flanked by towering outcrops, Lamoille Canyon is alive with a rich diversity of plants and wildlife. Sunflowers, paintbrushes, bluebells, and oceansprays are just a few of the colorful wildflowers that carpet this secluded garden of Eden. Himalayan snowcocks hide in the tall grasses; brook and rainbow trout swim in the crystal-clear mountain lakes; and bighorn sheep and mountain goats navigate the steep cliffs.

A 12-mile scenic road leads travelers through the canyon and around Ruby Dome, at 11,387 feet the highest peak in the Ruby Mountains. Ending at the 8,400-foot-high Roads End Trailhead, the route offers a series of breathtaking views. Forty-five miles of hiking trails, ranging from easy to difficult, give visitors of all ages the opportunity to experience the natural treasures of Nevada.

FOR MORE INFORMATION:
Nevada Commission on Tourism, Capitol Complex, Carson City, NV 89710; 702-687-4322 or 800-638-2328.

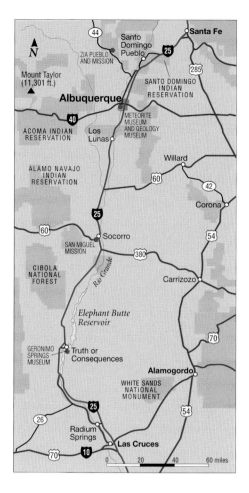

Native American pottery is displayed along with contemporary paintings and sculptures, left, at the Geronimo Springs Museum.

A river is the lifeblood of a people. Where its path flows, water is abundant, fish thrive, and transportation routes develop. Nowhere are these blessings greater boons than in New Mexico, an arid, sun-baked region of canyons, desert plateaus, and pasturelands. Here glistens the mighty Rio Grande, its life-sustaining power uncontested as it courses down the center of the state.

Early Spanish explorers appreciated the river's importance, for its name means "large river." The Mexicans call it Rio Bravo del Norte, which translates as "bold river of the north." Both names are accurate, for the Rio Grande is the fifth-longest river in North America, winding for 1,885 miles through the Southwest. On its path from Santa Fe down to Las Cruces, the river is paralleled by Interstate 25—a stretch of highway that snakes alongside the water, offering excellent views of the Rio Grande Valley and its settlements.

PUEBLO COUNTRY

Between Santa Fe and Albuquerque, a short detour along Hwy. 44 leads to Zia Pueblo and Mission, situated on a barren mesa. The Zia people—a word derived from the native name *Tseja* meaning "unknown"—have been living in the pueblo since A.D. 1250. A Spanish mission was established here in the early 17th century. Today the Zia inhabit a 119,537-acre reservation and are renowned for their elegantly designed pottery, which is sought by collectors worldwide. An ancient Zia sun symbol adorns the New Mexico state flag. At the Zia Pueblo Cultural Center, visitors can watch contemporary potters at work.

Worlds away from Zia Pueblo is the Meteorite Museum in Albuquerque. Founded in 1944 as part of the University of New Mexico's now-famous Institute of Meteoritics, the museum preserves a collection of meteorites found around the world. Examples include the one-ton Norton County—the second largest meteorite ever discovered, which fell in Kansas in 1948—and a 500,000-year-old fragment found in Arizona's Winslow Meteor Crater. At the Geology Museum, also run by the University of New Mexico, New Mexico's geological past is showcased. Displays range from fluorescent minerals and gems to fossils of phytosaurs (crocodilelike reptiles), duck-billed dinosaurs, and—perhaps most oddly—of ancient sharks.

I-25 offers a glimpse of the area's Spanish heritage at Socorro. The town's name means "help" and stems from an incident in 1598, when Native Americans saved a Spanish expedition led by Don Juan de Onate by providing them with corn. Two Franciscan priests built the Mission of San Miguel. Visitors can tour the church, which was completed in 1626, and admire the five-foot-thick adobe walls and carved corbels. According to accounts of the time, an Indian uprising in 1680 forced priests to bury the silver communion rail and tabernacle, which remain hidden to this day.

South of Socorro, I-25 meanders past the broad desert basin called Jornada del Muerto, or "journey of the dead." The nearby town of Truth or Consequences earned its name by winning a nationwide competition—a promotional stunt that the popular 1950's radio show of the same name sponsored on its 10th anniversary. The town, formerly known as Hot Springs, got its original name from the hot mineral waters that are reputed to cure arthritis, rheumatism, and other aches and pains. Even the great Apache warrior Geronimo bathed with his warriors in the life-giving waters of the Rio Grande Valley.

This journey ends in Las Cruces, situated on El Camino Real. The town was named for the crosses that mark the graves of travelers who lost their lives during the Apache raids of 1787.

FOR MORE INFORMATION:

New Mexico Tourism Dept., 491 Old Santa Fe Trail, Santa Fe, NM 87503; 505-827-7400 or 800-733-6396.

The thick adobe walls and red tile roof of Socorro's San Miguel Church, below, proclaim its Spanish heritage. Silver extracted from local mines was used to decorate the interior.

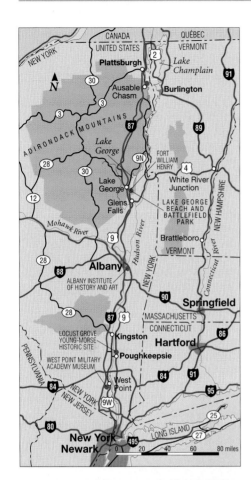

The torrents of the Ausable Chasm, near Plattsburgh, right, have been attracting visitors since it opened to the public in 1870. It is one of the oldest tourist destinations in the nation.

West Point, above, has produced such illustrious graduates as Robert E. Lee, Ulysses S. Grant, John J. Pershing, and Dwight D. Eisenhower.

Starting at the tip of New York State, Interstate 87 runs parallel to the Hudson River, tours the lowlands of the Adirondack Mountains, and heads north toward the Canadian border. Along the way travelers can enjoy art, history, and military lore.

The town of West Point, located about 40 miles north of New York City, is the seat of the United States Military Academy, found-ed in 1802 to train the nation's military commanders. The academy's museum is the oldest and largest military museum in the nation. Its collection of 45,000 objects includes George Washington's pistols, a sword that belonged to Napoleon, and a gold-plated pistol belonging to Adolf Hitler. Dioramas depict important battles, and a display chronicles the development of flight technology from Civil War balloons to the shuttles used in the space program.

About 20 miles north of West Point on I-87 is exit 18 for the Mid Hudson Bridge, which leads to the town of Poughkeepsie just on the other side of the Hudson River. Near the river in Poughkeepsie lies the 1830 manor of Samuel F. B. Morse, the painter and inventor of the telegraph and Morse code. The Locust Grove Young–Morse Historic Site houses a replica of the original telegraph, and visitors can practice sending messages using a telegraph key. Surrounding the house are 150 acres of gardens originally designed and laid out by Morse himself.

I-87 brings visitors to Albany, the state capital and home of the Albany Institute of History and Art. Operating under various guises since 1791, the institute focuses on the history, art, and culture of Albany and the Upper Hudson Valley region. Works by artists of the Hudson River School, Hudson Valley portraits of the early 18th century, and 18th- and 19th-century silver are among the 16,000 objects in the collection. Also housed in the institute is the McKinney Library, with an outstanding collection of more than 1 million items, including books, periodicals, photographs, artists' sketchbooks, and manuscripts.

BATTLEFIELD PARK

Leaving Albany, I-87 heads north toward Lake George. Bordering the southern end of Lake George, the 93-acre Lake George Beach and Battlefield Park has a tranquil setting that belies its history of bloodshed. Erected in 1755, Fort William Henry was built in preparation for an anticipated French advance from Canada into the American colonies. Two years later, the Marquis de Montcalm and 10,000 French and Indian troops swept across Lake George to attack Colonel Munro at Fort Henry; Munro surrendered six days later. The French burned the fort, and scores of British soldiers were killed in the massacre that followed. Musket balls, pottery shards, cannons, coins, rifles, and surgical instruments are on display at the restored fort. During the summer, members of the Fort William Henry Artillery Crew demonstrate 18th-century artillery drill and the manu-facture of musket balls.

Just south of Plattsburgh, visitors can explore an enchanted chasm, created by melting glaciers 500 million years ago. Bright lichens, soft mosses, evergreens, and ferns adorn Ausable Chasm's sand-stone cliffs. Stairs and steel bridges guide walkers past stone formations chiseled out of the cliffs by the action of flowing water. Pulpit Rock, Jacob's Ladder, Elephant's Head, and the Cathedral are among these craggy sculptures. A boat ride along the Grand Flume takes in the Sentry Box and Broken Needle, formed in cliffs scarcely 20 feet apart. The boat travels through a series of rapids and Whirlpool Basin, and then glides to a landfall at the chasm's lower end.

FOR MORE INFORMATION:
New York State Travel Information Center, 1 Commerce Plaza, Albany, NY 12245; 800-225-5697.

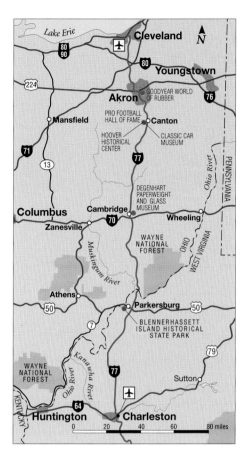

S licing through the nation's industrial heartland, the stretch of Interstate 77 running from Akron, Ohio, to Charleston, West Virginia, is studded with household names, such as Hoover and Goodyear. At the Goodyear World of Rubber in Akron, displays include an artificial heart, Indianapolis 500 race cars, and tires that were used on vehicles sent to the moon. Exhibits related to the history of blimps and the trucking trade reveal the rubber industry's influence on modern transportation and technology.

Visitors can tour a simulated rubber plantation and learn how rubber is made and tires are built. A replica of Charles Goodyear's workshop depicts his discovery of vulcanization—the process of treating rubber with sulfur to increase its elasticity. Founded in 1898, the Goodyear Tire and Rubber Company was named in honor of the inventor 38 years after his death.

A brief jaunt along I-77 leads to Canton, where an 1850 Italianate farmhouse shelters the Hoover Historical Center. Inside

The reconstructed mansion of Harman Blennerhassett, right, is located within Blennerhassett Island Historical Park. The original structure was built around 1800.

William H. Hoover's boyhood home, exhibits trace the changes in carpet cleaning from 1850 to the present. Although the Hoover Company began as a manufacturer of leather goods, Hoover quickly saw the potential in an electric cleaning machine invented by James Murray Spangler and began to manufacture vacuum cleaners. The original 40-pound "suction sweeper" of 1908 appears among a collection of brooms, early vacuum cleaners, and high-tech Hoovers.

The Canton Classic Car Museum stands just off Lincoln Highway, America's first transcontinental freeway. Period advertising and photographs capture the romance of the open road, but it is the museum's vintage automobiles that fire the imagination. Speedsters, phaetons, and coupes are on display, as well as a 1911 Ford Model T roadster, a 1937 Studebaker President police flyer, and a 1959 Cadillac Eldorado Biarritz convertible. Celebrity vehicles include Amelia Earhart's 1916 Pierce Arrow, the Lincoln used by the British royal family on their 1939 tour of Canada, and a vehicle from the 1969 movie *Those Daring Young Men in Their Jaunty Jalopies.*

FOOTBALL HALL OF FAME
A football-shaped dome announces Canton's biggest highlight: the Pro Football Hall of Fame. Opened in 1963, the 83,000-square-foot showplace celebrates the sport's heroes. Super Bowl videos and treasured relics, such as Dutch Clark's warm-up jacket and the cigar-singed desk of former

National Football League commissioner Bert Bell, are also on display. Visitors are greeted by a bronze statue of Jim Thorpe, onetime member of the Canton Bulldogs. Rows of bronze heads glow against a blue background in the enshrinement gallery, where a niche features an action mural and brief biography of each honoree. Elsewhere, football fans can watch NFL action on a huge Cinemascope screen, play electronic quiz games, and view photographs of great NFL moments.

Leaving Canton behind, I-77 leads to the Degenhart Paperweight and Glass Museum near Cambridge. The one-story museum was established at the bequest of Elizabeth Degenhart, who cofounded the Crystal Art Glass Company with her husband, John Degenhart, in 1947. An exquisite collection of paperweights made by John Degenhart includes some that are composed of swirls of colored glass; others contain butterflies and flowers. Exhibits focus on glass-making techniques, as well as Degenhart Crystal Art Glass novelties. In 1975 Ohio's governor proclaimed Elizabeth Degenhart the First Lady of Glass.

In Parkersburg, West Virginia, visitors can board a sternwheeler for Blennerhassett Island Historical State Park. A ride along the graceful Ohio River leads to an island rich with hardwood forests, verdant fields, and pioneer history. In 1800 Harman Blennerhassett, a wealthy Irish aristocrat, built an estate on the wilderness island. Blennerhassett then became caught up in a dubious military undertaking with Aaron Burr in 1806. Pres. Thomas Jefferson accused them of plotting to build an empire in the Southwest. Although the two men were later found innocent of treason, their lives were ruined by the accusations.

Visitors can tour the reconstructed mansion, which was rebuilt after a fire destroyed it in 1811, and travel around the island in horse-drawn wagons. Famous travelers who once visited this tranquil island include King Charles X of France, Walt Whitman, and Johnny Appleseed.

From here I-77 leads to the charming city of Charleston, which retains the old-world elegance of a bygone era.

FOR MORE INFORMATION:
Ohio Division of Travel and Tourism, P.O. Box 1001, Columbus, OH 43266-1001; 614-466-8844.
West Virginia Division of Tourism, 2101 Washington St. E., Bldg. 17, Charleston, WV 25305; 304-558-2200.

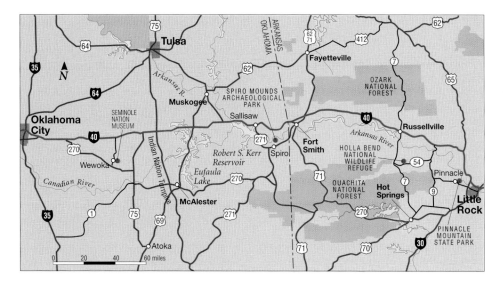

Although countless artifacts buried at Spiro Mounds were stolen by looters in the 1930's, many treasures, like the pierced shell gorget pictured above, have been recovered and are displayed at the site's visitor center.

Interstate 40 runs from coast to coast, but the segment that connects the capitals of Oklahoma and Arkansas follows the gentle undulations of the Arkansas River for much of the way. This portion of I-40 offers visitors the opportunity to sample natural and man-made wonders, and to glory in the tranquil beauty of the Ozarks.

Leaving Oklahoma City, I-40 leads to the Seminole Nation Museum in Wewoka. Driven from their homes in Florida by the federal government, members of the Seminole Nation relocated in Oklahoma, then called Indian Territory, in the 1830's. Exhibits on display in the museum include personal objects ranging from canes to teapots that the Seminoles carried with them during their forced exodus along the Trail of Tears. Photographs, art, patchwork clothing, and other artifacts bring this tragic tale to life. Also on display at the museum is a replica of a *chickee*—a traditional dwelling built from logs and palm leaves—and a

reconstruction of the facade of the Wewoka Trading Post.

Although the plight of the Seminoles is well documented, the history of the Spiro Moundbuilders remains shrouded in mystery. One of the most significant prehistoric Native sites east of the Rockies, the 140-acre Spiro Mounds Archaeological Park is home to 12 structural and burial mounds. Erected between the 7th and 15th centuries, these eerie, grass-covered tombs are the last remnants of a thriving culture. While experts believe that Spiro was a center for elaborate rituals and burials, they are uncertain why it was abandoned. Many of the treasures buried here, including copper breastplates, effigy pipes shaped like humans and animals, and engraved conch shell bowls, are on display at the visitor center. Trails wind through the park, passing the ancient mounds including the massive Craig Mound, a 300-foot-long giant that holds the remains of up to 1,000 tribesmen.

Located on the Arkansas River just 100 miles from Spiro's haunting stillness, the Holla Bend National Wildlife Refuge is alive with more than 240 species of birds. Ruby-throated hummingbirds, yellow-bellied sapsuckers, blue-gray gnatcatchers, and green-backed herons are just some of the species found in the refuge. Regal bald eagles gaze from their solitary perches; belted kingfishers plunge into the lakes in search of food; and northern harriers and American kestrels visit the refuge from December through February.

Pinnacle Mountain State Park is named for the massive cone-shaped peak that towers more than 1,000 feet above the Arkansas River valley. Whether strolling through bottomland forest or scrambling across boulder fields in the rugged ascent of Pinnacle Mountain, hikers will find a trail suitable to their level of experience.

Little Rock contains a wealth of historic buildings, including the Arkansas State Capitol, which is similar in design to that of the capitol in Washington, D.C.

FOR MORE INFORMATION:
Oklahoma Department of Tourism & Recreation, Travel & Tourism Division, 2401 North Lincoln Blvd., Oklahoma City, OK 73105; 800-652-6552.
Arkansas Division of Parks & Tourism, One Capitol Mall, Little Rock, AR 72201; 501-682-7777.

A shaded oasis in Arkansas' Pinnacle Mountain State Park, left, is the perfect spot to cast a fishing line. Catfish and bass are especially plentiful in the park's lakes and rivers.

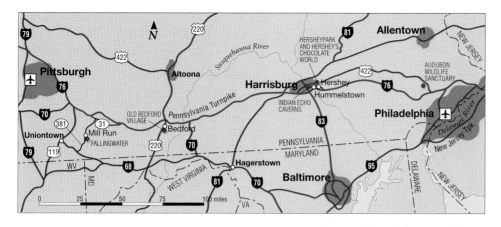

It's a rare traveler who can drive from Pittsburgh to Philadelphia along Interstate 76 without being lured off the highway by wayside adventures. A house built over a waterfall, a tour of a chocolate factory and a pioneer village, a famous bird sanctuary, and mysterious caverns are all too good to miss.

About 50 miles from Pittsburgh, near the town of Mill Run, stands a house that was designated "the best all-time work of American architecture" by the American Institute of Architects in 1991. Set over a stream, Fallingwater was built by architect Frank Lloyd Wright in 1937 for the family of Pittsburgh department store magnate Edgar J. Kaufmann, who used the house as a weekend retreat until 1963. Constructed of sandstone quarried on the property, Fallingwater's bold geometry is strangely harmonious with the rugged beauty of its surroundings. Inside, the clean lines of the Kaufmanns' original furnishings and artwork complement the house's modernist style. Brown sandstone floors and continuous expanses of window in Cherokee red steel casements add a softening effect to the interior of the house.

Nestled in the curve of the Pennsylvania Turnpike, Old Bedford Village is a pioneer village complete with historic houses, barns, and a covered bridge. Roughly one-third of the structures are the workshops and homes of skilled craftspeople, who use traditional methods to make iron implements, leather goods, tinware, quilts, baskets, and brooms. A cook mixes cornbread by an open hearth, and potters pound clay. Open since 1976, the village contains a pioneer farmstead, an octagonal-shaped Quaker schoolhouse, and picnic places.

I-76 leads to Indian Echo Caverns, near Hummelstown. Beneath the land where the Susquehannock tribe once lived, visitors wind through dark passageways covered with rock formations and flowstone. While eerie geological shapes glow in the dim

One of the most famous intersections in Hershey, above, leaves little doubt as to the town's primary industry. Tours of Chocolate World show how raw cocoa beans are transformed into chocolate.

light, a cavern echoes softly with the sound of moisture dripping from a massive stalactite into a dank pool below. During a 45-minute tour through the caverns, guides recount the tale of William Wilson, the "Pennsylvania Hermit" who lived in the cool chambers for 19 years.

In the town of Hershey, chocolate is a way of life. The roads of Chocolate Town, U.S.A. are lined with lamps shaped like Hershey's Kisses, hedges spell out "Hershey Cocoa," and giant walking Hershey Bars stroll the streets of Hersheypark.

The town was concocted by Milton S. Hershey, following the completion of the world's largest chocolate factory in 1905. Born a poor farm boy in 1857, Hershey built a chocolate empire out of a candy shop that he had started when he was only 19 years old.

Visitors learn about Hershey's life in the Hershey Museum, then wander through stunning rose beds in Hershey Gardens, or watch bison roam in ZooAmerica. Heart-pounding roller coasters, a splashdown ride, an antique carousel, and live shows entice pleasure-seekers to Hersheypark.

Guests are treated to a tour of the candy-making process in Hershey's Chocolate World. After eyeing conveyor belts bearing hundreds of chocolate bars, visitors are never in a hurry to leave this sweet town.

AUDUBON'S LEGACY

As I-76 nears Philadelphia, visitors should take a detour to Mill Grove, the first American home of artist and naturalist John James Audubon. Surrounded by the Audubon Wildlife Sanctuary, the tawny fieldstone mansion overlooks Perkiomen Creek and the land that sparked Audubon's lifelong fascination with birds and wildlife.

Audubon grew up in France, but at age 18 was sent to supervise Mill Grove by his father, Jean Audubon. Arriving in 1803, young Audubon spent three years at Mill Grove, sketching and banding birds in the nearby woods. He was a pioneer in the study and drawing of wildlife and was unsurpassed in his attention to detail.

Decorated with period furnishings, Mill Grove displays all of the naturalist's major works—most notably *Birds of America,* a rare set of copperplate engravings published between 1826 and 1838. A tour of the house includes the attic, which Audubon used as a studio and taxidermy room.

In the sanctuary, quiet trails are dotted with flowering shrubs, nesting boxes, and feeding stations. Rambling through fields and woods, visitors may encounter descendants of the birds that caught Audubon's eye almost two centuries ago.

I-76 now enters Philadelphia—the birthplace of American independence and home to the Liberty Bell and Independence National Historic Park.

FOR MORE INFORMATION:
Pennsylvania Department of Commerce, Office of Travel and Tourism, Forum Bldg., Rm. 453, Harrisburg, PA 17120; 800-VISITPA.

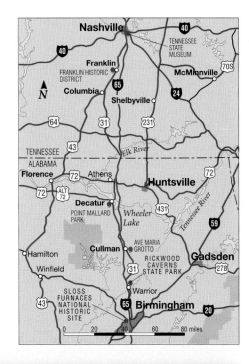

A Benedictine monk surveys the miniature city of Jerusalem, above, at the Ave Maria Grotto. This tiny city includes a replica of the Temple, where the Ark of the Covenant was housed.

The blacktop link between the birthplace of the Grand Ole Opry in Nashville, Tennessee, and a major site in the civil rights movement in Birmingham, Alabama, Interstate 65 has seen its share of happiness and heartache. Approximately 175 miles in length, this short stretch of highway offers varied rewards for adventurers.

Much of Tennessee's colorful past is preserved in the Tennessee State Museum in Nashville. Daniel Boone's knife, Davey Crockett's rifle, and the felt hat Andrew Jackson wore to his inauguration are just some of the fascinating articles on display.

Less than 20 miles down I-65, picturesque Franklin is a blend of the old and the new. Here, in the midst of bustling commercial enterprises, the 15-block original downtown area contains dozens of magnificent Victorian and antebellum buildings. The Old Franklin Ice House harks back to a time before refrigeration. Just down the street, the Gothic-style Hiram Masonic Lodge was where Pres. Andrew Jackson negotiated the Chickasaw Treaty of 1830. But much of Franklin's history is rooted in tragedy. On November 30, 1864, on the outskirts of town, Union and Confederate forces clashed in a Civil War confrontation that was marked by its brutal ferocity. After five bloody hours, more than 8,000 men lay dead or wounded. Travelers can visit the bullet-scarred Carter House, which served as a Union command post during the battle. The Historic Carnton Plantation was a makeshift Confederate field hospital, with the bodies of four slain Southern generals laid out on its porch. The dark bloodstains visible on the floorboards are a poignant testament to the horrors of war.

WATER WORLD

Although it doesn't reach as far back in time as Franklin, Point Mallard Park in Decatur also enjoys historical significance. In 1970 the nation's first wave pool was unveiled here. Four hydraulic fans blasting air into tunnels of water send gentle swells of water cascading through the 16,000-square-foot pool. A veritable water world, the 750-acre park offers aquatic adventures for the whole family. Children can splash in the shallow waters of the Duck Pond and Squirt Factory with its raindrop umbrella, tire swings, and miniature waterslides. For thrill-seekers, a ride down the 40-foot waterslide on an inner tube sends them hurtling into the Olympic Pool at speeds of up to 30 miles an hour. Tennis courts, baseball diamonds, and a championship golf course let visitors enjoy themselves while keeping their feet dry. Hiking trails, biking paths, and a 175-site campground offer visitors other opportunities to experience the park's natural charms.

For recreation of a less physical nature, travelers need go no further than the Ave Maria Grotto. Nestled on a terraced hillside on the grounds of the St. Bernard Abbey off I-65 at Cullman, the grotto contains about 150 scale models of famous churches, shrines, and other buildings from around the world. Built by Brother Joseph Zoettl over a 46-year span, this Lilliputian fairy-land includes replicas of everything from the ancient cities of Jerusalem and Rome to miniatures of the Statue of Liberty and the Alamo. Using photographs for reference, Brother Joseph painstakingly pieced together each building in incredible detail, creating a minuscule world renowned for its remarkable architectural accuracy. As well as working with cement and limestone, Brother Joe used children's marbles, cold cream jars, bits of tile, seashells, and an old bird cage in the construction of his magical miniatures. Visitors can stop at the Abbey Cemetery to see the grave of this tireless builder, who died in 1961 at the age of 83.

BURIED TREASURE

From the tranquillity of the grotto, visitors can plumb the mysterious region beneath the earth's surface at Rickwood Caverns State Park. Formed more than 260 million years ago, this extensive network of caves and tunnels includes the Miracle Mile—a series of deep subterranean chambers. Magnificent passages carved through the limestone wind their way eerily toward the earth's core, transporting amateur spelunkers 175 feet below ground, where delicate beads of water patter from stalactite to stalagmite. The Diamond Room is alive with sparkling limestone; the inky water of the underground lake is home to frogs, salamanders, and a unique transparent sightless fish. Once the bed of an ancient ocean, the cavern walls are encrusted with tiny remnants of seashells and the fossilized remains of prehistoric marine life.

Exploiting the earth's buried treasures made Birmingham a center of industry, as witnessed by the Sloss Furnaces National Historic Monument. Combining limestone, coal, and ore at high temperatures, these massive ironworks produced high-quality pig iron from 1881 to 1971. Former blast-furnace workers, who give tours of the ovens, casting areas, and boiler rooms, impress upon visitors the grit and determination that forged a civilization from this vast and untamed wilderness.

FOR MORE INFORMATION:

Tennessee Department of Tourist Development, P.O. Box 23170, Nashville, TN 37202-3170; 800-836-6200.
Alabama Bureau of Tourism & Travel, 401 Adams Ave., P.O. Box 4309, Montgomery, AL 36103-4927; 800-252-2262.

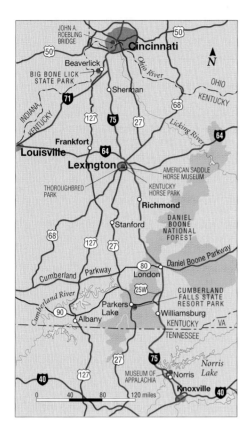

Big Tater Valley Schoolhouse, above, at the Museum of Appalachia gives visitors an impression of what schooling in the mountains was like during the 19th century.

From the rugged beauty of eastern Tennessee's mountain ranges to Kentucky's fertile farmlands and the cosmopolitan charm of Cincinnati, Ohio, this stretch of Interstate 75 ranks among the most beautiful drives in the nation.

For a look at the Appalachian region's colorful past, the 65-acre Museum of Appalachia is a perfect stop. With cords of firewood stacked neatly outside, dried beans and peppers on the tables, and cattle, sheep, and goats grazing peacefully in nearby pastures, this unique complex feels more like a village than a museum. Located just north of Knoxville, it holds some 250,000 artifacts, including a rocking chair built for two, pruning shears made from old bayonets, and one of the largest collections of pioneer relics in the world. Among the more than 30 original buildings that have been relocated to the museum grounds, the primitive Arnwine Cabin, built about 1800, is the oldest. The Cantilever Barn has an upper level with a 12- to 14-foot overhang that protected wagons and livestock from inclement weather.

Farther south on I-75 and nestled in the heart of the Daniel Boone National Forest, Cumberland Falls State Resort Park offers a variety of outdoor activities, including camping, canoeing, horseback riding, and white-water rafting. Nature trails lead to several waterfalls—the most famous of which is Cumberland Falls. Almost 70 feet tall and 125 feet wide, the "Niagara of the South" sends some 3,217 cubic feet of water per second thundering into the rocky gorge below. The cataract is one of only two worldwide that produces a moonbeam—a lunar rainbow created when moonlight hits the fine mist at the base of the falls.

PARADE OF BREEDS

Visitors can celebrate man's bond with his equine partner in Lexington. After touring Thoroughbred Park, travelers can proceed to the 1,032-acre Kentucky Horse Park just outside of town. At the International Museum of the Horse, the 58-million-year history of this magnificent animal is shown through art. Also on display are antique carriages and the Calumet Farm collection of gold, silver, and crystal trophies. The twice-a-day Parade of Breeds highlights the beauty of more than 40 different breeds. Also located on the grounds of the park is the American Saddle Horse Museum, dedicated to the American Saddlebred—the only breed native to Kentucky.

Before arriving in Cincinnati, motorists can visit Big Bone Lick State Park. Covered with mineral springs and swamps during the Ice Age about 12,000 to 20,000 years ago, the park's lush fields and woodlands hold the bones of mastodons, mammoths, ground sloths, and giant stag moose. Many of these fossilized bones are on display at the park's museum. A mile-long paved trail passes the last remaining salt-sulfur spring in the park, and winds through swampland with life-size models of a mastodon and a prehistoric bison.

As I-75 heads into Cincinnati, it crosses the Ohio River on the 1,056-foot John A. Roebling Bridge—the world's longest suspension bridge upon its completion in 1867.

FOR MORE INFORMATION:

Kentucky Department of Travel Development, 2200 Capital Plaza Tower, 500 Mero St., Frankfort, KY 40601; 800-225-8747.
Tennessee Department of Tourist Development, P.O. Box 23170, Nashville, TN 37202-3170; 800-836-6200.
Ohio Division of Travel and Tourism, P.O. Box 1001, Columbus, OH 43266-1001; 614-466-8844.

Charging toward the finish in a race that won't end, the thoroughbreds in this statue at the Thoroughbred Park, left, are frozen in time.

135

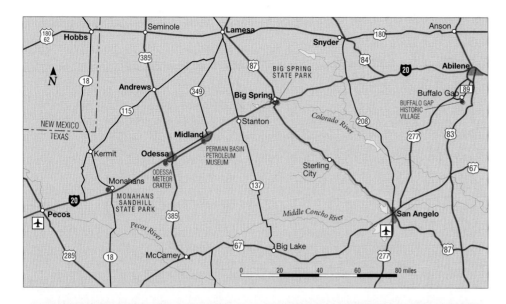

The golden glow of a Texas sunrise illuminates the limestone arch of the pavilion in Big Spring State Park, above. The pavilion was constructed by the Civilian Conservation Corps.

While the sheer immensity of Texas may make a sightseeing tour along Interstate 20 seem daunting, the best way to get to know the Lone Star State is one stop at a time.

Starting at Pecos—where the first rodeo in the nation was held in 1883—travelers heading east will come upon the towering sand dunes in the Monahans Sandhill State Park. An ancient seabed some 280 million years old, the park is now part of a vast field of undulating sandhills that stretches into New Mexico. Free to scale these giant wind-sculpted dunes—some of which can reach 70 feet in height—or rocket down them on rented surfing discs, visitors can also marvel at the wildlife that abounds in this arid landscape. Clustered around small, natural pools of water, scaled quail, Harris's hawks, and cactus wrens thrive among the reeds, willows, and Christmas cactus. Surprisingly, the park is home to one of the largest—and rarest—oak forests in the nation. Covering some 40,000 acres, the forest is populated with shin oaks, tiny trees that stand less than four feet tall.

One of the state's truly earth-shattering events occurred some 20,000 years ago, when a shower of meteorites fell from the sky. While the majority of these extraterrestrial hunks of rock were small, one massive chunk—estimated at 1,000 tons—plowed into the ground near present-day Odessa, blasting a hole in the bedrock some 100 feet deep and 550 feet across. Called the Odessa Meteor Crater, the site contains a self-guiding trail that passes exploratory shafts and trenches dug in the 1930's and 1940's, remnants of the futile attempts to locate the massive nickel comet. The crater explodes with wildflowers after each desert shower.

BLACK GOLD

In spite of the unforgiving desert, the land has been good to Texans. Nowhere is this more evident than at the Permian Basin Petroleum Museum in Midland. In the 1920's, land-owners struck it rich following the discovery of oil fields here. Audio-visual presentations, exhibits of industry artifacts and drilling equipment give travelers an idea of day-to-day life on an oil rig. Visitors can walk the main street of a re-created boomtown, and view the simulated explosion of an oil well as it is ripped asunder by a buildup of natural pressures deep within the earth. A replica of an ancient coral reef, complete with some 200,000 models of prehistoric marine creatures, conveys a vivid impression of the life forms that once thrived where oil rigs now churn black gold. Thousand-year-old reed mats, Native American tepees, cowboy artifacts, and historical paintings are also on display.

Continuing east on I-20, visitors to the Big Spring State Park will find natural riches of a different sort. Capping the 200-foot bluff called Scenic Mountain, the 343-acre park is home to cottontails, jackrabbits, ground squirrels, roadrunners, and prairie dogs. A three-mile scenic drive around the mesa's ridge provides joggers, hikers, drivers, and casual strollers with dramatic views of the rolling plains.

Ten miles southwest of Abilene—home of the only zoo between Fort Worth and El Paso—Buffalo Gap Historic Village's collection of 20 buildings preserves the frontier spirit of late–19th-century Texas. A log cabin built in 1875, railroad depot, two-room schoolhouse, and the 1879 Taylor County Courthouse and Jail are just some of the buildings open to the public.

FOR MORE INFORMATION:
Texas Department of Commerce, Tourism Dept., P.O. Box 12728, Austin, TX 78711-2728; 512-462-9191 or 800-888-8839.

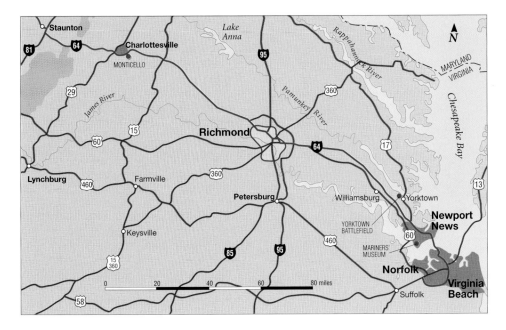

Moored in the James River, these three fishing boats, above, are a testament to the rich maritime tradition of Newport News, Virginia.

History resonates in every nook and cranny of Virginia. This beautiful state was the site of the first permanent English settlement in the New World, as well as the place where the first rebellion against royal British authority took place. Starting with the birthplace of Thomas Jefferson in Charlottesville, Interstate 64 links together some of the nation's most hallowed historic places.

Author of the Declaration of Independence, a founder and tireless promoter of the University of Virginia, and third president of the United States, Thomas Jefferson is one of Virginia's favorite sons. His mountaintop home, Monticello, is located just off I-64, some five miles east of Charlottesville. Jefferson blended French and Italian designs to create this neoclassical masterpiece. An avid horticulturist, he also laid out the plantation's inviting gardens, including two fruit orchards, a vineyard, and flower and vegetable gardens.

Driving east on I-64, travelers soon reach picturesque Richmond, one of the most historic cities in the nation. Founded in 1607, it was made state capital in 1780 and named the capital of the Confederacy in 1861. Monument Avenue, lined with stately mansions tucked away behind wrought-iron gates, features five monuments to Civil War heroes. Once the most fashionable neighborhood in town, the Court End district contains seven national historic landmarks, including the John Marshall House, named after the chief justice of the U.S.

Vivid colors adorn the storefronts in Richmond's Uptown District, right.

Supreme Court, who built it in 1791. The city is also home to the Museum of the Confederacy, with the largest collection of Confederate artifacts in the world.

COLONIAL HERITAGE

Heading toward the coast, I-64 passes close to the Yorktown Battlefield, site of the last major conflict of the Revolutionary War. Here, just east of Williamsburg, British General Cornwallis surrendered to George Washington in 1781. Visitors can view the battlefield from an observation deck or tour the museum, where the American troops' field tents are on display.

Before ending the journey along I-64 at the historic seaport of Norfolk, travelers can bone up on maritime history at the Mariners' Museum in Newport News. From the models of the tiny wooden craft in which man first kept afloat to the steel behemoths that patrol the ocean today, exhibits celebrate the culture of the sea. The museum's elaborate Venetian gondola is matched only by the Crabtree Collection of miniature ships. Ship modelers demonstrate their skill, and interpreters recount some of the great legends of the sea. Ship figureheads, scrimshaw, and maritime paintings are also on display.

Norfolk is a fitting end to this historic journey. Founded in the 1680's, the seaport was an important trading center between Virginia, the West Indies, and England.

FOR MORE INFORMATION:

Virginia Division of Tourism, 901 East Byrd St., 19th Fl., Richmond, VA 23219; 804-786-2051 or 800-847-4882.

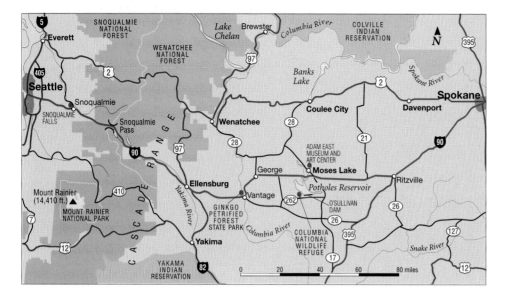

From the rainy shores of Puget Sound to the dry Palouse country around Spokane, Interstate 90 presents a panorama of Washington State. In between, the route negotiates some of the continent's mightiest mountain ranges, and offers visitors a blend of the majestic and the offbeat.

After enjoying the cosmopolitan charm of Seattle, travelers can return to nature by taking a short drive down I-90. Within the towering Cascade Mountains is the unspoiled beauty of Snoqualmie Falls. Plunging 268 feet, the cataracts are 100 feet higher than Niagara Falls. Home to the world's first underground power station, this thundering cascade is best seen from the observation platform above the Snoqualmie River. Arriving by a trail at the falls' base, visitors feel dwarfed by this mighty cataract. Pristine mountain waters filled with steelhead trout make the river below the falls an ideal spot for fishermen. Just a few minutes away, the Snoqualmie Winery offers daily tours and tastings. Located on a grassy plateau, the winery's picnic area affords panoramic views of Mount Si, which rises 4,100 feet above the valley floor.

About 15 million years ago, molten lava covered much of central Washington. Through the centuries, natural processes have revealed a vast petrified forest. Today Ginkgo Petrified Forest State Park harbors more than 200 species of these mineralized trees and is the only place on earth with petrified specimens of the rare ginkgo tree. Several trails lead up the steep hills to par-

tially excavated trees. Sharp-eyed hikers may spot deer, elk, coyotes, and a variety of snakes and lizards among the wildflowers and sagebrush. At the comprehensive visitor center, exhibits of petrified wood and Native American petroglyphs carved into black basalt slabs are on display. The park also offers excellent opportunities for fishing on the Columbia River.

Outside the town of Vantage on a barren hilltop just off I-90, a sculpture depicts 18 wild mustangs seemingly charging toward the Columbia River. Visible from five miles away, this monumental work represents a Native American creation scene in which the Great Spirit frees the exuberant colts. Titled *Grandfather Cuts Loose the Ponies*, the 250-foot-long sculpture is breathtaking in its immensity.

Art on a smaller scale can be found at the Adam East Museum and Art Center in

Moses Lake. With exhibits that change on a monthly basis, the center usually features the work of two Northwest artists. Much of the museum is dedicated to local history, regional arts, and Native American history of the Moses Lake region. The permanent collection displays approximately 8,000 Native American artifacts.

CANYONS AND BUTTES

Farther down I-90, the 23,200-acre Columbia National Wildlife Refuge is a must-see for nature lovers. Created over millions of years, the bizarre landscape of water-filled canyons, rocky buttes, and craggy cliffs is the result of bubbling lava flows, rock-crushing glaciers, buffeting winds, and man's inadvertent intervention. With the completion of the O'Sullivan Dam in the 1950's, the rising water table flooded numerous glacier-carved depressions. Today the area, which also encompasses the Potholes State Park, is awash with hundreds of lakes, ponds, and marshes. As fishermen plumb the waters in hope of hooking rainbow trout, perch, crappie, bass, walleye, and bluegill, bird-watchers glimpse great blue herons, white pelicans, sandhill cranes, hawks, and eagles. Deer, badgers, beavers, and rabbits are also found in this refuge.

Having viewed nature's bounty, motorists can end their jaunt along I-90 in Spokane—a city of tasteful modern architecture and lovingly restored older structures.

FOR MORE INFORMATION:
Washington Tourism Development Division, P.O. Box 42500, Olympia, WA 98504-2500; 360-753-5600 or 800-544-1800.

Visitors gathered at the base of Snoqualmie Falls, right, enjoy the brilliant rainbow created by its mist.

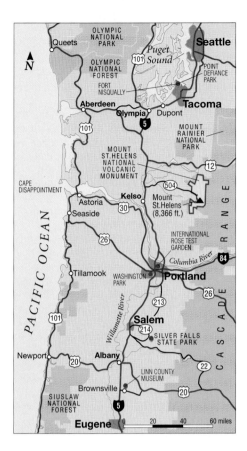

Sandwiched between the dramatic mountain vistas of the Cascade Range and the cool spray of the Pacific Ocean, Interstate 5 wends its way from Tacoma to Eugene. In Tacoma, the towering spectacle of Mount Rainier dominates the eastern horizon. The city's early settlers had remarkable foresight: in 1888, with vast tracts of the Western frontier still unexplored, they set aside as public parkland an area on the northern edge of the city with old-growth forests, saltwater beaches, and stunning views of the Puget Sound. A century later, the 698-acre Point Defiance Park protects one of the country's largest slices of urban green space.

The park features extensive gardens, an aquarium, and a zoo. Also on its grounds is Fort Nisqually, a restored Hudson's Bay Company trading post founded in 1833. For the next six years, it served as a crucial outpost in the expansion of the fur trade across North America. Originally located at DuPont on the Nisqually River, Fort Nisqually was moved to its present site during the early 1930's. The fort's granary is one of the oldest standing structures in the state.

The blasted trees and razed earth near Mount St. Helens, right, testify to the awesome power produced by the volcano's 1980 eruption.

Less than 80 miles south of Tacoma, I-5 crosses the Toutle River. On May 18, 1980, the temperature of its waters reached more than 100°F due to the violent eruption of Mount St. Helens some 40 miles upstream. The volcano, which had rumbled for two months, spewed 540 million tons of ash across the Pacific Northwest. Forests surrounding the site were seared and flattened, and an area of nearly 150,000 acres was rendered lifeless. Congress declared the site a national monument in 1982, but recurring volcanic activity kept the area closed to the public until the following year. Today access roads and hiking trails provide spectacular views of the colossal crater, as well as the chance to witness one of the planet's newest ecosystems. Visitor centers located around the site provide information on the volcano's explosive history.

CROSSING INTO OREGON

As I-5 crosses the Columbia River into Oregon, Portland comes into view at the confluence of the Columbia and Willamette rivers. Like Tacoma, Portland has greenery galore: with more than a dozen public gardens, the city is a feast of botanical delights. In manicured Washington Park, one of the sites of the city's annual Rose Festival, numerous seasonal displays and exotic flower beds compete for attention. In the summer months, a train carries visitors through the beautiful park to the famed International Rose Test Garden.

The reconstructed South Bastion of Fort Nisqually, above, is a silent reminder of the fur-trade era.

East of Salem, Silver Falls State Park encompasses lush forests and cascading waterfalls—a landscape formed 15 million years ago. With 10 waterfalls and an endless variety of plant life along its seven miles of trails, Silver Falls is an all-season park, featuring brilliant color in autumn and a more ethereal beauty in winter, when the falls freeze into dazzling ice sculptures.

Travelers can tour the Linn County Museum in Brownsville, where Oregon's pioneer past comes to life. The town's prosperity was aided by the arrival of the railway in 1880. Appropriately enough, the museum is located in the old Brownsville Depot and in nine antique railroad cars. Exhibits include a turn-of-the-century general store and dressmaker's shop, as well as one of only three authentic Oregon Trail wagons used by settlers as they traveled west. This trip along I-5 ends in Eugene—a picturesque city on the Willamette River.

FOR MORE INFORMATION:

Washington Tourism Development Division, P.O. Box 42500, Olympia, WA 98504-2500; 360-753-5600 or 800-544-1800.
Oregon Tourism Division, Oregon Economic Development Dept., 775 Summer St. NE, Salem, OR 97310; 800-547-7842.

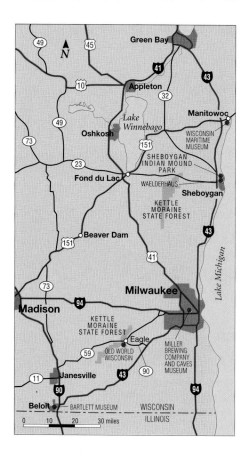

Neatly attired in period clothing, a costumed interpreter in Old World Wisconsin, left, patiently weaves a basket on the porch of a German farmstead.

A rich blend of ethnic cultures and American traditions, the Badger State offers unique rewards for those explorers willing to poke around. Stretching south from Green Bay—home of the NFL's Packers—Interstate 43 is the perfect route to follow for this voyage of discovery.

Renowned for producing elegant schooners in the 19th century, Manitowoc was once known as the Clipper City. During World War II, its shipyards produced landing craft, minesweepers, and 28 submarines. More than a hundred years of Great Lakes history is celebrated here at the Wisconsin Maritime Museum, where a wide range of shipping artifacts are on display, including old diving equipment. Films, photographs, and a reconstructed street of an old Great Lakes port town help bring the region's days of glory back to life. Hand-crafted model ships and a full-scale reproduction of the midship section of a 19th-century schooner illustrate the evolution of shipping from sailboats and steamers to diesel freighters and luxury yachts. Moored alongside the museum, the submarine USS *Cobia* gives visitors the chance to tour the cramped confines of an "iron fish" from the control room and ward to the torpedo room and crew's quarters.

Following I-43 down the windswept coast to Sheboygan, visitors will come upon

Waelderhaus, a replica of an Austrian chalet commissioned by Marie C. Kohler, sister of the former governor of Wisconsin, Walter J. Kohler. Modeled on the family home in the Alps, Waelderhaus contains its original furnishings, including wrought-iron door hinges, stained-glass windows, detailed carvings, and woodcuts. Dedicated to the Girl Scout movement, the Baden-Powell room contains a large frieze depicting the coats of arms of each country that had Girl Scout troops in 1931, and a large chandelier on which each hand-made section represents a merit badge.

Farther down I-43, the Sheboygan Indian Mound Park offers visitors a look into the region's mysterious Native American past. Situated on a short nature trail, a cluster of 18 flat-topped effigy mounds rises from the ground. Some of the 1,000-year-old mounds are oval or linear and a number of them have been fashioned to resemble deer and panthers. Earlier excavations of other sites in the area revealed that each mound was the burial place for one or two people, as well as artifacts such as projectile points. One of the mounds has been equipped with a window that reveals artifacts and the body of an adult.

Milwaukee is synonymous with beer, and visitors to the city can tour the facilities of the Miller Brewing Company, its largest

brewery. Following a video presentation on the history of brewing, visitors can watch a production line in action as it packages approximately 200,000 cases of beer daily. The brewhouse, which is complete with modern computerized brew kettles, may also be toured.

One of the highlights of the tour is a visit to the Caves Museum for a unique look into the history of brewing. In the mid-19th century, before the advent of mechanical refrigeration, the Miller firm excavated a series of deep, cool caverns to use as storage areas to age their beer. Today the massive 44-inch-thick brick-and-limestone walls are used to house antique bottles, huge wooden kegs, and cooper's tools. Numerous period advertisements and a miniature replica of the original Plank Road Brewery transport visitors back to a bygone era.

PIONEER DAYS
Old World Wisconsin, a 576-acre outdoor museum, is located just off I-43 in the south unit of Kettle Moraine State Forest. More than 55 structures built between 1830 and 1915 have been relocated here to form a series of working farms and a country village. Constructed by early immigrants who settled here, the buildings reflect the Old World architecture of Germany, Norway, Ireland, Denmark, Finland, and England. Whether treading the floorboards of a quaint one-room Norwegian cabin or admiring the half-timber construction of a German farmhouse, visitors take a 150-year step back in time. The interiors of these homesteads display period furnishings. Costumed interpreters demonstrate plowing, baking, and other daily activities using traditional techniques. Horse-powered grain threshing, dairy farming, and celebrations of ethnic holidays are also reenacted.

Perched upon the Wisconsin-Illinois border, the industrial town of Beloit is a perfect spot to end this tour along I-43. Here the Bartlett Museum and its extensive collection of Native American artifacts give visitors a look into the lives of the people who first inhabited this great land.

FOR MORE INFORMATION:
Wisconsin Department of Tourism, P.O. Box 7976, Madison, WI 53707; 800-432-TRIP.

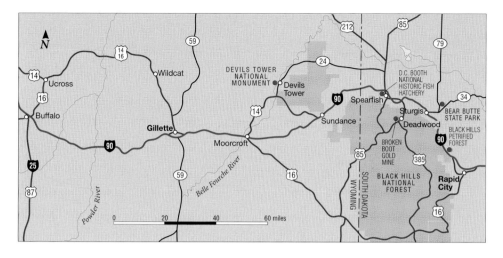

The weathered-looking Saloon Number 10 in Deadwood, South Dakota, above, is where Wild Bill Hickock was shot in 1876.

The segment of Interstate 90 that passes through eastern Wyoming's high plains to the ancient Black Hills of South Dakota leads travelers to quirky towns, scenes of stunning natural beauty, and plenty in between.

Leaving Buffalo—the favorite watering hole for Butch Cassidy and the Sundance Kid—eastbound travelers come to Devils Tower. The immense monument, which rises abruptly above a pine forest, thrusts out of the earth like a fragment of a prehistoric age. The tower is actually a column of hardened magma formed 60 million years ago. In 1906 the federal government proclaimed the 867-foot monolith the country's first national monument. Sacred to Native Americans, the Tower is a world-renowned recreational climbing venue.

Following I-90 across the South Dakota state line, travelers come upon the D.C. Booth National Historic Fish Hatchery. Founded in 1899 to bring trout to the streams of the Black Hills region, the facility harvested its first crop in 1900. Today about 30,000 fish are reared annually. Visitors can view rainbow and brown trout through windows in the underwater viewing area.

GOLD FEVER

Visitors to Deadwood and her sister city Lead relive the gold fever that swept the Black Hills in the late 1800's. When John Pearson discovered gold here in 1875, he set in motion one of the most frenzied episodes in American history. By 1876 some 25,000 fortune seekers had flooded the area, and the town of Deadwood was born. Scouring local streams with picks, shovels, sluice boxes, and gold pans, prospectors had to mine the hillsides once the easy pickings were depleted. Reopened in 1954, the Broken Boot Gold Mine, named for an old miner's boot that was left in the shaft more than 50 years ago, has changed little from those heady days. Its 840-foot main drift penetrates deep into the hillside and opens into a spacious stope where miners once searched for precious pockets of gold. Mining demonstrations revive the excitement of the gold rush.

Bear Butte is a large tepee-shaped bubble of hard volcanic rock, or laccolith, that stands 1,200 feet above the plains. It is revered as a sacred site by many Native Americans, particularly the Cheyenne. Artifacts dating from 10,000 years ago are on display at the visitor center in Bear Butte State Park.

Before reaching Rapid City, visitors can return to the age of the dinosaur in the Petrified Forest. A sandstone trail is lined with petrified cypress trees, relics of the tropical forest that covered the region more than 120 million years ago. Exhibits on display in the museum recount the history of the Black Hills, and, like other stops on I-90, bring a slice of history to life.

FOR MORE INFORMATION:

Wyoming Travel Commission, College Dr., Cheyenne, WY 82002; 307-777-7777 or 800-225-5996.
South Dakota Division of Tourism, 711 East Wells Ave., Pierre, SD 57501-3369; 800-732-5682.

A Native American legend claims that Devils Tower, left, was created as a sanctuary for young girls pursued by attacking bears.

INDEX

PICTURE CREDITS

Cover photograph by
R. Lassila/Réflexion/Camerique
2 Michael Collier
5 Martha McBride/Unicorn Stock Photos

THE EAST COAST
8, 9 Brian Vanden Brink
10 (upper right) Alan Briere
10 (lower left) Robert Perron
12 Mark E. Gibson/Stock Market
13 (left) Paul Rocheleau
13 (right) Eliot Cohen
14 Thomas Mark Szelog
14, 15 François Gohier
15 (right) Paul Rocheleau
16 (left) Gerry Ellis/Ellis Nature Photography
16, 17 Brian Vanden Brink

APPALACHIAN ADVENTURE
18, 19 David Muench
20 (left) Ron Blakeley/Réflexion/Camerique
20 (right) Kathy Adams Clark
22, 23 (both) Pat & Chuck Blackley
24 (upper) Lynn Seldon Jr.
24 (lower) Joe Goldfus
25 William B. Folsom
26 Réflexion/Camerique
26, 27 William B. Folsom
27 Kathy Adams Clark
28 (upper) John Skowronski
28 (lower) Jodi Cobb/ Woodfin Camp
   & Associates
29 (upper) John Skowronski
29 (lower) Sepp Seitz/ Woodfin Camp
   & Associates

THE OLD SOUTH
30, 31 Tom Till
32 (upper) Lawrence Dolan/ Transparencies
32 (lower) John Elk
34 (upper) Dennis O'Kain
34 (lower) Janice S. Sauls
35 H. Kaiser/Réflexion/Camerique
36 (both) John Elk
36 (lower) David Muench
37 Tom Till
38 M. Timothy O'Keefe
38 John Elk
38, 39 Ric Ergenbright

PIONEER ILLINOIS
40, 41 Willard Clay
42 John Patsch/Third Coast Stock Source

44 James P. Rowan
44, 45 Richard Hamilton Smith
45 Richard Day/Daybreak Imagery
46, 47 (both) Richard Day/Daybreak Imagery
47 (upper) Mitchell Museum at Cedarhurst
   Gift of John R. and Eleanor R. Mitchell
48 Kevin O'Mooney/Odyssey/Chicago
49 (upper) Gerry Ellis/Ellis Nature
   Photography
49 (lower) James P. Rowan

THE HIGH PLAINS
50, 51 Larry Ulrich
52 (upper left) Courtesy of the Minnesota
   Office of Tourism
52 (lower right) Larry Ulrich
54 (upper right) Tim Thompson
54 (lower left) Greg Ryan - Sally Beyer
55 Richard Day/Daybreak Imagery
56 (upper) Susan Day/Daybreak Imagery
56 (lower) James P. Rowan
57 Richard Day/Daybreak Imagery
58 (upper left) Richard Day/Daybreak Imagery
58 (lower right) T. Rumreich/Frozen Images
59 François Gohier

CHISHOLM TRAIL
60, 61 Jonathan Wallen
62 (upper left) Tim Thompson
62 (lower right) Zigy Kaluzny
64 Tim Thompson
65 (left) Laurence Parent
65 (right) John Elk
66 (upper) Michael Bodycomb/Kimbell
   Art Museum
66 (lower) Laurence Parent
67 (upper left) Laurence Parent
67 (lower right) Tim Thompson
68 (both) John Elk
69 Tim Thompson
70 Jonathan Wallen
70, 71 John Elk
71 Jonathan Wallen

THROUGH THE ROCKIES
72, 73 Laurence Parent
74 (upper left) Buzz Morrison
74 (lower right) Ric Ergenbright
76 Michael Collier
76, 77 James Prout
77 David Wilkins
78 (both) Michael Collier
79 Marc Muench

80 (upper left) John Elk
80 (lower right) Michael Collier
81 François Gohier

DESERT DISCOVERY
82, 83 Laurence Parent
84 (upper left) Richard Cummins
84 (lower right) James P. Rowan
86 (left) Bob Miller
86 (upper right) James P. Rowan
86 (lower left) Merlin D. Tuttle/Photo
   Researchers
87 Chuck Place
88 John Elk
89 (upper) John Elk
89 (lower) James P. Rowan
90 (upper) Richard Cummins
90 (lower) Chuck Place
91 Richard Cummins
92 (upper right) John Elk
92 (lower left) Richard Cummins
93 Chuck Place

PANORAMIC NORTHWEST
94, 95 David Jensen
96 (upper left) David Jensen
96 (lower right) Brian S. Sytnyk/Masterfile
98 Scott T. Smith
98, 99 Ric Ergenbright
99 Mark Turner
100 (upper) David Jensen
100 (lower) Steve Bly
101 (upper) Scott T. Smith
101 (lower) William H. Mullins
102 John Elk
102, 103 Steve Bly
103 John Elk

GOLDEN STATE DRIVE
104, 105 Larry Ulrich
106 (upper right) Ron Garrison/Zoological
   Society of San Diego
106 (lower left) Chuck Place
108 (left) Richard Cummins
108 (right) Robert Holmes
109 John Elk
110 Chuck Place
110, 111 Frank S. Balthis
111 Chuck Place
112 (both) Frank S. Balthis
113 Lee Foster

GAZETTEER
114 Ken Laffal
115 (left) David Muench
115 (right) George Wuerthner
116 (left) Lee Foster
116 (right) Larry Ulrich
117 Aneal F. Vohra/Unicorn Stock Photos
118 John Elk
119 (upper right) James P. Rowan
119 (lower left) Réflexion/Camerique
120 (upper right) Bob Miller
120 (lower left) Ken Laffal
121 James P. Rowan
122 John Elk
123 (both) John Elk
124 (upper) Greg Ryan - Sally Beyer
124 (lower) James P. Rowan
125 Aneal F. Vohra/Unicorn Stock Photos
126 (upper) James P. Rowan
126 (lower) Jonathan Wallen
127 Dave G. Houser
128 Larry Prosor
129 (upper left) Greg Ryan - Sally Beyer
129 (lower right) Kent & Donna Dannen
130 (upper left) Jonathan Wallen
130 (lower right) Buddy Mays/Travel Stock
131 (upper) Tom Bean
131 Jonathan Wallen
132 (upper left) Jim Argo/Spiro Mounds
   Historic Parks
132 (lower right) Dennis Thompson/Unicorn
   Stock Photos
133 Jean Higgins/Unicorn Stock Photos
134 Courtesy of the Alabama Bureau of
   Tourism and Travel
135 (upper) Jonathan Wallen
135 (lower) Andre Jenny/Unicorn
   Stock Photos
136 Laurence Parent
137 (upper) Dave G. Houser
137 (lower) Nik Wheeler
138 Wolfgang Kaehler
139 (upper right) James P. Rowan
139 (lower left) Lee Foster
140 James P. Rowan
141 (upper right) Dave G. Houser
141 (lower left) Andre Jenny/Unicorn
   Stock Photos

Back cover photograph by Pat
& Chuck Blackley

ACKNOWLEDGMENTS

Cartography: Map resource base courtesy of the USGS; shaded relief courtesy of Mountain High Maps® Copyright © 1993 Digital Wisdom, Inc.

The editors would also like to thank the following: Sonia Di Maulo, Lorraine Doré, Dominique Gagné, Pascale Hueber, Brian Parsons, and Cynthia Shannon.